*Jacob Arminius*

# Jacob Arminius

*Theologian of Grace*

KEITH D. STANGLIN

AND THOMAS H. McCALL

OXFORD

UNIVERSITY PRESS

# OXFORD
UNIVERSITY PRESS

Oxford University Press is a department of the University of Oxford.
It furthers the University's objective of excellence in research,
scholarship, and education by publishing worldwide.

Oxford   New York

Auckland   Cape Town   Dar es Salaam   Hong Kong   Karachi
Kuala Lumpur   Madrid   Melbourne   Mexico City   Nairobi
New Delhi   Shanghai   Taipei   Toronto

With offices in

Argentina   Austria   Brazil   Chile   Czech Republic   France   Greece
Guatemala   Hungary   Italy   Japan   Poland   Portugal   Singapore
South Korea   Switzerland   Thailand   Turkey   Ukraine   Vietnam

Oxford is a registered trade mark of Oxford University Press
in the UK and certain other countries.

Published in the United States of America by
Oxford University Press
198 Madison Avenue, New York, NY 10016

© Oxford University Press 2012

Library of Congress Cataloging-in-Publication Data
Stanglin, Keith D.
Jacob Arminius: theologian of grace /Keith D. Stanglin and Thomas H. McCall.
p.   cm.
Includes bibliographical references (p. ) and index.
ISBN 978-0-19-975566-0—ISBN 978-0-19-975567-7
1. Arminius, Jacobus, 1560–1609. 2. Theology, Doctrinal—History—16th century.
3. Theology, Doctrinal—History—17th century. 4. Arminianism
I. McCall, Thomas H. II. Title.
BX6196.S73   2012
230′.49092—dc23     2012001907

*To*
*John and Beverly Stanglin*
*Randy and Marilou Lawhead*
*Thomas† and Carol McCall*
*Edward† and Thalya Coleman*

# Contents

# *Preface*

IN OUR FORMER lives as Ph.D. students at Calvin Theological Seminary, we first discussed the idea of writing a book on Arminius and Arminianism. After focused publications in the areas of historical and systematic theology, we thought the time was right to return to this project. We now both teach at institutions affiliated with evangelicalism, and we regularly field questions from students and colleagues about Arminianism. We struggle to find one good volume to recommend. In addition, we have taught seminars on Calvinism and Arminianism and also have trouble finding appropriate textbooks for upper-level undergraduate and graduate students.

The most widely read book on Arminius is the classic biography by Carl Bangs. Bangs's work is based on good historical records and is accessible to any interested reader. Its primary task is strictly biographical, which is its strength. Bangs also weaves some theology into the narrative, and he includes a brief chapter summarizing Arminius's theology. Since theology is not its primary purpose, however, Bangs's book is necessarily limited when it comes to exposing Arminius's thought. There are other books available that deal with Arminianism but have little or nothing significant to say about Arminius himself. These and other popular-level books are of varying quality. But they are mostly written from an overtly apologetic-polemical perspective, and none gives full attention to Arminius. Moreover, there are recent, quality studies devoted to Arminius himself, but they are technical monographs. These contributions appeal primarily to scholars in historical theology and focus much of their attention on narrow aspects of Arminius's ideas.

Thus our book recommendations have always been accompanied by necessary caveats. We desired a book that would serve as the best "one-stop" source of information for ministers and theologians interested in Arminius and the movement that he inspired, as well as a book that would be accessible to the extensive audience of interested laity (perhaps especially those who self-identify as "Arminians" or "Calvinists"). We wanted a book that would have the opposite aim of Bangs's biography—one that would give some attention to the life of Arminius but would spend most of the space providing a clear, accessible exposition of Arminius's theology. Since we could not find the textbook we wanted, we decided to try writing it ourselves.

The method we have chosen for providing this overview of Arminius's theology focuses on the theological topics, rather than attempting a chronological story or an account that focuses on particular treatises. First of all, although there is some discernible development throughout the course of Arminius's writings, such developments are minor and, for the purposes of this survey, render a chronological account of his thought unnecessary. Moreover, attention to distinct writings works well for some topics (such as predestination), but it does not work as well for other topics. Thus there is no need to protect the integrity of each treatise at all cost. We have opted for a topical presentation that draws from the breadth of his writings without ignoring their original setting.

The nature of this book demands heavy reliance on primary sources. We have cited all of Arminius's writings (as well as nearly all older sources) from the original Latin or Dutch texts (most of which are found in the *Opera*). The three-volume London edition of Arminius's works in English has also been used and, where possible, cited in the footnotes as *Works*, though for the sake of accuracy we have altered existing translations in many quotations. Public and private disputations of Arminius have been cited only according to disputation and thesis numbers, and they can easily be found in the *Opera*, *Works*, and *Missing Disputations* (ed. Stanglin). Important vocabulary from the original languages has been included in various places along the way. We have more frequently included in footnotes the original language excerpts from the works that are absent from the *Opera* and thus generally more difficult for readers to acquire (especially the Dutch of *Dec. sent.* and Latin of *Exam. Gom.* and *Disp. pub.* XXVI–LXI). In translating, we have attempted to observe gender neutrality but have also given priority to renderings that adhere closely to the original texts. When these goals seem to conflict (for example, when *homo* or *mensche* is followed by other singular personal pronouns), we have generally chosen the more literal rendering.

Before proceeding further, we would like to acknowledge the debts that we have accumulated in writing this book. Mark Mann, Mark Bilby, Mike

Lodahl, and Sam Powell read portions of an earlier draft of the manuscript and offered helpful suggestions. We also wish to thank Jessica Wilson (a very promising scholar) for her excellent work in helping to prepare this manuscript. A section in the Introduction appeared in an earlier version as "The New Perspective on Arminius: Notes on a Historiographical Shift," *Reformation & Renaissance Review* 11/3 (2009): 295–310, (c) Equinox Publishing Ltd (2011). Our thanks go to the editors for permission to use this article in a new format. The portrait of Arminius on the book cover was anonymously painted ca. 1620. It is used by the gracious permission of the Remonstrantse Gemeente Rotterdam, where the original is housed. Thanks to Marijke Tolsma and Tjaard Barnard for their help in acquiring this image. We would also like to thank Cynthia Read (executive editor at Oxford University Press in New York, who worked with us from the beginning stages of this project) as well as the production team for their help along the way.

My (Stanglin's) part of the work began in 2010 during a summer Research Fellowship at the H. Henry Meeter Center for Calvin Studies at Calvin College and Theological Seminary in Grand Rapids. I am grateful to that institution for its generosity and accommodations, and to Paul Fields, Karin Maag, and the staff of the Meeter Center for their assistance. It was a treat once again to scratch the surface of their library's wonderful collection (both rare and recent). This project was concluded in San Diego, where I have spent the summer and autumn of 2011 as a Visiting Scholar in the Wesleyan Center at Point Loma Nazarene University. My family and I are grateful for the university's support in accommodating us, and for the numerous ways in which the staff has gone out of their way to make us comfortable in such a beautiful location during these seven months. It has been a great pleasure to work with Mark Bilby, Mark Mann, Lydia Heberling, and Sharon Bowles. My family's time in both of these cities was well spent, thanks to our friendship with the Bidigare, Bilby, Gailey, Gunnells, and Medawar families, as well as with Sherley Cooper, Macky Harlan, and Janet Klein. Finally, I am thankful to the administrators at Harding University who granted my sabbatical in the autumn of 2011, which made the extended time of research and writing possible.

I (McCall) am grateful to those scholars from whom I have learned much regarding the theology of Arminius (and historical theology more generally): Bill Ury, Richard Muller, and Keith Stanglin have been very helpful in many ways. I am also thankful for the sabbatical in the autumn of 2010 granted by the Regents and Administration of Trinity Evangelical Divinity School—and to the many wonderful students with whom I have been blessed at Trinity. I routinely have better students than I deserve, and their insightful questions, friendly objections, and cheerful friendship leave me in their debt.

We both want to express our utmost gratitude to our families. Amanda, Paul, Isaac, and Rachel Stanglin, and Jenny, Cole, Josiah, Madelyn, and Isaac McCall bring more joy than we could have imagined. We dedicate this book to our parents and in-laws: John and Beverly Stanglin, Randy and Marilou Lawhead, Thomas (d. 2009) and Carol McCall, and Edward (d. 2003) and Thalya Coleman. We will forever be grateful to you.

Keith Stanglin
San Diego, California
Tom McCall
Deerfield, Illinois
16 October 2011

# Abbreviations

| | |
|---|---|
| *Apologia* | Arminius, *Apologia adversus articulos quosdam theologicos in vulgus sparsos* |
| *Art. non.* | Arminius, *Articuli nonnulli diligenti examine perpendendi* |
| *Cap. VII Rom.* | Arminius, *De vero et genuino sensu cap. VII Epistolae ad Romanos dissertatio* |
| *Cap. IX Rom.* | Arminius, *Analysis cap. 9. ad Romanos ad Gellium Snecanum* |
| *Collatio* | Arminius, *Amica cum D. Francisco Iunio de praedestinatione collatio* |
| *Dec. sent.* | Arminius, *Verklaring (Declaratio sententiae)*, ed. Hoenderdaal (1960) |
| *Disp. priv.* | Arminius, *Disputationes privatae, de plerisque Christianae religionis capitibus* |
| *Disp. pub.* | Arminius, *Disputationes publicae* (I–XXV in *Opera* and *Works*; XXVI–LXI in Stanglin, *Missing Public Disputations*) |
| *Ep. ecc.* | *Praestantium ac eruditorum virorum epistolae ecclesiasticae et theologicae* |
| *Epistola* | Arminius, *Epistola ad Hippolytum a Collibus* |
| *Exam. Gom.* | Arminius, *Examen thesium D. Francisci Gomari de praedestinatione* (1645) |
| *Exam. Perk.* | Arminius, *Examen modestum libelli, quem D. Gulielmus Perkinsius . . . edidit* |
| *Opera* | Arminius, *Opera theologica* (1st ed., 1629) |
| *Oratio de dissidio* | Arminius, *Oratio de componendo dissidio religionis inter Christianos* |
| *Oratio de sacerdotio* | Arminius, *Oratio de sacerdotio Christi habita a Arminio cum doctor crearetur* |

| | |
|---|---|
| *Oratio prima/secunda/tertia* | Arminius, *Orationes tres de theologia* |
| *PG* | Migne, ed., *Patrologia Graeca cursus completus* |
| *PL* | Migne, ed., *Patrologia Latina cursus completes* |
| *PRRD* | Muller, *Post-Reformation Reformed Dogmatics*, 4 vols. (2003) |
| *Quaestiones* | Arminius, *Quaestiones numero novem cum responsionibus et anterotematis* |
| *ST* | Thomas Aquinas, *Summa theologiae* |
| *Works* | Arminius, *The Works of James Arminius*, London edition (1825–1875; reprint, 1986) |

# Chronology

*Jacob Arminius*

# Introduction

*Arminianism still needs a critical confrontation with its founder.*

—CARL BANGS, 1963

## I. Neglect of Arminius

The reputation of the Dutch theologian Jacob Harmenszoon (1559–1609)—who would later follow academic custom and latinize his name to Arminius (after the German chieftain who defeated Varus's legions in A.D. 9)—has been established on his status as the most renowned of the so-called anti-Calvinists. He is remembered primarily as an opponent of the predestination taught by John Calvin (1509–1564) and as a proponent of free will—such is the extent of popular familiarity with Arminius. Since Arminius's brand of Protestant theology is often portrayed as the alternative to Calvin's, one's personal fondness for Arminius is often inversely proportional to one's fondness for Calvin. Arminius, therefore, is a famous figure in many popular-level discussions, being idolized as a hero and derided as a heretic. He has been the object of veneration and vitriol, and, in both cases, he has often been misunderstood, misrepresented, and misjudged (and misspelled). In his own day, and in the four centuries since his death, the name "Arminius" has been a lightning rod for controversy.

And this is the reputation that is dominant among those who *have* heard of Arminius. Yet, there are surely even more Christians who have never heard of Arminius. Not only are "Arminius" and "Arminianism" not household words for most Protestants, neither are they part of the vocabulary of most churches and some seminaries. For a theologian who inspired a distinct trajectory within Protestantism and whose name became synonymous with this movement, the neglect is surprising. The dearth of scholarly attention given to Arminius has become the subject of a common lament, even to the present day.[1]

The importance of Arminius will become clear in the course of this book. For now, though, why has there been such misunderstanding and neglect of this figure? In addition to all kinds of cultural and religious reasons, including a general lack of historical perspective and a declining interest in doctrine, two reasons may be mentioned. One reason for the neglect has to do with the *nature of his writings*. First of all, compared with other theological luminaries, he did not write much. It is true that the first Latin edition of his collected works contains 966 (mostly) double-columned pages, and that there are many other works not published in that collection. His works, however, pale in comparison to the voluminous output of, say, Martin Luther (1483–1546) and John Calvin. Although he was by all accounts a talented theologian with a gifted intellect, Arminius was not primarily a writer. He was a minister and teacher who had little ambition for writing,[2] and he was a professor for only the last six years of his relatively short life.

In addition, what Arminius did write tended to have a narrow scope. Most of his writings are of an apologetic-polemical nature, or they are simply trying to seek the truth in conversation with an interlocutor. In any case, they were not written for general publication. There were also documents he wrote for academic use—namely, orations and disputations; disputations were the only documents printed during his lifetime. Though he had vague intentions of doing so, he did not write a systematic theology. Neither did he publish any full commentaries on Scripture. His writings, therefore, are not as pastoral and constructive as they are academic and controversial. He has no clear magnum opus, nothing as defiant as Luther's *Bondage of the Will* or as celebrated and far-reaching as Calvin's *Institutes of the Christian Religion*. To a degree, this neglect plagues most other Protestant scholastics as well, and for similar reasons. As a group, the Protestant scholastics—that is, the theologians who followed the

---

1. Carl Bangs noted this back in 1958, in "Arminius and Reformed Theology" (Ph.D. diss., University of Chicago, 1958), p. 11. See similar statements in Richard A. Muller, *God, Creation, and Providence in the Thought of Jacob Arminius: Sources and Directions of Scholastic Protestantism in the Era of Early Orthodoxy* (Grand Rapids, MI: Baker, 1991), p. 3; Roger E. Olson, *The Story of Christian Theology: Twenty Centuries of Tradition and Reform* (Downers Grove, IL: IVP, 1999), p. 455; Keith D. Stanglin, *Arminius on the Assurance of Salvation: The Context, Roots, and Shape of the Leiden Debate, 1603–1609*, Brill's Series in Church History, vol. 27 (Leiden: Brill, 2007), pp. 1–2.

2. This was also observed by Lowell M. Atkinson, "The Achievement of Arminius," *Religion in Life* 19/3 (1950): 423.

reformers and systematized Protestant theology—are neither known nor read for their novelty, humor, or witticisms.

Despite the neglect of Arminius, the dissemination of his thought throughout the European Continent, Great Britain, and North America, along with the appeal of his ideas in current Protestant evangelical spheres (whether rightly understood or misunderstood), continues to be the subject of both scholarly and popular discussion. The range of the impact of Arminianism has arguably equaled, if not surpassed, the influence of any other Protestant system of thought. But it is, in many ways, an anonymous impact, which leads to the second reason for the neglect of Arminius. Although there seem to be so many Arminians, nevertheless *no one owns Arminius*. First of all, not all who are Arminians know that they are, and, thus, most of these anonymous Arminians do not answer to that name. Few denominations, and few members within them, have a consciousness of their Arminian heritage. Moreover, those groups who do claim Arminius as a theological forebear have, for various reasons, failed to inspire serious study of the reformer. The Remonstrants, the theological descendants of Arminius in The Netherlands, are small and decreasing in number and have minimal influence outside their homeland. Their present theological tendencies owe more to later Remonstrants than to Arminius. In the Anglo-American world, Methodists and other Wesleyan churches acknowledge their affinities with Arminian theology. When they engage in historical work, however, these groups have typically devoted their energy and resources to John Wesley (1703–1791) and subsequent Methodists. Other Protestant evangelical groups, whose theology is essentially and tacitly Arminian, simply see themselves as going back to the Bible, though it is read through an Arminian lens. Still other Christians reject the label of Arminian and self-identify as Calvinist or Reformed, yet they are, unwittingly, actually Arminian in their beliefs. Otherwise informed Christians remain ignorant about Arminianism. Unlike the case for Luther, Calvin, and Wesley, there is no learned society or seminary that bears the name of Arminius, no study group or center devoted to researching his legacy, and no systematic attempt to publish and translate his works.

In 1963, while reviewing a collection of essays on Arminianism, Carl Bangs concluded his article with these words: "Arminianism still needs a critical confrontation with its founder."[3] In other words, as the varieties of

---

3. Carl Bangs, "Recent Studies in Arminianism," *Religion in Life* 32/3 (1963): 428. The book that Bangs reviewed was Gerald O. McCulloh, ed., *Man's Faith and Freedom: The Theological Influence of Jacobus Arminius* (New York: Abingdon Press, 1962).

Arminianisms have been acknowledged and explored, yet so many Christians still have a vague and perhaps conflicting sense of what it means to be Arminian, it is time to investigate Arminius himself and to improve on the situation just described. Much has been written since Bangs penned those words nearly half a century ago. Bangs's own biography of Arminius has been followed by numerous specialized studies of the Dutchman's theology. There has yet to appear, however, an overview of Arminius's thought, one that is conversant with the whole range of scholarly discussion on Arminius and at the same time is accessible to the general reader. This is the goal of the present book. If progress is made toward this lofty goal, then this book will help dispel some of the ignorance about Arminius, enabling a wider audience to grasp both the complex thoughts expressed in his writings, as well as the new insights provided by recent scholarship. It is our hope that this examination will help Arminians and non-Arminians alike come to grips with Arminius.

## II. Received Perspectives

There has never been complete scholarly consensus about Arminius's theology and its meaning. Over the last four centuries, a number of perspectives have shaped and continue to shape accounts of Arminius, each offering its own narrative. Moreover, the last three decades have witnessed a new perspective emerging in the study of Arminius that has accompanied a mild resurgence of scholarly interest in Arminius the theologian. Our purpose here is to describe various older narratives of Arminius the theologian that are driven by dogmatic concerns and decontextualized depictions. The older perspectives will then be contrasted with the new perspective, and the superiority of the latter will be demonstrated.[4] This survey will help set the context for the approach of this book.

## A. Old Perspectives on Arminius

Because Arminius has been a controversial figure from his own day until the present, he has had his fair share of both detractors and champions. The average church member today who knows something about "TULIP" or "Calvinism versus Arminianism" probably has formed some opinion about Arminius, whether or not she has ever actually read Arminius. Such preformed opinions are often based on a body of literature that places a theological bias above accurate understanding. Some of these narratives,

---

4. In most cases, illustrations of both perspectives will be provided in the footnotes.

whether oral or written, popular or scholarly, produce what we may call *dogmatic perspectives* of Arminius, inasmuch as they are dominated more by theological evaluation than historical investigation. Other narratives are dominated by perspectives that are not as overtly dogmatic as they are straightforwardly inaccurate, though they may also serve a dogmatic agenda. Each narrative, with its respective governing perspective, serves as a lens through which the evidence from or about Arminius is then read and interpreted. Although there are many possible variations within each perspective, we will classify the approaches of older scholarship into four main categories. The first two are openly dogmatic portrayals of Arminius aimed at theological evaluation, and the latter two are simply inaccurate, but dominant, portrayals of Arminius. As we develop each type briefly, it is important to remember that these perspectives have been a guiding force in older scholarship, and that they still function in various forms as models for discussions that continue to be influenced by the older scholarship. No attempt is made here to provide an exhaustive account of Arminius historiography, but only to offer notable illustrations of each perspective.[5]

### A.1. Arminius the Heretic

This perspective of Arminius is common among those who have judged Arminius's theology to be wrong or even heretical. Already in his own day, Arminius was accused of resurrecting the ancient "anthropocentric" heresy of Pelagianism.[6] Through his indirect influence, he has been known as the harbinger of Enlightenment rationalism and even anti-Trinitarianism.[7]

---

5. For supplementary accounts of the history of scholarship on Arminius, see Keith D. Stanglin, "Arminius and Arminianism: An Overview of Current Research," in *Arminius, Arminianism, and Europe: Jacobus Arminius (1559/60–1609)*, ed. Th. Marius van Leeuwen, Keith D. Stanglin, and Marijke Tolsma, Brill's Series in Church History, vol. 39 (Leiden: Brill, 2009), pp. 3–24; idem, *Arminius on Assurance*, pp. 1–9; Muller, *God, Creation, and Providence*, pp. 3–14; William Gene Witt, "Creation, Redemption and Grace in the Theology of Jacob Arminius" (Ph.D. diss., University of Notre Dame, 1993), pp. 187–210.

6. Pelagianism affirmed an optimistic anthropology which allowed human free will to play the decisive role in salvation. Augustinianism, in contrast to Pelagianism, emphasized the negative effects of the fall on human nature and the inability of human free will to play any role in salvation. For more on the charge of Pelagianism, see chapter 4 of this volume.

7. The association with anti-Trinitarianism is due in part to the Christological controversy with which he was involved in Leiden with his colleague, Lucas Trelcatius, Jr. On this controversy, see chapter 1 and chapter 2 in this volume, and Richard A. Muller, "The Christological Problem in the Thought of Jacobus Arminius," *Nederlands archief voor kerkgeschiedenis* 68 (1988): pp. 145–163. On putative links between Arminius and Socinianism, see Carl Bangs, "Arminius and Socinianism," in *Socinianism and Its Role in the Culture of the XVIth to XVIIth Centuries*, ed. Lech Szczucki (Warsaw: Polish Academy of Sciences, 1983), pp. 81–84.

This viewpoint is apt to lead to a negative evaluation not only of Arminius's theology, but also of his moral character and intellectual abilities. During his lifetime, for example, he was accused of being surreptitiously sympathetic to the Roman Church, its doctrine, and its pope, an accusation that impugned his integrity as well as his religious and political allegiances.[8] He has since been portrayed as disingenuous or outright deceptive in his dealings with opponents.[9] This portrayal is often based on a statement he made publicly that it is sometimes prudent not to say everything one believes about a particular theological topic.[10] This picture of a devious heretic becomes the lens through which everything about Arminius is read. Regardless of what Arminius might have done or said to counter such claims, it will be insufficient to mitigate the overriding anxiety that he was a Pelagian or Jesuit incognito.

## A.2. Arminius the Saint

The other common dogmatic perspective views Arminius as a saint, and this narrative is thus hagiographic or reverential in tone. Arminius becomes the champion of religious toleration and enlightened, latitudinarian thought in the church. This perspective is especially prominent among

---

8. This constitutes, in some sense, the most significant controversy that surrounded Arminius and is connected to the more well-known controversy of predestination. For example, Franciscus Gomarus, *Waerschouwinghe over de vermaninghe aen R. Donteclock* (Leiden: Jan Jansz. Orlers, 1609), pp. 35–51, repeatedly claims that "papism" is the source of Arminius's disputed teachings. A survey of related accusations may be found in Eric H. Cossee, "Arminius and Rome," in *Arminius, Arminianism, and Europe*, pp. 73–85.

9. For example, Abraham Kuyper, *De Leidsche professoren en de executeurs der Dordtsche nalatenschap* (Amsterdam: J. H. Kruyt, 1879), p. 36, calls Arminius a "looze vos" (crafty fox). See also Louis Praamsma, "The Background of the Arminian Controversy (1586–1618)," in *Crisis in the Reformed Churches: Essays in Commemoration of the Great Synod of Dort, 1618–1619*, ed. Peter Y. De Jong (Grand Rapids, MI: Reformed Fellowship, 1968), p. 28. Similar assessments are documented in Carl Bangs, "Arminius and the Reformation," *Church History* 30/2 (1961): 156, 170 n. 3.

10. Arminius makes this statement in writing in *Ep. ecc.* 78, p. 147. He was not attempting to deceive, for he said the same thing publicly at the oral disputation in question, as reported by Franciscus Gomarus, *Bedencken over de lyck-oratie van Meester P. Bertius*, in *Verclaringhe, over de vier hoofstucken, der leere, waer van hy met sijn weerde mede—Professore D. Iacobo Arminio, gheconfereert heeft, voor de E. E. moghende Heeren Staten van Hollandt ende Westvrieslandt: overghelevert den achtsten Septembris* (Leiden: Jan Jansz. Orlers, 1609), p. 44. For a discussion of this statement and its implications, see Keith D. Stanglin, *The Missing Public Disputations of Jacobus Arminius: Introduction, Text, and Notes*, Brill's Series in Church History, vol. 47 (Leiden: Brill, 2010), pp. 92–94; Jan Hendrik Maronier, *Jacobus Arminius: Een biografie* (Amsterdam: Y. Rogge, 1905), pp. 222, 354.

Dutch Remonstrants and others who cherish these values.[11] Arminius is also remembered fondly as a biblical theologian who used divine Scripture to refute his opponents and their human confessional standards. This perspective is prominent among American evangelicals who prize such use of the Bible over creedal formulae.[12] Regardless of which aspect is positively underscored, in either case, Arminius is made to be the theological hero.

Before proceeding to the next two perspectives, some remarks about these two dogmatic perspectives are in order. First of all, each perspective is as old as (church) history itself. Dogmatic perspectives are not peculiar to the historiography of Arminius. More important, the main problem with dogmatic perspectives that dominate the investigation is their tendency to skew the evidence, whether consciously or unconsciously. If one has already judged Arminius to be a "Pelagian"—and therefore wrong—it is difficult to look beyond the initial evaluation and allow it to be challenged on historical grounds. All the evidence appears one-sided; it is read or presented in such a way as to confirm the predetermined judgment.

The problem, therefore, is not with evaluation per se, but with giving it priority over understanding that is open to the true complexity of Arminius's thought. Anyone who reads theology with personal interest as a Christian knows that a judgment can and should be made. Evaluations of orthodoxy or heterodoxy, however, cannot precede the task of understanding the authors on their own terms. Accurate, descriptive understanding is requisite for, and leads to, fair evaluation. One may ultimately regard Arminius as either a saint to be emulated or a heretic to be avoided, but this judgment should not be made until the evidence from all sides

---

11. That there is discontinuity between Arminius and later Arminians, especially Dutch Remonstrants, is a truism acknowledged by all parties. Yet the later Remonstrant emphasis on toleration and Enlightenment is traced with appreciation back to Arminius, if not earlier antecedents. Alexander Schweizer, commenting on the connection between Sebastian Castellio and Arminianism, can be cited in this regard. Alexander Schweizer, "Sebastian Castellio als Bestreiter der calvinischen Prädestinationslehre, der bedeutendste Vorgänger des Arminius," *Theologische Jahrbücher* 10 (1851): 12: "er ist recht eigentlich Vorläufer der Arminianer, einer Partei also, die durch humanistische Bildung, nüchterne Exegese, Freisinnigkeit, Toleranz und Entwicklung des vernünftigen Denkens in Sachen der Religion." The same point is made in D. Tjalsma, *Leven en strijd van Jacobus Arminius* (Lochem: Uitgave de Tijdstrrom, 1960), pp. 86–88.

12. For example, Donald M. Lake, "Jacob Arminius' Contribution to a Theology of Grace," in *Grace Unlimited*, ed. Clark H. Pinnock (Minneapolis: Bethany Fellowship, 1975), p. 230, without explanation labels Arminius a "biblical theologian." Cf. H. Y. Groenewegen, *Jacobus Arminius op den driehonderd-jarigen gedenkdag van zijnen dood* (Leiden: Van Doesburgh, 1909), p. 27, who opposes biblical Christianity to speculative dogmatics.

has been taken into account. Too many narratives about Arminius have given their judgments without bothering to look at the facts.

Along with these two contradictory depictions, there are two alleged characteristics of Arminius that have become part of the mythos, both of which are common to—and employed in the service of—the two otherwise distinctive dogmatic perspectives.

### A.3. Arminius the Anti-scholastic

Arminius is frequently depicted as an anti-scholastic. Scholasticism (medieval or early modern) is properly a method of teaching for addressing disputed questions by means of appealing to biblical and patristic authorities, drawing philosophical distinctions, providing precise definitions and causal descriptions, and answering objections. In contrast to the burgeoning scholastic theology typical of late sixteenth- and early seventeenth-century Protestant thought, Arminius is represented as a theologian who resisted such developments.[13] Rather than getting caught up in the scholastic method—with its Aristotelian categories, philosophical distinctions, and alleged speculation—Arminius is said to have been devoted above all to the simple language and categories of Scripture. This putative feature cuts across both dogmatic perspectives. Some later detractors claimed that his reluctance to use the scholastic method is due to his incompetence in matters philosophical.[14] More often, though, his admirers have claimed that the biblical and practical emphases in his theology simply rendered the scholastic method unnecessary, if not irrelevant. Given this assumption, then, it is no surprise how seldom older scholarship has bothered to

---

13. In addition to those cited above who identify Arminius as a biblical theologian in contrast to a scholastic theologian, note Howard A. Slaatte, *The Arminian Arm of Theology: The Theologies of John Fletcher, First Methodist Theologian, and His Precursor, James Arminius* (Washington, DC: University Press of America, 1978), pp. 34, 63, who opposes Arminius's theology to the cold Greek (presumably scholastic) rationalism of Calvin. See also Mark A. Ellis, "Introduction," in Simon Episcopius, *The Arminian Confession of 1621*, trans. Mark A. Ellis (Eugene: Pickwick, 2005), p. vii, who describes the Remonstrant "rejection of Reformed scholasticism as a theological method," adding that "certainly Arminius viewed himself this way." Ellis (ibid., p. xi n. 13) also quotes with approbation the assessment of W. R. Bagnall, in *The Writings of James Arminius*, American edition, trans. James Nichols and W. R. Bagnall, 3 vols. (Grand Rapids, MI: Baker Book House, 1956), 1: v: "Yet it will be found, we think, on the perusal of his writings, that he [Arminius] was less scholastic in his style and more practical and scriptural both in his views and in his mode of presenting them than most of his contemporaries."

14. This was the claim of William Twisse, according to James Nichols, in *The Works of James Arminius*, London edition, trans. James Nichols and William Nichols, 3 vols. (1825, 1828, 1875; reprint, Grand Rapids, MI: Baker, 1986), 1: 251–252.

investigate Arminius's scholastic antecedents and his own use of the method.

The chief problem with viewing Arminius as anti-scholastic is that it is contrary to fact. First of all, no contemporary peer of Arminius ever accused him of philosophical incompetence or lack of scholastic proficiency. On the contrary, there are several instances of his contemporaries praising his intellectual prowess.[15] Second, and more important, it has been demonstrated that he used scholastic categories just as often as his "Reformed" colleagues on the theological faculty. In a scholastic context such as the university, Arminius employed as many fine distinctions of Aristotelian causality as did anyone else.[16]

The myth that Arminius was anti-scholastic is driven by two mistakes. One mistake is the erroneous assumption that the use of scholastic method determines theological content. Thus, if Arminius's opponents who taught absolute predestination defended it by means of scholastic definitions and categories, then it is assumed that Arminius, who taught conditional predestination, could not have relied on a similar scholastic method.[17] The truth is that, although scholastic method can influence the theological content and can conceivably narrow the options, the method itself does not necessarily determine the theological outcome. Arminius articulated his alternative version of predestination with a thoroughly scholastic method comparable to that of his colleagues.

---

15. While a student in Leiden, Arminius was publicly praised by Leiden professor Lambert Daneau, and as he concluded his studies in Basel, he was offered the title of "doctor," which he respectfully declined due to his youth. See Petrus Bertius, *De vita et obitu reverendi et clarissimi viri D. Iacobi Arminii oratio. Dicta post tristes illius exsequias XXII. Octob. Anno M.D.C.IX.*, in *Opera theologica* (Leiden: Godefridus Basson, 1629), fols. 002ᵛ–003ʳ; *Works* 1: 21, 24. See also the glowing evaluation of Arminius's aptitude in philosophy and theology given by Matthias Martinius, *Ep. ecc.* 133, p. 238; *Works* 1: liii. Similar contemporary testimonies were given about Arminius by luminaries such as Theodore Beza and Josephus Scaliger. Other testimonies to Arminius's erudition can be found throughout Bertius's funeral oration, and James Nichols has collected many in *Works* 1: xxxvii–lxiv. See also Stanglin, *Arminius on Assurance*, pp. 30, 64.

16. For specific claims and statistical analysis, see Stanglin, *Arminius on Assurance*, pp. 63–67, 262–265. Cf. Muller, *God, Creation, and Providence*; Evert Dekker, *Rijker dan Midas: Vrijheid, genade en predestinatie in de theologie van Jacobus Arminius, 1559–1609* (Zoetermeer, The Netherlands: Boekencentrum, 1993); idem, "Was Arminius a Molinist?" *Sixteenth Century Journal* 27/2 (1996): 337–352.

17. This assumption is made explicit in G. J. Hoenderdaal, "The Life and Struggle of Arminius in the Dutch Republic," in *Man's Faith and Freedom*, p. 23: "Supralapsarian predestination guards very well the idea of the absolute sovereignty of God, even though it is an outcome of Scholastic thinking. Arminius' opposition to it took him into the anti-Scholastic world which in turn led to the modern philosophy of the West and all the dangers of rationalism."

A second reason that Arminius is mistaken for an anti-scholastic is the confusion of popular with academic genre. The documents of Arminius that are read most often are not his academic, scholastic materials but the more popular-level works directed to laity, especially his *Declaration of Sentiments, Letter to Hippolytus à Collibus*, and *Apology against Thirty-one Articles*. When these certain writings are compared to the more overtly scholastic and academic works of a Reformed theologian such as François Turretin, Arminius indeed comes away looking less scholastic. This mistake, then, has to do with the selection of sources and, in this case, the neglect of Arminius's fully scholastic and academic disputations.

### A.4. Arminius the Anti-predestinarian

This perspective views Arminius basically as a Reformed, or "Calvinist," theologian who dissented on one chief point: predestination. In its most careless form, this account says that Arminius simply rejected predestination.[18] Those interpreters who strive for some degree of accuracy will clarify that he rejected the doctrine of absolute, or unconditional, predestination but retained his own brand of conditional predestination. Once this single contribution of Arminius has been described, there is not much left to say about him as a theologian.[19] According to his detractors who subscribe to this narrative, his doctrine of predestination is sufficient by itself to disqualify him from the Reformed camp. For some admirers, Arminius is Reformed in every other way and should not be disqualified from the group for this one doctrine.[20] In either case, Arminius is viewed

---

18. E.g., G. C. Berkouwer, *Faith and Justification*, trans. Lewis B. Smedes, Studies in Dogmatics (Grand Rapids, MI: Eerdmans, 1954), p. 161, classifies "Arminianism" among those systems that "have denied election."

19. According to Peter White, *Predestination, Policy, and Polemic: Conflict and Consensus in the English Church from the Reformation to the Civil War* (Cambridge: Cambridge University Press, 1992), p. 13, "Arminianism was nothing if not a doctrine of predestination." Similarly, see F. Stuart Clarke, "Arminius's Understanding of Calvin," *Evangelical Quarterly* 54 (January–March 1982): 30: "In fact, Arminius himself was obsessed with the doctrine of predestination, more so than Calvin."

20. "Calvinist" and "Reformed" are slippery terms. As with most scholars, we understand "Calvinist" to be a narrower term than "Reformed," and a label that is inaccurate in the sense that most Reformed theologians were not self-conscious of practicing a slavish devotion to Calvin's theology. "Reformed" is a more proper label for the broader tradition of which Calvin was a part. Arminius's relationship to the Reformed tradition will be considered briefly in the conclusion of this volume. For the sake of ease, throughout this book we juxtapose Arminius's thought to the "Reformed," by which we mean the mainstream theology among his opponents.

as an anti-Calvinist on this one point, with the undemonstrated assumption that the remainder of his theology is amenable to that of Calvin.[21]

This view underestimates the breadth of Arminius's theology taken as a whole, as well as the extent to which one difference affects Arminius's total system. Arminius cannot be understood simply by means of a reductionistic "central dogma" approach, as if his opposition to absolute predestination equals the sum of his thought. Such an approach makes him to be a controversialist only, and it unduly ignores his doctrines of God, creation, providence, assurance, and the church, all of which are distinct from the typical Reformed options of his time.

As with other inaccuracies, this narrative of the anti-predestinarian Arminius is sustained by the narrow use of primary sources by modern theologians who tend to look only at the controversial materials. Because of the times in which he lived and his context in Amsterdam and Leiden, Arminius indeed spent much of his energy writing apologetic and polemical material to vindicate his contested beliefs about predestination. These documents are the ones that tend to be read first, and they function as a fine introduction to Arminius's thought. By no means, though, should one stop here. In the absence of any full-orbed system of theology, Arminius's public and private disputations provide the best window into the full breadth of his theology. These very disputations, however, are often neglected.

Such is a brief sketch of the dominant perspectives that have shaped opinions and literature about Arminius. Certainly these are not the only perspectives, and those depictions that are not mutually exclusive with one another can be and are mingled together. Most of the older and some of the more recent work on Arminius bears the marks of these narratives. Some authors are guilty of flagrant caricature and grossly one-sided narratives, while others perpetuate the myths more subtly or unwittingly, paying lip service to the contrary evidence without allowing it to inform or balance the one-sided perspective. It is not that there is no grain of truth to each portrayal; a proponent of a given perspective can produce a passage or demonstrate a characteristic that seems to fit, thereby reinforcing the misleading narrative. After all, Arminius did engage with, and draw upon, Roman

---

21. G. J. Hoenderdaal approaches this view in his constant appeal to the similarities between Arminius and Calvin. See G. J. Hoenderdaal, "De theologische betekenis van Arminius," *Nederlands theologisch tijdschrift* 15 (1960): 90–98. Hoenderdaal implies that Arminius and Calvin would have enjoyed cordial relations had Arminius lived fifty years earlier (96). On this point, see also G. J. Hoenderdaal, "Arminius en Episcopius," *Nederlands archief voor kerkgeschiedenis* 60 (1980): 213.

Catholic (especially Jesuit) philosophical theology. He did promote unity among Christians and an end to dissension. He did want to subject the Reformed confession and catechism to Scripture and revise them if necessary. He did spend much effort opposing unconditional predestination. But each picture offered by these narratives is insufficient by itself to do justice to the full range of Arminius's contributions as a theologian.[22]

## B. New Perspective on Arminius

Over the last three decades, the field of historical theology has seen a new perspective on Arminius emerge. Its precursor in Arminius studies was the biography written by Carl Bangs, who situated Arminius within The Netherlands at the dawn of the Golden Age (seventeenth century) and called for the study of Arminius "not as a hero, not as a heretic, and not as a forerunner."[23] But the explicit call for a new perspective on Arminius's theology was pioneered and brought to fuller realization especially by the historical theologian Richard A. Muller. Though a shift has certainly taken place, this new perspective has remained largely undefined in Arminius studies, and to a certain extent has gone unnoticed outside the work of early modern historians.[24] The following characteristics of this new perspective, anticipated by the critiques of the older perspectives submitted above, are offered here in an attempt to define the spirit of this recent scholarship. Vis-à-vis those older perspectives, we may mention three features of this new perspective as correctives to the older narratives.

### B.1. Objective

In the venerable spirit of Gottfried Arnold, who coined the phrase "impartial church history" in the late seventeenth century, and in the more recent spirit of Heiko A. Oberman's historiography,[25] this new perspective on

---

22. Richard A. Muller, *The Unaccommodated Calvin: Studies in the Foundation of a Theological Tradition*, Oxford Studies in Historical Theology (New York: Oxford University Press, 2000), pp. 3–14, points out similar problems as these in Calvin scholarship.

23. Carl O. Bangs, *Arminius: A Study in the Dutch Reformation*, 2nd ed. (Grand Rapids, MI: Zondervan, 1985), p. 19.

24. In many ways, this new perspective parallels and is influenced by a similar shift in the broader field of historical study of early modern theology over the last half-century or so.

25. Hans J. Hillerbrand, "Was There a Reformation in the Sixteenth Century?" *Church History* 72/3 (2003): 527, goes on to note that Arnold was indeed partial to the traditional losers, making them the new winners. On Oberman, who was more successful in this regard than Arnold, see ibid., 532.

Arminius eschews overtly dogmatic agendas. The study of Arminius should not be theologically driven but historically driven. The historical perspective need not preclude any dogmatic judgment about the man and his teaching, but such values must come subsequent to the historical investigation without tainting the full scope of the historical record. Unmitigated objectivity, or neutrality, is surely not possible, and perhaps not desirable, in historiography.[26] But the goal is fairness—to allow the historical Arminius to speak for himself before the historians and theologians drown him out.

### B.2. Contextual

Second, the new perspective seeks to contextualize Arminius. In addition to recognizing the complex socio-political, pastoral, and academic settings of Arminius, part of this contextualization means fully acknowledging his scholastic context. Arminius was indeed a participant in and contributor to the early scholastic movement in Protestant theology.[27] The use of scholastic method as a vehicle for systematizing theological content was emerging among Protestant thinkers, simultaneously with the process of confessionalization and codification. This new era of Protestant scholasticism was part of the transition that began in the 1560s with the deaths of prominent Protestant theologians (for example, Philip Melanchthon [1497–1560], Peter Martyr Vermigli [1499–1562], Wolfgang Musculus [1497–1563], and Calvin), the final gatherings of the Council of Trent (1545–1563), and the proliferation of new Protestant universities. Late sixteenth-century Protestant theology, if it would survive the Catholic Counter-Reformation, demanded an academically respectable method for articulating its positive content and the differences with Rome and among fellow Protestants. Older perspectives that tended to remove Arminius from this development and to see him only as a "prescholastic" Dutch Protestant also missed some of the influences on which he built his theology. The new perspective seeks not only his native Dutch influences,

---

26. See Carl R. Trueman, *Histories and Fallacies: Problems Faced in the Writing of History* (Wheaton, IL: Crossway, 2010), pp. 27–28, 62–68, who distinguishes between objectivity and neutrality, noting that the former is the historian's goal, but the latter is impossible.

27. On Arminius's use of scholastic method, see Richard A. Muller, "Arminius and the Scholastic Tradition," *Calvin Theological Journal* 24/2 (1989): 263–277; idem, *God, Creation, and Providence*, pp. 31–51, 269–281, passim; Stanglin, *Arminius on Assurance*, pp. 58–69.

but also examines his reliance on medieval scholastics and contemporary Jesuit philosophers.[28]

Another example of historical contextualization would be the attention given to the academic setting in which Arminius found himself. From the beginning there was tension, an ambience of strife mixed with moments of collegiality. His appointment as professor of theology at Leiden University was initially opposed by the regent of the Theological College, Johannes Kuchlinus (1546–1606), and the other member of the theological faculty, Franciscus Gomarus (1563–1641). Although they conceded and seemed convinced that they could work with Arminius, it took less than a year for Gomarus—and later, Kuchlinus and the other faculty member, Lucas Trelcatius, Jr.—to voice their opposition in various ways. Their differences were not confined to predestination, but it is significant that all three of Arminius's colleagues held to a supralapsarian doctrine of absolute predestination.[29] Knowing what Arminius faced every day when he came to work helps to illumine his passionate rejection of those beliefs. To whatever degree Arminius's doctrine may have been a reaction to any person(s), it was not as much to his former teacher, Theodore Beza (1519–1605),[30] as it was to the more proximate and quotidian opposition that he faced in

---

28. With respect to contextualization, Bangs contributed most directly to a better understanding of the social and cultural milieu of Arminius. Other works, though not directly focused on Arminius, nevertheless help set the socio-political context. Worthy of special mention are A. T. van Deursen, *Bavianen en slijtgeuzen: Kerk en kerkvolk ten tijde van Maurits en Olde[n]barnevelt* (Assen: Van Gorcum, 1974); Christine Kooi, *Liberty and Religion: Church and State in Leiden's Reformation, 1572–1620*, Studies in Medieval and Reformation Thought, vol. 82 (Leiden: Brill, 2000). The most comprehensive overview of the social context is Jonathan Israel, *The Dutch Republic: Its Rise, Greatness, and Fall, 1477–1806* (Oxford: Clarendon Press, 1995). As to Arminius's scholastic background, Muller and Dekker have contributed most to this new understanding. Stanglin has shown how his church ministry and university teaching contexts contributed to his doctrine.

29. Supralapsarianism was regarded by Arminius as the most extreme doctrine of predestination. Infralapsarianism was less extreme, but still problematic. For a fuller discussion of supra- and infralapsarianism, see chapter 3 and the Appendix p. 140.

30. Cf. the imaginative description in Nathan Bangs, *The Life of James Arminius, D. D., Compiled from His Life and Writings, as Published by Mr. James Nichols* (New York: Harper and Brothers, 1843), p. 38: "Arminius parted from the supralapsarian doctrines, which he had imbibed in his very boyhood, and which were afterward confirmed and fixed in him by the authority and persuasive eloquence of the venerable Beza, who had magnified them into such importance, as to make the recognition of them, and of all their eventful consequences, a *sine qua non* to salvation." Cf. also the more succinct—though no less dubious—claim found in White, *Predestination*, p. 13: "Arminianism was conceived as a direct response to Beza's doctrine."

Leiden.[31] Arminius reasoned that if supralapsarianism could be embraced by his colleagues who subscribed to the Reformed confessions, whose texts incline to an infralapsarian point of view, then his own version of infralapsarian, conditional predestination ought to be considered acceptable as well.

### B.3. Comprehensive

The new perspective on Arminius seeks to take into account, as much as possible, all his relevant works and the entire scope of his theology. The most popular work of Arminius, *Declaration of Sentiments*, which is a good place to begin, is not a constructive account of his whole theology. Most of its text is devoted to the latest ecclesiastical matters of synods and conferences, as well as the focused refutation of what became known as supralapsarianism. In addition to the significant apologetic and more overtly occasional material, such as *Declaration of Sentiments*, the new perspective gives greater attention to the full corpus of public and private disputations. Although they resemble outlines more than long expositions, these disputation exercises, authored by Arminius himself, are the best substitute in the absence of a systematic theology. The disputations reveal his opinion on matters that, although not always the subject of outright controversy, sometimes illumine other controversial doctrines. They help to fill in the gaps in our access to his thought, revealing a more complete theology than has often been acknowledged.[32]

After surveying these three characteristics of the new perspective, there are two points worth noting. First, perhaps no single work can perfectly balance and fulfill these three desiderata. Even so, they remain legitimate goals for anyone wanting to make a scholarly contribution to this field. A second and related point is that there exists a continuum between older perspectives and the new perspective. In the time of transition to a new perspective, it is to be expected that older models will continue to wield their influence on scholarly contributions. Such works inhabit the vast gray area between black and white—that is, old and new—and may defy

---

31. See Stanglin, *Arminius on Assurance*, pp. 32–34, 92.

32. See Stanglin, *Missing Disputations*, pp. 31–41.

easy categorization.[33] If the three features of the new perspective are indeed methodologically superior to the older perspectives, then all contributions should be measured according to these criteria. Of course, few historians would object to any of these three goals. What distinguishes the new perspective is its renewed, deliberate attempt to prioritize these goals. To the degree that any historical analysis strives for and attains these goals, even if imperfectly, scholars should welcome these contributions as steps toward a common end of right understanding.

So far, the new perspective tends to find in Arminius a theologian who was not simply a Calvinist or Reformed theologian who changed one doctrine. Though Arminius's theology is born of Reformed theology and resembles it enough that he remained within the Dutch Reformed Church during his lifetime, the new perspective has shown that his theology, in more ways than one, follows a different trajectory from that of his Reformed opponents. These paths run parallel much of the way, but they diverge in more places than older scholarship generally admitted, again, due to a narrowly conceived "central dogma" approach to both Arminius and Reformed orthodoxy.

The new perspective has already contributed a great deal to correcting popular misconceptions. The final word, however, has not been spoken. Since the goals of greater contextualization and comprehensiveness are almost never exhaustively achieved, and to the degree that this perspective is still "new," much remains to be done in Arminius studies. In addition to working more closely with the primary texts that are now widely available, more attention should be concentrated on Arminius's letters and

---

33. Take, for instance, a study that employs the largely undefined notion of "Christocentric" and then proceeds to evaluate Arminius's theology as immature and weak when it does not meet this sole criterion and mature and strong when it does. See F. Stuart Clarke, *The Ground of Election: Jacobus Arminius' Doctrine of the Work and Person of Christ*, Studies in Christian History and Thought (Waynesboro, GA: Paternoster, 2006), pp. 38–39, passim. On the ambiguity of such a method, see Richard A. Muller, "A Note on 'Christocentrism' and the Imprudent Use of Such Terminology," *Westminster Theological Journal* 68 (2006): 253–260. Another study tends to neglect Arminius's primary contexts and proposes an "all-determining leading motive" that, in the end, fails to account for his whole theology. See William A. den Boer, *God's Twofold Love: The Theology of Jacob Arminius (1559–1609)*, trans. Albert Gootjes, Reformed Historical Theology, vol. 14 (Göttingen: Vandenhoeck & Ruprecht, 2010), p. 279, passim. See also a detailed review of the original Dutch version in Keith D. Stanglin, "Review of William den Boer, *Duplex Dei Amor: Contextuele karakteristiek van de theologie van Jacobus Arminius (1559–1609)* (Apeldoorn: Instituut voor Reformatieonderzoek, 2008)," *Church History and Religious Culture* 90/2–3 (2010): 420–425; and idem, "Methodological Musings on Historiography (A Rejoinder)," *Church History and Religious Culture* 92 (2012): 121–129.

lectures available only in manuscript. These documents will lend greater insight into biographical, pastoral, and academic matters, as well as his relationship to ecclesiastical and political controversies.

In sum, the new perspective presents a more complex and nuanced narrative of Arminius than is commonly found in the older scholarship. No longer can he be casually invoked as a heretic or a hero without knowledge of what he actually believed and wrote. No longer can a scholar look at one document or doctrine of Arminius and presume an adequate comprehension. No longer can the full range of his disputations be ignored. No longer can Arminius be regarded merely as a controversialist, or anti-Calvinist, with only one important thing to say. Rather, Arminius must be interpreted in light of the dynamic mélange of factors, experiences, and influences that shaped him. The historical Arminius was raised by a single mother; his father died before he could remember. He was a personal victim of the Spanish atrocities in the early years of the Dutch Revolt: his immediate and much of his extended family was massacred during his adolescence. He was a student of J. J. Grynaeus and Theodore Beza, he was a Dutch Reformed pastor in Amsterdam, and later a professor at the oldest and premier university of the northern Netherlands. He was a husband and the father of a dozen children, nine who survived him, three who did not. He was skilled in mathematics, logic, and the scholastic method, an admirer of both Aristotle and Ramus. He was a voracious reader of Erasmus, Melanchthon, Bullinger, and Calvin. As a constructive theologian, he was the recipient of a long and complex tradition—the patristic tradition that included, among many others, Basil the Great, John Chrysostom, Ambrosiaster, and Augustine; the Catholic scholastic tradition that included Bernard, Aquinas, Duns Scotus, and Molina; the Protestant tradition that included Bucer, Musculus, Hemmingsen, and Junius; and the Dutch tradition that included Veluanus, Coolhaes, Herberts, and Wiggertszoon. He was irenic in his call for Christian unity and his toleration of other Christians besides the Reformed, but he was also an ardent and sincere defender of his faith, especially the Protestant version against the Roman Catholic. He was biblical, humanistic, and scholastic. From at least 1604, he intermittently suffered the effects of tuberculosis, to which he finally succumbed five years later. He was under pressure from the States of Holland; he was under the scrutiny of his ecclesiastical and faculty colleagues, but he was strengthened by the support of friends and students. He was not afraid to speak his mind, though he rarely did so without political circumspection.

There is nothing particularly unusual about this multifaceted portrait of Arminius. He was highly regarded for his qualities and abilities, but the presuppositions, afflictions, and eclecticism that made up his life and thought were typical in the early modern period. He was a child of his age. Neither should there be anything extraordinary about the new perspective on Arminius. It is merely a description of what historians ought to be doing and what theologians appealing to history ought to be aware of. What is unfortunate, but sadly not unusual, is how often theologians have pigeonholed Arminius, focusing on one aspect to the neglect of many others. Each of the characteristics mentioned above must be taken into account to gain the fuller understanding sought by the new perspective.

Finally, it is worth reiterating the place of evaluation in the new perspective. Having rejected so-called dogmatic perspectives, it could appear that the new perspective is somehow incompatible with theological evaluation. Such exclusion, however, is not the intention. The new perspective underscores the historical task of description; it does not prevent the historian or theologian from then proceeding to evaluation and even prescriptive tasks. Whatever positive evaluation and prescription may be offered in the theological portrait that follows, the intention is to base it all in an accurate portrayal of Arminius. Simply put, the "Arminius of faith" must take seriously the "Harmenszoon of history."

## III. Our Approach

In order to clarify this book's purpose, it may be easier to begin by eliminating a couple of possible expectations. First of all, this book is not a defense of Arminian theology. The primary purpose is to provide an account of Arminius's theology; therefore the flow of argument in the chosen topics will stick fairly closely to his own mode of presentation. Although we think that there is much to be commended in Arminius's theology—a fact we do not seek to hide—there will be no long discourses on debated biblical passages or current developments in systematic and philosophical theology in order to answer every possible objection.[34]

---

34. While we readily admit that we are generally more sympathetic to Arminius's theology than to that of his critics, we do not endorse either all of his views or all of his arguments. At any rate, our purpose here is not the criticism, modification, and defense of Arminius's theology. Our purpose is to explicate it as clearly as possible.

This book is not a meticulous treatment of Arminius's life or theology. The burden of this book is not to offer an exhaustive or definitive system of Arminius's thought or to provide an account of everything that he believed and discussed in his writings. Some topics of his theology, particularly the ones that have not been regarded as central to his legacy, will not be covered here. In omitting protracted analyses of his prolegomena, Christology, ecclesiology, and eschatology, we do not mean to leave the impression, as so much of older scholarship has, that Arminius was a one-dimensional thinker who was interested only in predestination. But in our attempt to produce an introductory overview of his theology, we must restrict ourselves to the topics that Arminius spent most of his time handling, to the themes that recent scholarship has found to be central, and to a finite number of pages. Such is the nature of this beast.

Along these same lines, neither will there be any attempt to present a thorough description of Arminius's remote and proximate influences or a comparative analysis with his contemporaries on every doctrine. Where these have been done, and whenever we find these influences and comparisons to be most relevant, we will note them.

Instead, this book is meant to provide an overview of Arminius's theology that is methodologically rigorous and informed by the latest scholarship and, at the same time, accessible to the interested theologian, student, or layperson who is not a specialist in historical theology. The book will therefore examine and summarize the main contours of Arminius's theology in an attempt to show what "makes him tick." Perhaps it can best be described as a constructive synthesis of the somewhat disparate condition of current Arminius studies. Presently, there is a chasm between, on the one hand, the technical, scholarly discussions of Arminius and, on the other, the popular-level appeals to his thought. The book will seek to bridge the scholarly and general discussions by providing an account that is helpful to the seasoned scholar as well as comprehensible and relevant to the beginning student, based on interaction with all the primary sources and latest secondary research. In this scholarly yet accessible format, we will describe key elements of Arminius's theology with careful attention to his own thought in its proper context; we will also explore the broader theological implications of his views. Just as this text is written with the non-specialist in mind, at the same time we will point interested readers to possibilities for further reading in the footnotes.

In some ways, the goal of this book may be described as a counterpart to Carl Bangs's classic biography, *Arminius: A Study in the Dutch Reformation*.

Instead of focusing on the life with a little attention to the thought of Arminius, we will focus attention on his theology, while including some necessary biographical details. As Bangs is the place to go for biography, this book is intended to be the place to go for an introduction to Arminius's theology, which will then point readers to the more technical and detailed studies that have been done, as well as inspire new examinations of neglected topics.

One of the goals of surveying Arminius's thought is to challenge some of the common misrepresentations of his theology. Of the many labels and caricatures (both appreciative and pejorative) attached to Arminianism, perhaps none is more prevalent than the charge that Arminius undermined the Reformed doctrine of grace, thus elevating autonomous human free will and introducing anthropocentrism into Protestantism. On the contrary, those who study Arminius or get a glimpse of his thought in this volume know that he was no enemy of grace.

Bangs notes that many "Wesleyan-Arminian" theologians have maintained that Arminius was in fact a "theologian of grace."[35] Although grace should not be taken as any sort of "central dogma" for Arminius, it is a recurring theme and very important to his theological and indeed pastoral concerns. Grace is, for Arminius, grounded in the being of God, and it is always expressed in a manner fully consistent with the divine nature. Humans have fallen into sin and have brought destruction upon themselves; thus grace is absolutely necessary for redemption. God's grace is extended to all, but it is not irresistible. The fact that some sinners reject it and finally perish, however, is due only to their stubborn persistence, and it cannot be traced back to divine intention or action. Arminius's doctrine of grace, which declares that God's sufficient grace is extended to all, is different but no less central and dynamic than that of his Reformed counterparts. Throughout his theological formulations, Arminius, as much as his contemporaries, was exercised to uphold the necessity (due to human finitude and especially human sin) and sufficiency of grace, and demonstrating this commitment of his is one of our primary tasks.

To these ends, chapter 1, "The Making of a Theologian," lays a biographical foundation for the book by providing a historical overview of Arminius as a student, pastor, and professor. This biographical sketch gives attention to the various experiences and realities that shaped his life,

---

35. Bangs, "Arminius and Reformed Theology," p. 28. Bangs's list includes H. C. Rogge, Richard Watson, W. B. Pope, John Miley, James Nichols, A. W. Harrison, and H. O. Wiley.

particularly the pastoral, exegetical, and scholastic contexts, and, of course, the major controversies. After a brief summary of the context and content of his writings, we provide a description of the most important influences on his theology. This preliminary description of the factors that shaped Arminius should help modern readers understand his theology, but it will also reveal some of the complexities involved in interpreting Arminius.

The topic of chapter 2 is God and creation. Like his fellow Protestants, Arminius's doctrine of God was based on biblical grounds and was informed by medieval scholastic developments. Arminius held to a "classical" doctrine of God's essence, attributes, and Trinitarian nature. Special attention is given in this chapter to divine simplicity, perfection, goodness, omniscience, and will. The next part of the chapter examines Arminius's doctrine of the Trinity, including the Christological controversy in which he was involved. Finally, his doctrine of creation is summarized, noting that God's love for creation and his desire for relationship with humanity provided Arminius with a different theological starting point from that of his opponents. Throughout this chapter, it will be shown that the main differences between the thought of Arminius and his Reformed contemporaries are based on his distinctive doctrine of God and creation.

Chapter 3, "Providence and Predestination," investigates the most defining controversy of Arminius's career. Far from rejecting God's providence and predestination, Arminius's description of the eternal decrees of God reflected his thoroughly Reformed context. He affirmed a meticulous divine providence, yet one that allows for human freedom and contingency. Focusing especially on the *Declaration of Sentiments*, the *Analysis of Romans 9*, and his responses to Junius, Perkins, and Gomarus, this chapter goes on to explain his opposition to the most extreme accounts of predestination in Reformed theology. Arminius's doctrine of predestination diverges from that of his opponents on the basis of his doctrine of God and creation and his use of middle knowledge. If reprobation is unconditional and sin occurs because of God's active decree, as his opponents argued, then God created people simply to destroy them, and he is the author of evil and sin. Even unconditional election, accompanied by irresistible grace, destroys the true intention of grace and a loving relationship with God. God's love, rightly understood, cannot coexist with unconditional predestination. Arminius's own account of the conditional nature of predestination is thoroughly theocentric.

Chapter 4, "Sin and Salvation," considers Arminius's teaching on some of the central doctrines of the Protestant Reformation. His views of original sin and fallen humanity are explored first. Arminius's doctrine of salvation was, in many ways, consistent with typical Protestant Reformed theology. His teaching on the grace of God was foundational to his theology. His views on God, predestination, and the nature of grace particularly affected his understanding of the role of faith and assurance in salvation, as well as the life of sanctification. The claim that grace is resistible means that God's gift of salvation is never irrevocable in this life; but the acknowledgment that God loves all people for salvation, and that he has given grace sufficient for redemption, means that there can be true assurance.

The conclusion is a summary of the trajectories and impact of the distinctive emphases of Arminius's thought. We summarize the subsequent history of Arminianism, review some of the most important features of Arminius's theology, and consider various aspects of his legacy for today.

*I*

# The Making of a Theologian

*In Holland there was a man: those who knew him could
not adequately esteem him; those who did not esteem him,
never adequately knew him.*

—PETRUS BERTIUS, 1609

BEFORE EXAMINING THE theology of Arminius in the following chapters, it is appropriate first to lay a biographical foundation. Since the purpose of this book is to provide an overview of his thought, only the barest account of his life will be given here. Yet familiarity with his life, writings, and influences is a prerequisite for understanding Arminius and the contexts of his ideas.

## *I. Life*

Jacob Harmenszoon (Arminius) was born around 1559 in the small town of Oudewater in South Holland.[1] His early life was spent in the midst of a tumultuous and difficult period that was perhaps a foreshadowing of things to come in his own life. Politically, The Netherlands would soon be involved in a bloody and costly revolution that would last for decades. On the religious front, Reformed theology was supplanting other brands of Protestantism as the dominant stream, a process that also would take decades, and one in which he was to play a leading role. The personal

---

1. The first synopsis of Arminius's life was the funeral oration composed by Petrus Bertius, Arminius's long-time friend and the controversial regent of the Theological (Staten) College at Leiden University. Bertius, *Oratio*, in *Opera*, fols. 001–0004; ET, *Works* 1: 13–47. On Bertius, see L. J. M. Bosch, "Petrus Bertius (1565–1629)" (Ph.D. diss., Katholieke Universiteit te Nijmegen, 1979). Over a century later, the next biography of Arminius, written by the Arminian (Remonstrant) minister Caspar Brandt, was published posthumously in 1724. Caspar Brandt, *Historia vitae Iacobi Arminii* (Amsterdam: Martinus Schagenius, 1724); ET, *The Life of James Arminius, D.D.*, trans. John Guthrie, with an intro. by T. O. Summers (Nashville: E. Stevenson and F. A. Owen, 1857).

trials for Arminius began before he could remember. His father, a weap-
onsmith, died either in Arminius's infancy or before he was born.[2] In
either case, Arminius never knew his father. The local priest, Theodore
Aemilius, took personal responsibility for young Jacob's education. With
the financial support of Aemilius, he moved to Utrecht and spent his
early teenage years studying there. As was typical of late medieval and
early modern students, Arminius would spend his teenage and early
adult years studying in several different schools and universities. Utrecht
was merely the first stop on his educational journey. When Aemilius
died, probably in early 1575, the scholar Rudolph Snellius (1546–1613)
from the University of Marburg met Arminius on a visit to Utrecht.
Having been impressed with the adolescent's potential, as well as his
financial need, Snellius took Arminius back with him and, as his bene-
factor, enrolled him at Marburg. Based on archival research, Bangs suggests that both of these benefactors, Aemilius and Snellius, were probably

---

The next major biography was written in Dutch by J. H. Maronier, *Arminius*. The first full-
scale biography of Arminius in English was that by Carl Bangs, *Arminius*, first published in
1971, which added significant details to the previous biographies by means of archival
research and attention to the Dutch social context. (Previous accounts in English are merely
derivative. E.g., the appendices in volume one of James Nichols's translation are mostly
dependent on C. Brandt. And Nathan Bangs, *Life of Arminius*, merely summarizes Nichols.
The biographical account given below is dependent on these four main biographies, but will
note any unique contributions to Arminius's story.)

Besides these four main biographies, other noteworthy accounts of Arminius's life and
works, some of which add accounts of the early Remonstrants, include Philip van Limborch,
*Historical Relation Concerning the Origin and Progress of the Controversies in the Belgic League,
upon Predestination and Its Connected Heads*, in L.W. P., "Arminian Controversy in the Low
Countries," *Methodist Review* 26 (1844): 425–460, 556–587; Gerard Brandt, *The History of the
Reformation and Other Ecclesiastical Transactions in and about the Low-Countries*, 4 vols. (London: T. Wood for Timothy Childe, 1720–1723), 2: 25–63; G. J. Hoenderdaal, "Jacob Arminius,"
in *Orthodoxie und Pietismus*, ed. Martin Greschat (Stuttgart: W. Kohlhammer, 1982), pp.
51–64; A. W. Harrison, *The Beginnings of Arminianism to the Synod of Dort* (London: University of London Press, 1926), pp. 16–130; Carl O. Bangs, "Introduction," in *Works* 1: vii–xxix;
Kooi, *Liberty and Religion*, pp. 132–161; Dekker, *Rijker dan Midas*, pp. 19–53; Stanglin, *Arminius
on Assurance*, pp. 19–70; and W. Stephen Gunter, *Arminius and His Declaration of Sentiments: An Annotated Translation with Introduction and Theological Commentary* (Waco: Baylor
University Press, 2012). For a Counter-Remonstrant account, see *Acta synodi nationalis, in
nomine Domini nostri Iesu Christi . . . Dordrechti habitae anno M.DC.XVIII. et M.DC.XIX*
(Dordrecht: Isaac Elzevir, 1620), fols. 001ʳ-00003ʳ; ET, *The Articles of the Synod of Dort, and
Its Rejection of Errors: With the History of Events which Made Way for That Synod*, trans.
Thomas Scott (Utica, NY: William Williams, 1831), pp. 7–77. For a Roman Catholic account,
see Salomon Theodotus, Ἑνωτικον *dissecti Belgii, in quo historica relatio originis et progressus
eorum dissidiorum continentur* (Ursel: Wendelinus Iunghen, 1618), pp. 1–93.

2. Bangs, *Arminius*, pp. 25–26, demonstrates that Arminius's father died before 1559, so
Arminius must have been born before the traditional date of his birth, 10 October 1560.

relatives of Arminius and thus had a special obligation to care for him as guardians.[3]

Not long after settling in Marburg, Arminius heard the news that the Spanish had invaded his hometown of Oudewater. He returned to the place of his birth, while the town was still under Spanish occupation, to find that his mother, siblings, and much of his extended family had perished in the massacre.[4] After grieving the loss of his family, the teenager traveled back (on foot) to Marburg to continue his studies. Having studied for several months in Marburg, Arminius decided to return to his homeland. Leiden University, the oldest university in the northern Netherlands, was established in 1575 as a reward for the city's courageous victory in the face of Spanish siege; it was also seen as the Protestant competitor to the older Roman Catholic university in Leuven.[5] On 23 October 1576, "Jacobus Hermannus," as he signed his name at that time, enrolled in the new university, the twelfth student to matriculate. He declared himself a student of liberal arts, not theology.[6] This program of study, however, allowed him to study theology, and by the end of his stay in Leiden he was studying under the Reformed theologian Lambert Daneau.

Arminius completed his time as a student in Leiden in 1581. He journeyed from there to the Academy in Geneva, where the following year he would begin his training under John Calvin's successor, Theodore Beza. Arminius's initial stay in Geneva was brief and was tainted by a minor controversy over his admiration for the method of Pierre de la Ramée (Ramus) (1515–1572), whose philosophy was influential on Snellius and at

---

3. Bangs, *Arminius*, pp. 384–386. For more on Snellius, see Dekker, *Rijker dan Midas*, pp. 259–260.

4. Bangs, *Arminius*, p. 42.

5. Albert Eekhof, *De theologische faculteit te Leiden in de 17de eeuw* (Utrecht: G. A. J. Ruys, 1921), pp. 10*–11*. The siege of Leiden in 1574 was, according to Israel, *Dutch Republic*, p. 181, "the costliest, hardest fought, and most decisive" siege of the war. On the founding of Leiden University, see Bangs, *Arminius*, pp. 45–49. See also Willem Otterspeer, *Groepsportret met Dame I. Het bolwerk van de vrijheid: De Leidse universiteit, 1575–1672* (Amsterdam: Bert Bakker, 2000), the first volume in a multi-volume series on the university's history; Henrike L. Clotz, *Hochschule für Holland: Die Universität Leiden im Spannungsfeld zwischen Provinz, Stadt und Kirche, 1575–1619* (Stuttgart: Steiner, 1998). Firsthand reports and archival transcripts are printed in P. C. Molhuysen, *Bronnen tot de geschiedenis der Leidsche Universiteit*, 7 vols. (The Hague: Martinus Nijhoff, 1913–1924).

6. W. du Rieu, ed., *Album studiosorum Academiae Lugduno Batavae MDLXXV–MDCCCLXXV, accedunt nomina curatorum et professorum* (The Hague: Martinus Nijhoff, 1875), col. 1.

Marburg.[7] There were no apparent negative repercussions concerning Arminius's alleged Ramism, but he left very soon for the University of Basel. By September 1582, Arminius was already defending disputations under Johann Jacob Grynaeus at Basel, and did so through 1584.[8] After studying in Basel for about two years, Arminius had returned to Geneva by October 1584 for a second and final stay. At the conclusion of his studies in Geneva in 1586, he took a trip to Italy, and was later accused by his enemies of fraternizing with the Jesuit Robert Bellarmine (1542–1621) and also kissing the pope's toe, rumors which had no basis in reality.[9] Besides a few disputations that he defended as a student, the only literary output from Arminius during this period of his life are poems that he composed in Latin.[10]

By 1587, coming highly recommended by Beza himself,[11] Arminius was back in his homeland to stay, and he passed the examinations for ministry in the Dutch Reformed Church. He was called and committed to ministry in Amsterdam, which was quickly becoming a booming commercial center,[12] and whose consistory (local church council) had been funding his education in Geneva. In 1588, he was ordained as a minister in the Old Church (*Oude Kerk*) in Amsterdam, embarking on a fifteen-year ministry there. In 1590, Arminius married Lijsbet Reael, and they started a family soon thereafter.

A story has circulated since the time of Bertius's funeral oration, and is sometimes still perpetuated, that Arminius was once a supralapsarian Calvinist when it came to his doctrine of predestination, and that he made a

---

7. As noted in Bangs, *Arminius*, p. 63, some strict Calvinists were just as "Ramist" as Arminius; the philosophical method, in this case, did not determine theological content. Contra F. Stuart Clarke, "Arminius's Use of Ramism in His Interpretation of Romans 7 and 9," in *Interpreting the Bible: Historical and Theological Studies in Honour of David F. Wright*, ed. Anthony N. S. Lane (Leicester: Apollos, 1997), pp. 131–146. Clarke suggests that the widespread influence of Ramist method exacerbated the controversies of the late sixteenth century, not to mention the playoff brackets in "modern sport," where there is severe competition and only one winner (pp. 136–137).

8. This differs from the chronology of Bangs. See Keith D. Stanglin and Richard A. Muller, "*Bibliographia Arminiana*: A Comprehensive, Annotated Bibliography of the Works of Arminius," in *Arminius, Arminianism, and Europe*, pp. 265–266 n. 8. Cf. Dekker, *Rijker dan Midas*, p. 24.

9. See Bangs, *Arminius*, pp. 78, 113.

10. These were published as *Quelques poésies de Jacques Arminius composées pendant son séjour en Suisse*, ed. H. de Vries de Heekelingen (The Hague: Martinus Nijhoff, 1925).

11. Beza's recommendation letter, written in 1583, is recorded in *Ep. ecc.* 12, pp. 26–27.

12. According to Israel, *Dutch Republic*, p. 328, Amsterdam's population doubled from 1570 to 1600, from about 30,000 to 60,000. On the emerging Dutch society following the most violent years of the early revolt, see ibid., pp. 328–360.

dramatic about-face early in his Amsterdam ministry. Bertius claims that Arminius was asked to refute the infralapsarian position of the ministers of the city of Delft, who in turn had refuted the conditional predestination of the humanist Dirck Coornhert. Arminius, so the story goes, was invited to write a treatise that would defend the supralapsarianism of his former teacher, Beza. Arminius never produced such a treatise because, as Bertius claims, Arminius's honest study of the doctrine led him to embrace the views that he was invited to refute. Bangs has questioned the validity of this story, pointing out that Arminius probably never held to the supralapsarianism of Beza.[13] Not only did Beza never require his students to agree with his precise predestinarian views, but Arminius never gives any hint that he had a change of heart. It is just as likely that Arminius, as an heir of the early Dutch Reformation, always held to a sort of conditional predestination.[14]

The more probable impetus of Arminius's deeper study of predestination came in the context of his church ministry. The controversy began during his Amsterdam years as he was preaching through the Epistle to the Romans, a series of sermons he had initiated soon after his ordination in 1588. When he came to Romans 7, a classic and controversial text describing from a first-person perspective the losing battle against sin, Arminius interpreted this text as a depiction of one not yet regenerate. The typical—albeit not uniform—Reformed interpretation was that the apostle Paul was actually describing himself, a man already regenerate, yet still struggling with sin. Petrus Plancius, another Reformed minister in Amsterdam, accused Arminius of Pelagianism on the grounds that only a Pelagian anthropology could acknowledge an unregenerate man who knows and desires to do the good. By 1592, Arminius was called before the consistory in Amsterdam. The following year, 1593, when he began preaching on Romans 9, he again appeared before the consistory to face his accusers. Arminius was acquitted on both occasions, and those specific debates eventually settled down.[15] Thereafter, he enjoyed an effective and uncontroversial ministry for the remainder of his tenure in Amsterdam. Nearly a decade after the controversies, at the end of his time in Amsterdam, he wrote in appreciation of the "emphatic love and fondness of the

---

13. Bangs, "Arminius and Reformed Theology," pp. 1–12; idem, *Arminius*, pp. 138–141.

14. On the general character of the early Dutch Reformation, including its remarkable diversity, see Israel, *Dutch Republic*, pp. 74–105, 367–372.

15. For fuller accounts of these controversies, see C. Brandt, *Life*, pp. 67–71, 86–98; Nichols, *Works* 1: 100–118; Bangs, *Arminius*, pp. 142–150.

church towards me," a sentiment corroborated by the testimonies of the church and classis (regional governing body of clergy and elders).[16] After those early controversies, however, some persistent opponents would peg him as a provocateur and a heterodox teacher.

The plague came to the Low Countries in 1601, and by 1602 it had taken two of the three theological faculty members in Leiden University's Staten College. The purpose of the Staten, or Theological, College, established at the university in 1592, was the training of ministers within the Reformed Church. It consisted of a regent, a sub-regent, and three members of the theology faculty.[17] With the passing of Lucas Trelcatius, Sr., and Franciscus Junius (1545–1602),[18] only Franciscus Gomarus remained as teaching faculty.[19] Although Arminius never sought the position, and he confessed his insufficiency for the task, the university nevertheless sought him to fill one of the vacant spots. The curators of the university, the magistrates, and the students were overwhelmingly in favor of appointing Arminius; there was some resistance to his nomination, however, particularly from vocal church ministers. The most important opposition came from Arminius's former Amsterdam colleague and the present regent of the Staten College, Johannes Kuchlinus (his uncle by marriage),[20] and from Gomarus. Arminius's strongest advocate in this particular controversy, as in all others, was his best friend, Johannes Uytenbogaert (1557–1644), who was a minister in The Hague and chaplain to Maurits (Prince

---

16. Cf. *Ep. ecc.* 56 (1 October 1602), p. 107; *Works* 1: 180; with Bertius, *Oratio*, in *Opera*, fols. 004ʳ–0001ʳ; *Works* 1: 34–36.

17. For more on the Staten College, see Stanglin, *Arminius on Assurance*, pp. 20–23; Otterspeer, *Bolwerk*, pp. 151–163, 175–176; and Clotz, *Hochschule für Holland*, pp. 67–76.

18. On Trelcatius, Sr., and Junius, see G. Brandt, *History*, 2: 18–21. See also B. A. Venemans, "Junius, Franciscus (François du Jon)," in *Biografisch lexicon voor de geschiedenis van het nederlandse protestantisme*, ed. D. Nauta, et al., 6 vols (Kampen: Kok, 1978–2006), 2: 275–278; Tobias Sarx, *Franciscus Junius d.Ä (1545–1602): Ein reformierter Theologe im Spannungsfeld zwischen späthumanistischer Irenik und reformierter Konfessionalisierung*, Reformed Historical Theology, vol. 3 (Göttingen: Vandenhoeck & Ruprecht, 2007).

19. On Gomarus, see Gerrit Pieter van Itterzon, "Gomarus, Franciscus," in *Biografisch lexicon voor de geschiedenis van het nederlandse protestantisme*, 2: 220–225; *Franciscus Gomarus* (The Hague: Martinus Nijhoff, 1929).

20. On Kuchlinus, see A. J. Lamping, "Kuchlinus (Cuchlinus), Johannes," in *Biografisch lexicon voor de geschiedenis van het nederlandse protestantisme*, 5: 317–319; Keith D. Stanglin, "Johannes Kuchlinus, the 'Faithful Teacher': His Role in the Arminian Controversy and His Impact as a Theological Interpreter and Educator," *Church History and Religious Culture* 87/3 (2007): 305–326.

of Orange and military commander).[21] Arminius and Uytenbogaert had been friends since their student days in Geneva, and perhaps as far back as their teenage years in Utrecht. His support of Arminius played a key role in his call to Leiden. Most importantly, though, Arminius thrived in the interviews, satisfying all questions, and was even examined by Gomarus himself, who ended up supporting his call. Following the custom of universities to bestow the title of doctor on those who excelled in their discipline (especially in theology, which was at that time considered the chief of the academic disciplines),[22] Leiden University conferred the doctoral degree on Arminius, by the approval of his examiner Gomarus, after a public disputation on the nature of God on 10 July 1603. By September 1603, 27 years after matriculating as a student there, he began his duties as a full professor (*ordinarius*) at Leiden alongside Gomarus and the newly appointed Lucas Trelcatius, Jr.[23]

Arminius's time at Leiden University would prove to be even more controversial than his ministry in Amsterdam, and it would be a period of gradually declining health. Throughout their time together, both of Arminius's faculty colleagues, along with the regent Kuchlinus, resisted him in various ways. For example, Trelcatius was known to complain about Arminius, and Kuchlinus attempted to schedule his own lectures at the same hour as Arminius's in order to keep his students away from the latter's influence.[24] But Gomarus, described by G. P. van Itterzon as having a "fiery temperament," was the most contentious.[25] In 1604 he was involved in the first true outbreak of controversy during Arminius's tenure as a professor. In February, as part of the normal curriculum and cycle of theological topics, Arminius wrote and a student defended a disputation on predestination. Gomarus was scandalized by Arminius's theses, so he responded in October with an ad hoc disputation of his own on the same topic. This disputation was outside the normal cycle of disputations, and its

---

21. On Uytenbogaert, see *Works* 1: 194–202; H. C. Rogge, *Johannes Wtenbogaert en zijn tijd*, 3 vols. (Amsterdam: Y. Rogge, 1874–1876); Bangs, *Arminius*, passim. As Nichols observes, before translating a poem about Uytenbogaert, his is "a name highly unpoetical" (*Works* 1: 251).

22. C. Brandt, *Life*, p. 182.

23. On the curriculum in the Staten College, see Otterspeer, *Bolwerk*, pp. 162–163.

24. G. Brandt, *History*, 2: 33, 46. Otterspeer, *Bolwerk*, p. 159: "Cuchlinus verzette zich met hand en tand tegen de invloed van Arminius."

25. Van Itterzon, *Gomarus*, pp. 376–379.

oral presentation by Gomarus included thinly veiled attacks on Arminius.[26] As news of unrest spread to the churches, the theological faculty and their regent Kuchlinus, attempting to put the churches at ease, all signed a statement declaring that "they did not know of any difference among the professors of the Faculty of Theology, so far as related to fundamental points of doctrine."[27] This statement is indicative of the relationships within the faculty: there were times of conflict and even confrontation, mixed with moments of collegiality.[28]

From 1605 to 1606 there arose a Christological dispute that took place indirectly between Arminius and Trelcatius, Jr. It was sparked by a student who heard competing opinions from the two professors. Trelcatius's student learned from his teacher that the Son of God may be properly described as αὐτόθεος (literally, "God [from] himself"). This same student confronted Arminius during a lecture when he heard Arminius deny the Son this attribute. Arminius appealed not only to the ancient church, but also to Gomarus, when he affirmed that the Son's deity is communicated to him by the Father, who alone has his deity from himself. At the same time, Arminius acknowledged that, inasmuch as the Son shares fully in the Father's deity, God the Son may be called αὐτόθεος. Thus, Arminius drew a distinction that was not clear in Trelcatius's teaching: if the word means "truly God," it applies to the Son; if it means "one who is God from himself," it does not. Despite his attempted clarification of the issue, however, Christological heresy and subordinationism within the Trinity would be added to the accusations that Arminius faced for the remainder of his life.[29]

From February 1605 to 1606, Arminius served as the elected rector of Leiden University, a year-long term. Arminius's election to this position reflects the broad and deep respect he so quickly commanded among the

---

26. See G. Brandt, *History*, 2:31. Bangs, *Arminius*, pp. 263–264.

27. The original Dutch statement is preserved in Molhuysen, *Bronnen*, 1: 417*, and translations are found in Bertius, *Oratio*, in *Opera*, fols. 0002ʳ–0002ᵛ; *Works* 1: 39. For a discussion of this statement, see Stanglin, *Arminius on Assurance*, pp. 27–28.

28. For more on faculty working relationships, see Stanglin, *Arminius on Assurance*, pp. 23–35.

29. See Arminius's account and defense in *Ep. ecc.* 88, pp. 160–161; *Art. non.* III, in *Opera*, pp. 949–950; *Works* 2: 707–708; *Epistola*, in *Opera*, pp. 938–941; *Works* 2: 690–696; *Apologia*, art. 21 (1), in *Opera*, pp. 164–166; *Works* 2: 29–32; *Dec. sent.*, pp. 118–123; *Works* 1: 691–695. Secondary accounts may be found in C. Brandt, *Life*, pp. 257–261; Bangs, *Arminius*, pp. 281–282. For a theological analysis of this controversy, see Muller, "Christological Problem," pp. 145–163; and chapter 2 of this volume.

faculty outside of his college. Later, on 3 July 1606, Kuchlinus, the respected regent of the Staten College, died. As head of the theological college, he had held his faculty and students in check only with difficulty and had done his best to keep the theological disagreements from spilling over into the churches. His successor, the long-time sub-regent Bertius, was more divisive and less esteemed than his predecessor, and it is therefore no coincidence that the rhetoric within and outside the university became more polemical after 1606.[30] In 1607, Trelcatius also died, leaving the faculty responsibilities solely to Gomarus and Arminius.

By 1608, the theological debates and accusations against Arminius were escalating to such a degree that the magistrates of Holland could no longer ignore the situation. Connected with charges of teaching false doctrine was the ever-present suspicion that Arminius was a closet Roman Catholic. There were religious and political reasons for this accusation. First, the central point of doctrinal disagreement between the early reformers and the Roman Church was the issue of justification by grace alone through faith alone. For Luther, Zwingli, Calvin, and most of their associates, their rejection of salvation by merit of any kind entailed the doctrine of unconditional predestination. In other words, if any cooperation is ascribed to the human will as a condition of salvation, then this human contribution was viewed as a step back toward the Roman Catholic view of justification and the Pelagianism that it seemed to imply. As someone who would defend a role for human will in the process of salvation, Arminius freely acknowledged that he sided with the Church of Rome against Reformed supralapsarianism.[31] It is no wonder, then, that Arminius bore this accusation.

Along with the religious mistrust of the Roman Church, Dutch political resentment toward the Catholic Hapsburg dynasty was growing as well. Arminius was reared and lived most of his life in a socio-political environment that was growing more intense with each passing year. The seeds of discontent were being sown in the Hapsburg Netherlands as Charles V abdicated the throne in 1555, passing control to Philip II (1527–1598).[32] What the rest of Europe calls the Thirty Years' War is known in The Netherlands as the Eighty Years' War. From the late 1560s until the

---

30. See Stanglin, "Johannes Kuchlinus," pp. 309–311.

31. *Dec. sent.*, p. 94; *Works* 1: 640–642.

32. See Israel, *Dutch Republic*, pp. 129–154.

Peace of Westphalia, in 1648, the Dutch people were engaged in a revolt against the Spanish occupation, which sought to enforce Hapsburg sovereignty and religious uniformity. The revolt began in earnest after the Duke of Alva's army of 10,000 arrived in 1567 to put down the Protestant iconoclastic revolts. By 1572 war was in full swing, which would soon result in the emergence of a new state.[33] The ensuing war had more to do with the rise of the autonomous modern nation-state than with confessions of faith, and sides did not always divide neatly over religious lines. But for the new Spanish sovereign Philip II, religious conformity was the desired means to political conformity. Jonathan Israel writes, "Ultimately, Philip hoped to transform the Netherlands into a secure bastion of Spanish power which would simultaneously serve as a bulwark against the spread of heresy."[34] Thus the calls to arms on both sides were often religious in nature. In this period, as in other premodern societies, it was difficult for most people to distinguish religious from political allegiances. Politics were never absent from the theological controversies. In 1606 Arminius stated prophetically that any lover of peace "is esteemed a deserter of the common cause, an accomplice to heresy, a supporter of heretics, and an apostate who joins the enemy."[35] Arminius's followers who supported the Twelve Years' Truce (beginning in 1609) would be accused of these very things.[36] This also means that the charge of "papism" was much more than an allegation of doctrinal preference or even ecclesiastical communion; in early modern Protestantism, it always carried with it connotations of sedition.[37]

Thus, in an attempt to assuage the Protestant church's conflicts before they also began to disturb the peace, in October 1608 the magistrates invited Arminius to declare his theological opinions before them in The Hague. He was suspected by his opponents of teaching contrary to the

---

33. See Israel, *Dutch Republic*, pp. 155–230.

34. See Israel, *Dutch Republic*, p. 166. For a summary of this period, its conflicts, and the outcomes, see J. J. Woltjer and M. E. H. N. Mout, "Settlements: The Netherlands," in *Handbook of European History, 1400–1600: Late Middle Ages, Renaissance, and Reformation*, 2 vols., ed. Thomas A. Brady, Jr., et al. (Leiden: Brill, 1994–1995), 2: 385–415. See also the account in Frederick Calder, *Memoirs of Simon Episcopius, the Celebrated Pupil of Arminius, and Subsequently Doctor of Divinity* (London: Hayward and Moore, 1838), pp. 9–16.

35. *Oratio de dissidio*, in *Opera*, p. 77; *Works* 1: 451.

36. On the Twelve Years' Truce, see Israel, *Dutch Republic*, pp. 399–420.

37. Cf. Bangs, *Arminius*, p. 273.

confession and catechism of the churches, so this speech was an opportunity to clear his name in a very public way.[38] Though Arminius took advantage of the opportunity to justify himself before the magistrates, who were
largely in sympathy with him, his opponents were not mollified. Disappointed that he had not been initially invited, Gomarus presented his opposing declaration before the same group of magistrates later that year,
and his speech consisted largely of personal attacks against Arminius.[39]
Despite the best efforts of the magistrates, controversy continued to plague
Arminius, and a conference was called in August 1609. Both Arminius
and Gomarus were summoned once again to the gathering of the magistrates in The Hague, and each was accompanied by four companions. The
conference was to be carried out in writing and would debate such matters
as justification, predestination, and the perseverance of believers.[40] This
conference, however, was to be Arminius's last, for the physical symptoms
with which he had struggled for years returned. He was fighting a losing
battle with what was probably tuberculosis. As a result of the worsening
symptoms, he was forced to leave the conference early. He eventually
returned to his home in Leiden, where he spent a few weeks bed-ridden,
receiving visitors and setting his house in order, which included drawing
up a last will. His tranquil spirit during these last days made an impression
on those who visited him. Bertius recalls one of Arminius's final prayers:

> Lord Jesus, faithful and merciful high priest—you who were willing
> to be tempted as we are in all things without sin, so that, being taught
> by such experience how painful (*grave*) a thing it is to obey God in
> sufferings, you can be affected with the sense of our infirmities—
> have mercy on me; help me your servant who is lying ill and oppressed
> with so many maladies (*malis*). God of my salvation, render my soul
> fit for your heavenly kingdom, indeed [my] body for the resurrection.[41]

---

38. This is his famous speech known as *Declaration of Sentiments*. It was first published as
*Verclaringhe Iacobi Arminii saliger ghedachten, in zijn leven professor theologiae binnen Leyden:
aengaende zyn ghevoelen* (Leiden: Thomas Basson, 1610).

39. Joannes Uytenbogaert, *Kerckelicke historie, vervatende verscheyden gedenckwaerdige saecken*
(S. l., 1646), p. 462; G. J. Hoenderdaal, "Inleiding," in *Verklaring van Jacobus Arminius,
afgelegd in de vergadering van de staten van Holland op 30 Oktober, 1608*, ed. G. J. Hoenderdaal
(Lochem: De Tijdstroom, 1960), p. 20.

40. See Uytenbogaert, *Kerckelicke historie*, pp. 462–476; C. Brandt, *Life*, pp. 359–362.

41. Quoted in Bertius, *Oratio*, in *Opera*, fol. 0003ᵛ; *Works* 1: 44–45.

Arminius passed from this life on 19 October 1609, at around the age of 50. He was eulogized three days later by his friend, Bertius, who concluded his oration with these words: "In Holland there was a man: those who knew him could not adequately esteem him; those who did not esteem him, never adequately knew him."[42] The motto appearing on his seal, which well epitomized his life of seeking the truth despite the consequences, was "a good conscience is paradise" (bona conscientia paradisus).[43]

## II. Writings

Also preliminary to a discussion of his theology, it is necessary to provide a brief summary of some of Arminius's major writings, particularly since most of these writings are utilized as sources throughout this book.[44] Most of these works are available in the Opera theologica, though a significant portion were published later or have not been published at all. As Bangs reports, nearly 45 percent of the treatises later published in Arminius's collected works were actually written during his Amsterdam years.[45] Two of these works, the Dissertation on Romans 7 (Cap. VII Rom.) and Analysis of Romans 9 (Cap. IX Rom.), are the direct results of his preaching through Romans and the controversies that ensued. He also engaged in a lengthy correspondence with the Leiden professor Franciscus Junius discussing the latter's disputation on predestination (Collatio). And after reading a treatise on predestination by the Cambridge theologian William Perkins (1558–1602),[46] Arminius responded to Perkins point by point, and, though he later completed his response, he had not been able to finish it before Perkins's death in 1602 (Exam. Perk.).[47]

---

42. Bertius, Oratio, in Opera, fol. oooo4ᵛ; Works 1: 47.

43. G. Brandt, History, 2: 63. Cossee, "Arminius and Rome," 74, suggests that Arminius's motto may have originated with Theodore Aemilius.

44. For dates and publication information on all these writings, see Stanglin and Muller, "Bibliographia Arminiana," pp. 263–290. Individual analyses of these writings are most readily accessible in Bangs, Arminius, passim; and Dekker, Rijker dan Midas, pp. 29–53.

45. Bangs, Arminius, p. 186.

46. William Perkins, De praedestinationis modo et ordine: et de amplitudine gratiae divinae . . . desceptatio (Cambridge: John Legatt, 1598).

47. Bangs, Arminius, p. 209, calls Exam. Perk. "perhaps the most difficult of Arminius' writings," and hyperbolically refers to it as the "basic document of Arminianism." Dekker, Rijker dan Midas, p. 37, rightly observes that it is written in "a rather chaotic style." Despite its chaos, however, it is filled with a number of compelling passages and arguments.

In addition to these treatises, which were published a few years after his death, there are also over one hundred extant letters of Arminius, the earliest of which go back to his tenure in Amsterdam. As a window into Arminius's life and the development of his thought, these letters provide an invaluable, though neglected, wealth of information. His favorite correspondent was his friend Uytenbogaert. Some of Arminius's letters still have not been transcribed, but the majority of them were transcribed and collected with other letters of Remonstrant interest, the last edition of which was published in 1704.[48]

On the occasion of receiving his doctoral degree from Leiden in July 1603, Arminius delivered an address on the topic of the priesthood of Christ (*Oratio de sacerdotio*). Later that year, when he began his duties as a professor, he presented three theological orations on the nature of theology (*Orationes tres*). Besides these four orations, Arminius's other extant speech presented in the university context was given at the close of his term as rector in February 1606 (*Oratio de dissidio*). The address was on religious dissensions, in which, among other things, he called for a council that would irenically discuss the matters pertaining to controversies within the Protestant churches.[49]

Aside from the lectures and private instruction given to theology students, the other primary responsibility of teaching faculty was composing and presiding over practice disputations. Arminius composed sixty-one public disputations during his tenure at Leiden, each of which was printed for the occasion of its oral performance; these public disputations were his only writings published during his lifetime (*Disp. pub.*).[50] The later collection of his works, *Opera theologica*, reprinted twenty-five public disputations

---

48. *Praestantium ac eruditorum virorum epistolae ecclesiasticae et theologicae*, 2nd ed., preface by Philip van Limborch (Amsterdam: H. Wetstenium, 1684). In the second and third editions, the epistles are numbered, and throughout this volume they are cited with their respective numbers as *Ep. ecc.*, along with page numbers, from the second edition. James Nichols has provided many excerpts of the letters in English translation, but, as a corpus, the letters of Arminius have never been systematically translated.

49. This speech from 1606 is discussed in G. J. Sirks, *Arminius' pleidooi voor de vrede der kerk*, Referatenreeks uit Remonstrantse Kring, vol. ii (Lochem: Uitgave de Tijdstroom, 1960).

50. In a public disputation, a professor would present in printed form a number of theses on a specific theological topic; one student would be chosen to defend the propositions, and about three students selected to raise objections. Although disputations are not as exhaustive as a long treatise and do not answer all the possible questions about a topic, the disputations of Arminius are the best indicators of his constructive theology on non-controversial topics, particularly in the absence of the systematic theology he never completed.

of Arminius and seventy-nine private disputations (*Disp. priv.*); the thirty-six other public disputations have only recently been gathered and reprinted. Together, these public and private disputations cover most of the traditional theological topics, but not all.[51]

One of the renowned treatises of Arminius actually arose from the public disputation of his colleague, Gomarus, who composed his theses on predestination in opposition to Arminius on 31 October 1604. In response, Arminius wrote his *Examen thesium Gomari* (*Exam. Gom.*), a point-by-point refutation of Gomarus's supralapsarian view of predestination. Among Arminius's major treatises, this is the only one that did not appear in his collected *Opera*, but was finally published in 1645.

In addition to the lengthy treatises, Arminius composed brief responses to particular topics. In 1605, he provided responses to nine controversial questions relayed to him by the curators of Leiden University (*Quaestiones*). And sometime after 1606, he also recorded his thoughts and questions on a number of theological issues (*Art. non.*).

During the year 1608, Arminius wrote three great apologies defending himself against charges of heresy. The first was a letter written in April to Hippolytus à Collibus, an ambassador from the Palatinate who had heard negative reports about Arminius (*Epistola*). The second treatise was an apology against thirty-one articles that Arminius's opponents had circulated as representative of his teaching (*Apologia*). In this treatise, he exposed the articles either as misquotes or as quotations taken out of context, and he responded in detail to each point.

The third apologetic treatise of that year was a speech that Arminius delivered in Dutch before the States (magistrates) in The Hague. He was summoned by the States of Holland on 20 October 1608 to deliver the speech on Thursday, 30 October, giving him only ten days' notice. In the letter from the States to Arminius, he was asked to give his opinions on the controversial topics of the day, and to do so "briefly, plainly, and clearly" (*kortelijck, duydelijck, ende klaerlijck*) by mouth, and later in writing.[52] In this speech, more than simply giving a defense of his positions, he also went on the attack against opposing viewpoints. He spent most of the speech dismantling the Reformed view of predestination later known as supralapsarianism, especially explaining that this doctrine makes God the

---

51. For more information on disputations, see Stanglin, *Missing Disputations*, pp. 7–41; Otterspeer, *Bolwerk*, pp. 236–238.

52. The text of this letter is preserved in Uytenbogaert, *Kerckelicke historie*, p. 446.

author of sin and has been rejected by the great majority of the Christian tradition. He then presented his positive view of predestination and briefly addressed other important topics, including providence, free will, grace, assurance of salvation, perfection of believers, the divinity of Christ, and the justification of humanity. This *Verklaring* (Declaration) was later translated into Latin as *Declaratio sententiae (Dec. sent.)*. Because he delivered this speech to laymen in Dutch in a mostly non-technical presentation, the *Declaration of Sentiments* remains a very accessible introduction to the controversies surrounding Arminius's time in Leiden (compared to the more technical and academic disputations). And since it was given less than a year before his death, the speech represents his mature opinions on these issues. For these reasons, the *Declaration of Sentiments* is the best place to begin reading and understanding Arminius.

## III. Theological Influences

The question of theological influences is a complex matter but important for understanding a figure's theology. As stated above, Arminius was accused of excessive attraction to Roman Catholic authors. For example, his colleague Gomarus claimed that Arminius's distinctive teachings originated in the writings of Roman Catholic theologians, namely Thomas Aquinas, Gabriel Biel, Albert Pighius, Luis de Molina, Francisco Suárez, Robert Bellarmine, and the Council of Trent.[53] At the same time, he was accused of denouncing the writings of widely respected Reformed theologians of the previous generation, especially Calvin, Beza, Peter Martyr Vermigli, Girolamo Zanchi, and Zacharias Ursinus.[54] Putting polemics aside, though, who were Arminius's influences, and what is the true story? Arminius's thought is more than the sum of his theological influences, but it also would have been quite different without those same influences. To answer the question, one must begin by noting the authors whom Arminius explicitly cites and implicitly uses. It is also helpful to refer to his personal library collection, which contains the books to which he had easiest access.[55] The simple fact that he owned a

---

53. Gomarus, *Waerschouwinghe*, pp. 35–38, 49; idem, *Bedencken*, p. 48.

54. *Acta synodi Dordrechti*, fol. 002ʳ (ET, p. 11).

55. *The Auction Catalogue of the Library of J. Arminius*, a facsimile edition with an introduction by Carl O. Bangs (Utrecht: HES, 1985).

book does not necessarily mean that he agreed with or even read it, but it does give additional insight into his likely influences and the range of his interests.

First of all, there is no doubt that the Bible was the primary theological influence on Arminius. Like all fellow Protestants, he claimed Scripture to be the starting point for all theology. He affirmed that nothing but Scripture is the "norm of theological truth," and that no merely human writing (such as the Belgic Confession and Heidelberg Catechism) is self-authenticating ($\alpha\dot{v}\tauo\pi\acute{\iota}\sigma\tauo\varsigma$).[56] Only Scripture is. As the "infallible word of God,"[57] Scripture "must be read with reverence and submission of soul toward God."[58] Its authority is derived not from the church, but from its primary author, God.[59] Scripture is complete as a guide in doctrines necessary to salvation.[60] "These books contain in themselves all theological truth."[61] No discernible difference exists between Arminius's doctrine of Scripture and that of his Reformed colleagues. Some readers of older Protestant theology, including Arminius's works, might wonder why there is not more discussion of biblical texts. Two things must be kept in consideration. First, there are numerous quotations of and allusions to biblical passages in Arminius's works, even in those writings that are more topical than explicitly exegetical. Because the citations are often shoved into marginalia or brackets and not quoted in full, one can easily miss the degree to which his writings are saturated in the idiom of Scripture. Second, and more importantly, a long history of biblical exegesis—including Arminius's own sermons, lectures, and treatises on Scripture—is assumed behind every reference to Scripture and every philosophical distinction that is made. For example, when Arminius distinguishes between the antecedent and consequent will of God, he is not only appealing to a distinction that precedes him by centuries, but he is also seeking to resolve a problem raised by a close reading of Scripture itself (in this case, the declaration that God wants all people to be saved *and* that God will not

---

56. *Art. non.* I.1–4, in *Opera*, p. 948; *Works* 2: 706.

57. *Disp. priv.* V.5.

58. *Disp. pub.* XXVI.13. Arminius treats the topic of Scripture in *Oratio tertia*, in *Opera*, pp. 61–71; *Works* 1: 383–401; *Disp. pub.* I–II, XXVI–XXVII; *Disp. priv.* V–X; and *Art. non.* I, in *Opera*, p. 948; *Works* 2: 706.

59. *Disp. pub.* I.2; XXVI.9; XXVII.5; *Disp. priv.* VI.2, cor. 1.

60. *Disp. pub.* XXVI.5–6; XXVII.11, 16; *Disp. priv.* VII.1.

61. *Disp. pub.* XXVII.1.

save all). Thus, Arminius's theological arguments do not always include an explicit discussion of the biblical starting point, but it is tacitly assumed. And when a Scripture reference is tagged to a statement, it is not a mere "proof text" but is accompanied by a known history of reception (even if that interpretation was not unanimously held among Reformed theologians). In all these respects, Arminius is neither more nor less "biblical" than his contemporaries.

The conflicts between the theological perspectives of Arminius and his opponents were due to disagreements over the interpretation of Scripture, never explicitly over its authority. As Arminius admits, despite its overall clarity, Scripture itself, by its "figurative and ambiguous sentences," can become "an occasion for error and dissension."[62] This small gap of uncertainty, in which his opponents found room enough to build a case, is one reason that Arminius placed so much emphasis on church history as a subordinate but important voice in the controversies. His statement with reference to the topic of Christ's priesthood reflects his theological sources in general: doctrine should be considered "from the rule of Scripture, which ought to have precedence, and from the supporting guidance of the orthodox fathers."[63] He acknowledged that the fathers could err,[64] yet remained convinced that the great tradition was an invaluable tool for biblical interpretation. Like most of his contemporaries, Arminius did not desire to say anything novel. He was conscious of a long line of Christian tradition that extended all the way back to the church fathers, many of whom he invoked for corroboration of his own controversial views.[65] Although his opponents accused him of theological novelty, he was able to turn the charge of novelty back on them by citing church fathers.[66] One finds Arminius appealing to a number of early

---

62. *Oratio de dissidio*, in *Opera*, p. 79; *Works* 1: 454. This same point is acknowledged within the biblical canon (2 Pet. 3:16).

63. *Oratio de sacerdotio*, in *Opera*, p. 14; *Works* 1: 412.

64. *Oratio de dissidio*, in *Opera*, p. 85; *Works* 1: 466; *Disp. priv.* IX.12.

65. Appeals to the "tradition" here and in the remainder of this volume are not meant to conceal the fact that the Christian tradition is vast and complex. Notwithstanding the complexities, there are, on the one hand, central core beliefs that remained constant through the early church and the greater part of its subsequent history; on the other hand, there are disputed doctrines whose origins can be traced objectively to later church history and which, when considering Christianity globally and diachronically, represent a minority in the historical record. By "tradition," we refer to the former class.

66. E.g., see *Exam. Perk.*, in *Opera*, p. 638; *Works* 3: 273–274.

Christians, including Tertullian, Origen, Lactantius, Hilary of Poitiers, Ambrose of Milan, John Chrysostom, Jerome, Prosper of Aquitaine, and John of Damascus, to name a few. As a rule, Arminius preferred the earlier fathers over the later ones.[67]

Like his contemporaries, Arminius cited Augustine of Hippo (354–430) more than any other church father. Not only was Augustine the most respected father in the Western Church in general, but he was also cited particularly in the Protestant Reformation, whose most famous figure, Luther, had been an Augustinian monk. From their beginnings, the magisterial Reformations in (present-day) Germany, Switzerland, and England had an Augustinian flavor, and Protestants had to deal with the theology of Augustine, second only to Scripture. Regarding Augustine's success against the Pelagian heresy, the French Protestant Pierre du Moulin (1568–1658) wrote, "After God, we are indebted to the genius and industry of such a great man."[68] Most Protestants felt the same way about Augustine's contribution to a wide range of topics.[69] Though Arminius never cites Pelagius in a positive way, care had to be taken when disagreeing with Augustine, especially with his later, anti-Pelagian writings. Arminius usually cited Augustine favorably, but on some issues, such as Romans 7, he preferred the early Augustine to the later Augustine. In *Declaration of Sentiments*, after appealing to early ecumenical and local

---

67. E.g., Arminius cites Tertullian: "Whatever is most ancient is most true" (*antiquissimum quodque verissimum*). *Oratio tertia*, in *Opera*, p. 64; *Works* 1: 389. Tertullian's actual words are, "id esse verum, quodcumque primum." See Tertullian, *Adversus Praxeam* II, in *PL* 2: 157B.

68. Pierre du Moulin, *Anatome Arminianismi seu, enucleatio controversiarum quae in Belgio agitantur, super doctrina de providentia, de praedestinatione, de morte Christi, de natura et gratia* (Leiden: Abraham Picard, 1619), XLII, p. 348: "Debemus ergo, post Deum, viri tanti ingenio et industriae quod exitialis haec pestis ab Ecclesiae visceribus depulsa est." ET: *The Anatomy of Arminianisme: or The Opening of the Controversies Lately Handled in the Low-Countryes* (London: T. S. for Nathaniel Newbery, 1620), p. 422.

69. By way of an example in Arminius's own time, note the comments subjoined to the Lambeth Articles (1595) by the Archbishop of York, Matthew Hutton, in *The Works of John Whitgift, D. D.*, 3 vols., ed. John Ayre for the Parker Society (Cambridge: Cambridge University Press, 1851–1853), 3: 612–613 (emphasis added): "Hae theses ex sacris literis vel aperte colligi, vel necessaria consecutione deduci possunt, *et ex scriptis Augustini*." S. van der Linde, "De Dordtse Synode, 1619–1969." *Nederlands theologisch tijdschrift* 23/5 (1969): 341, speaks of the "uitbarsting van Augustinianisme" in the whole Reformation, especially in Luther and Calvin. On the reception of Augustine in the Reformation, see Arnoud S. Q. Visser, *Reading Augustine in the Reformation: The Flexibility of Intellectual Authority in Europe, 1500–1620*, Oxford Studies in Historical Theology (New York: Oxford University Press, 2011); Paul Rorem, "Augustine, the Medieval Theologians, and the Reformation," in *The Medieval Theologians*, ed. G. R. Evans (Oxford: Blackwell, 2001), pp. 365–372.

councils, he notes contemporary catholic disapproval of Augustine's more extreme statements.[70] These examples are typical of Arminius's appreciative but nuanced use of Augustine.[71]

Arminius also read and was shaped by medieval theologians. Arminius often cited figures such as Bernard of Clairvaux (1090–1153), and, as with most early modern theologians, tendencies from various strands of scholasticism are present in Arminius's theology, including categories inspired by John Duns Scotus (ca. 1265–1308). But no one from this period was more influential on his thought than Thomas Aquinas (1225–1274), "of whose genius and erudition," writes Arminius, "I have the highest opinion," despite the occasional disagreements.[72] Even when Arminius does not explicitly refer to Thomas, his impact is so evident throughout his theology that it is legitimate to refer to Arminius as a "modified Thomist."[73] With respect to the influence of medieval scholasticism, Arminius is hardly unique among his colleagues.

Closer to his own time, Arminius also read deeply from the works of reform-minded predecessors. First, he was inspired by the native Dutch influence. Foremost on this list is Desiderius Erasmus of Rotterdam (1466–1536), the best-known of the "Christian humanists," who remained a favorite author in the Low Countries throughout the sixteenth century.[74] His influence was rarely made explicit in Arminius's works,[75] yet a look at Arminius's library catalogue reveals that, of the "recent divines," Erasmus is the most well-represented Roman Catholic in his personal library, surpassed by only

---

70. *Dec. sent.*, pp. 73–74; *Works* 1: 620–621.

71. On Arminius's use of Augustine, see Aza Goudriaan, "'Augustine Asleep' or 'Augustine Awake'? Arminius's Reception of Augustine," in *Arminius, Arminianism, and Europe*, pp. 51–72; Keith D. Stanglin, "'Arminius *avant la lettre*': Peter Baro, Jacob Arminius, and the Bond of Predestinarian Polemic," *Westminster Theological Journal* 67 (2005): 65–66; Diana Stanciu, "Reinterpreting Augustine: Ralph Cudworth and Jacobus Arminius on Grace and Free Will," *Zeitschrift für antikes Christentum* 11/1 (2007): 96–114. Cf. Anneliese Bieber-Wallmann, "Remonstrantenstreit," in *Augustin Handbuch*, ed. Volker Henning Drecoll (Tübingen: Mohr Siebeck, 2007), pp. 627–633. In contrast to Arminius, cf. David C. Steinmetz, *Luther in Context* (Grand Rapids: Baker, 1995), p. 21, who states that Luther preferred the older Augustine over the younger.

72. *Exam. Perk.*, in *Opera*, p. 682; *Works* 3: 340–341.

73. See especially Muller, *God, Creation, and Providence*, pp. 271–272. Witt, "Creation, Redemption and Grace," p. 676, calls Arminius a "good 'Thomist.'"

74. Joseph Lecler, *Toleration and the Reformation*, 2 vols., trans. T. L. Westow (New York: Association Press, 1960), 2: 256.

75. Arminius quotes from Erasmus only once in the *Opera*, and he does so approvingly. *Cap. VII. Rom.*, in *Opera*, p. 902, in *Works* 2: 624.

a few Protestants.[76] One can also find passages in Arminius that appear to echo Erasmus.[77] The implicit influence of Erasmus was made clearer by those who opposed Arminius and his followers, the Remonstrants. Whereas many in The Netherlands revered the memory of Erasmus and his brand of flexible, irenic Christianity, Arminius's antagonists "scorned" this aspect of Erasmus.[78] Besides Erasmus, Arminius was influenced by other non-Calvinist Dutch reformers. Although Arminius never explicitly cites him, Anastasius Veluanus, often regarded as a forerunner of Remonstrantism, almost certainly had an indirect influence on him through his well-known writings.[79] Arminius favorably cited Dutch Reformed ministers who came into controversy over their doctrines of conditional predestination, including Caspar Coolhaes, Herman Herberts, Cornelius Wiggertszoon, and Tako Sybrants.[80] In addition to Dutch influences, Arminius also appealed to Lutheran predecessors who taught a similar doctrine of predestination, especially Philip Melanchthon and Niels Hemmingsen (Hemmingius; 1513–1600), whose works appear in his personal library.[81]

Among Reformed authors, Arminius also owned many books by his former teacher, Theodore Beza, as well as by Franciscus Junius and Heinrich Bullinger. But the number of books by Calvin surpassed them all. In a letter from 1607, Arminius denies the charge that he recommends his students read Jesuit theology instead of Reformed authors. Rather, he

---

76. See *Auction Catalogue*. The only sixteenth-century figures with greater representation are Calvin, Junius, Melanchthon, Beza, Bullinger, and Ramus.

77. For example, the view expressed by Erasmus on Romans 9 is similar to that articulated by Arminius in his treatise on the same topic. Cf. Desiderius Erasmus, *On the Freedom of the Will: A Diatribe or Discourse*, trans. E. Gordon Rupp, in *Luther and Erasmus: Free Will and Salvation*, Library of Christian Classics, vol. 17 (Philadelphia: Westminster Press, 1969), pp. 69–70; with *Cap. IX Rom.*, in *Opera*, pp. 778–800; *Works* 3: 485–519.

78. Israel, *Dutch Republic*, p. 392, specifically mentions Petrus Plancius and Franciscus Gomarus. Matthew Slade, an English Puritan preacher and Counter-Remonstrant in Amsterdam, disparaged Erasmus as being the spiritual forefather of Arminianism (ibid., pp. 429–430). H. C. Rogge, *Caspar Janszoon Coolhaes, de voorloper van Arminius en der Remonstranten*, 2 vols., new ed. (Amsterdam: Y. Rogge, 1865), 2: 15 n. 15, notes that "Arminius en zijne volgelingen hebben Erasmus altijd hoog geroemd."

79. See Gerrit Morsink, *Joannes Anastasius Veluanus (Jan Gerritsz. Versteghe, levensloop en ontwikkeling)* (Kampen: Kok, 1986), pp. 107–111; Stanglin, *Arminius on Assurance*, pp. 84–85 n. 47.

80. *Dec. sent.*, pp. 57, 96; *Works* 1: 601–603, 643. On all four of these ministers, see the biographical notices by James Nichols in *Works* 1: 602–605 n. See also Rogge, *Caspar Janszoon Coolhaes*; Lecler, *Toleration*, 2: 263–267; Israel, *Dutch Republic*, pp. 370–371.

81. *Dec. sent.*, pp. 94–95; *Works* 1: 642–643; *Auction Catalogue*.

claims that he recommends Calvin's commentaries above all other works on Scripture, for they contain a "certain extraordinary spirit of prophecy." In addition, Calvin's *Institutes of the Christian Religion* should be read after the (Heidelberg) Catechism as a fuller interpretation of it. He then adds that all of Calvin's works, like those of any human, should be read with caution.[82] Arminius is ambivalent in his endorsement of Calvin. His respect for Calvin's commentaries is clear. At the same time, though he recommends the *Institutes* to students, he does not claim wholesale agreement with its content, but only recommends the book specifically as a supplement to the catechism.[83]

If Arminius did not positively recommend that students read Jesuit theology, what then was his relationship to late medieval and early modern Roman Catholic theology? According to the library auction catalogue, Arminius did in fact own works by the very authors he was accused of recommending—namely, Biel, Molina, Suárez, Bellarmine, and the decrees of the Council of Trent. To be ignorant of these writings would have been unflattering for a theologian of Arminius's caliber. These writers were commonly found in Protestant collections and were read by Arminius's colleagues; the Jesuit Francisco Suárez (1548–1617), for example, was the most formidable and popular metaphysician of the day, an authority for anyone interested in philosophical theology. Arminius never refers to them positively by name, but some of the differences between Arminius and his Reformed contemporaries can be traced to the tacit influence of these writers. Luis de Molina (1535–1600), for instance, gave Arminius the language of divine middle knowledge (*scientia media*), which he then filtered through a Protestant context that enabled him to speak about divine knowledge and predestination in ways that were ostensibly consistent with earlier Lutherans such as Melanchthon and Hemmingsen, as well as with a host of other patristic, medieval, and Protestant theologians. Arminius, while never recommending these Roman Catholic writers or endorsing everything they advocated, was certainly influenced by some of their interpretations of Aquinas.

---

82. *Ep. ecc.* 101, p. 185; *Works* 1: 295–296.

83. For comments on Arminius's evaluation of Calvin, especially in light of the passage in *Ep. ecc.* 101, see William A. den Boer, "Met Onderscheidingsvermogen: Arminius' waardering voor en kritiek op Calvijn en diens theologie," *Theologia Reformata* 52/3 (2009): 260–273; Clarke, "Arminius's Understanding," 25–35; Bangs, *Arminius*, pp. 287–289.

This survey of his life, works, and influences indicates, among other things, the complexity of Jacob Arminius as a theologian and the challenge of reading and interpreting his influential works accurately. With these biographical and bibliographical backgrounds in mind, as well as the influence of Scripture and fifteen hundred years of Christian theological tradition that preceded him, we turn now to his doctrines of God and creation, providence and predestination, and sin and salvation, revealing the main contours of a theological system that changed the Protestant landscape.

## 2

# God and Creation

*God himself is the object of theology. . . . He is the best; that is, he is the first and highest good and goodness itself, and he alone is good, as good as goodness itself, ready to communicate it as far as it can be communicated; his great liberality is matched by the treasures he possesses. . . . He is the greatest, and he alone is great.*

—JACOB ARMINIUS, 1603

AS WE HAVE seen, Jacob Arminius is both a "scholastic" as well as a "biblical" theologian; his theology is self-consciously grounded in Holy Scripture while at the same time attentive to logical and metaphysical concerns.[1] His theology is also oriented toward pastoral sensitivities, and it is impossible to come to grips with his theology without understanding that these scholastic and pastoral elements are mutually reinforcing. This means that patience and care must be exercised when engaging his theology. It may be tempting simply to jump to the more controversial elements of his teaching, but we are likely to misunderstand that teaching and misconstrue his arguments if we are not sufficiently attentive to the broader theological foundation from which he works. The theology of Arminius cannot be reduced to an interpretation of, say, Rom. 9:1–23 (or Rom. 7:14–25). It cannot be grasped by modern interpreters who attempt to conform it to

---

1. The theology of Arminius bears important similarities with the doctrinal formulations offered by his Reformed contemporaries (and immediate predecessors). As Richard A. Muller explains, the scholastic Protestant doctrine of God at the turn of the seventeenth century retained the biblical grounding of the Reformers while also showing increased interest in the categories of scholasticism: "Whereas the Reformers' theology was primarily exegetical and discursive, even the *loci* drawn from Scripture by the orthodox have become methodologically stylized and thoroughly dialectical" with respect to "rational argumentation and metaphysical concerns." *God, Creation, and Providence,* p. 83. Right in line with this approach (and in agreement with his Reformed contemporaries on many issues, while also disagreeing with them on others), Arminius worked toward a theology that is biblically grounded and logically precise.

ready-made categories of "divine sovereignty versus free will." On the contrary, Arminius's positions on the controversial issues of his day can be understood only within the theological context of his doctrine of God, from which flowed the rest of his theology. More particularly, modern interpreters of Arminius will make sense of his views only when they understand the centrality and importance of Arminius's understanding of the simplicity, omniscience, and infinite goodness of the Triune God.

## I. The Divine Nature and Attributes

God is the primary object of theology. In the course of his writings, Arminius assumes the existence of God and proposes a number of arguments in favor of God's existence.[2] But the purpose here is to examine Arminius's beliefs about the divine attributes. Although the divine nature is one, humanity—in an attempt to understand and speak of God—must predicate or "attribute" certain qualities or characteristics to the one divine essence. In line with the Christian tradition, Arminius confesses, "We cannot know the nature of God in itself."[3] "It cannot be known *a priori*," but only in a slight measure that is "infinitely below what it is in itself."[4] We must, therefore, arrive at divine attributes in some way other than self-evident knowledge. As such, God has accommodated knowledge of himself to human capacity.[5] General revelation in nature and special revelation contained in Scripture are helpful, but they still allow humans to see only "through a mirror in an enigma," granting a perspective that is proper to "travelers and pilgrims" who are on their way but have not yet reached their goal.[6]

---

2. E.g., see his ten axioms and arguments in *Disp. priv.* XIV. For a summary and analysis of these arguments, see John E. Platt, *Reformed Thought and Scholasticism: The Arguments for the Existence of God in Dutch Theology, 1575–1650*, Studies in the History of Christian Thought, vol. 29 (Leiden: Brill, 1982), pp. 148–159. Among the figures surveyed by Platt, Arminius represents the first "genuine attempt at a systematic approach" to the arguments for God's existence (ibid., p. 156). See also Muller, *God, Creation, and Providence*, pp. 83–101.

3. *Disp. priv.* XV.2. E.g., see John of Damascus, *Expositio accurata fidei orthodoxae* I.i, in *PG* 94: 789A: "Therefore the deity is unspeakable and incomprehensible." *ST* Ia.ii.1 resp.: "we do not know the essence of God (*de Deo quid est*)."

4. *Disp. pub.* IV.2. Cf. *Disp. pub.* XXVIII.1. Cf. Muller, *God, Creation, and Providence*, pp. 60–61.

5. *Oratio prima*, in *Opera*, p. 30; *Works* 1: 328.

6. *Disp. pub.* IV.3.

In light of such limitations, the Christian tradition has generally held fast to the "negative way" (*via negativa*) of speaking about God, except in cases of being informed by divine revelation. By this *modus negationis* or *via negativa* (mode of negation or negative way), God's attributes are defined by negating the qualities of finite creatures, removing them from God. By the "mode of affirmation" or "way of eminence" (*modus affirmationis* or *via eminentiae*), however, perfections in the order of creation are acknowledged as gifts of God and therefore attributed analogically to God himself.[7] To these modes of predication Arminius adds the "mode of supereminence" (*modus supereminentiae*), by which the finite perfections of creatures are raised to an infinite degree and are attributed to God. In other words, "supereminence," as its name implies, involves adding infinite eminence, though these modes are often expressed negatively.[8] These modes of supereminence are proper to God, incommunicable to creatures, and without analogy.[9]

The history of theology reflects a number of ways of classifying various divine attributes.[10] In his public disputation on the nature of God (*Disp. pub.* IV), which is his most extensive discussion of God's essence and attributes, Arminius thinks of the divine attributes under two main headings: there are attributes of the divine essence, and there are attributes of the divine life, the first and second "moments" of the divine nature, respectively. Under the divine essence he discusses simplicity and infinity, and under the divine life he considers understanding and will. As Muller explains, "Simplicity and infinity yield, logically, eternity, immensity, omnipresence, impassibility, immutability, and incorruptibility. Understanding (*intellectus*) implies knowledge (*scientia*) and, by extension, wisdom (*sapientia*)—and will carries with it all the affective and relational attributes like goodness, love, mercy, and so forth."[11]

---

7. Arminius affirms the legitimacy of both of these modes of predication. *Disp. pub.* IV.4; *Disp. pub.* XXVIII.3.

8. *Disp. pub.* IV.4; *Disp. priv.* XV.2.

9. *Disp. pub.* IV.19; XXVIII.10. According to Muller, *God, Creation, and Providence*, pp. 104, 108–112, Arminius is following his Leiden predecessor Junius in his acceptance of this unusual category. Cf. *PRRD* 3: 220–221. In another disputation, these same modes are classified as attributes "of the first kind." See *Disp. pub.* XXVIII.

10. For a survey of the problems and options among the Reformed orthodox, see *PRRD* 3: 195–226.

11. Muller, *God, Creation, and Providence*, p. 113.

# A. The Divine Essence

Compared to his Reformed contemporaries, Arminius had worked out an unusually elaborate doctrine of God's essence (*essentia Dei*).[12] Arminius calls the divine essence the "first moment of the divine nature or deity."[13] God's essence is one and indivisible,[14] yet certain qualities can be attributed to it. Since the divine essence is independent of any other principle and cause, as well as free from all external limitation and boundary, to this essence can be attributed simplicity and infinity of nature.[15] Arminius is convinced that the doctrines of simplicity and infinity are vital to any proper understanding of the divine essence, and that these are indeed foundational to a proper understanding of the divine attributes as a whole.[16]

## A.1. Divine Simplicity

It would be hard to overestimate the importance of the doctrine of divine simplicity in Arminius's theology. The doctrine of divine simplicity, however much maligned in modern theology, is a staple ingredient not only of medieval Latin theology but also of patristic theology (Greek and Latin), on the one hand, as well as post-Reformation scholasticism on the other.[17] At base, the doctrine of divine simplicity maintains that God is not composed of parts or pieces, for that would mean that there is something prior to and more fundamental than God. Simplicity implies aseity (*aseitas*), that is, that God's own being is from himself (*a se*) and dependent on no other.[18] God is the ground of being, not one being among others. He is "being

---

12. See Muller, *God, Creation, and Providence*, pp. 103–112.

13. *Disp. pub.* IV.7; XXVIII.2.

14. *Disp. pub.* IV.21; XXVIII.11.

15. *Disp. pub.* XXVIII.4–5.

16. Arminius treats the topic of God's essence and attributes in *Disp. pub.* IV, XXVIII; *Disp. priv.* XV–XXIII; *Art. non.* II, in *Opera*, pp. 948–949; *Works* 2: 707; *Ep. ecc.* 60 and 65.

17. The doctrine of divine simplicity has not received due attention within the recent growth of patristic scholarship, but see Andrew Radde-Gallwitz, *Basil of Ceasarea, Gregory of Nyssa and the Transformation of Divine Simplicity* (Oxford: Oxford University Press, 2009); Lewis Ayres, *Nicea and Its Legacy: An Approach to Fourth-Century Trinitarian Theology* (Oxford: Oxford University Press, 2004); and the dated and somewhat less balanced study of Basil Krivocheine, "Simplicity of the Divine Nature and the Distinctions within God, According to St. Gregory of Nyssa," *St. Vladimir's Theological Quarterly* 21 (1977): 77–104. See also the discussion in *PRRD* 3: 38–44.

18. E.g., see *Disp. pub.* IV.9.

itself" (*entitas ipsa*).[19] In his affirmation of divine simplicity, Arminius is consistent with both his Reformed contemporaries and the broader Christian tradition.[20] But exactly what he means in his affirmation and defense of the doctrine warrants further consideration, and a brief explanation and look at the background may be helpful.

According to the classic statement of Aquinas, which is in continuity with the church fathers, God is not composed of extended parts; God is not, and does not have, a body.[21] Nor is God composed of substantial form and form-receiving matter. Within God there is no composition of his substantial form that makes him the kind of thing that he is, or form-receiving matter that would make him the particular thing that he is. Neither is God composed of act and potency. Furthermore, God is not composed of essence and existence. While there is a difference between the man Socrates and the essence *humanity*, there is no such difference between God and his essence. Nor yet is he composed of subject and accidents.[22] There are no properties outside the divine nature that enter into composition with that essence; God's goodness, God's wisdom, and God's power are all the same as the divine essence, and thus are the same thing as each other. Furthermore, God is not composed of essence and existence (*esse*)—*what God is* is no different from *that God is*. Finally, God does *not* enter into composition with anything outside God; he is not the "world-soul" or part of a larger complex (the "God-world"). All of this means that God is not made up of parts or pieces; God is not composed of either temporal or physical parts, nor is there any other kind of metaphysical complexity within God. There

---

19. *Oratio prima*, in *Opera*, p. 29; *Works* 1: 326.

20. On this and other doctrines, historic Reformed theology and Arminius's theology have more in common with each other than either does with much twenty-first century "Arminian" and "Reformed" theology. One theology textbook, for instance, rightly states that "most Christians have not even heard of the doctrine of divine simplicity," but then goes on to assert that the doctrine "has no real biblical basis and has in fact worked to defeat the resources of a full-fledged trinitarianism." Richard Plantinga, Thomas R. Thompson, and Matthew D. Lundberg, *An Introduction to Christian Theology* (Cambridge: Cambridge University Press, 2010), p. 104. For a recent explication and defense of the doctrine, see Jeffrey E. Brower, "Simplicity and Aseity," in Thomas P. Flint and Michael C. Rea, eds., *Oxford Handbook of Philosophical Theology* (Oxford: Oxford University Press, 2009), pp. 105–128.

21. *ST* Ia-IIae.xiii.3. For a brief summary, see also Augustine, *De civitate Dei contra paganos* VIII.vi, in *PL* 41: 231.

22. Cf. Christopher Hughes, *On a Complex Theory of a Simple God: An Investigation in Aquinas' Philosophical Theology* (Ithaca, NY: Cornell University Press, 1989), pp. 3–106; Eleonore Stump, *Aquinas* (New York: Routledge, 2003), pp. 92–130.

are no "real distinctions" (no distinctions between res or "things"); the only distinctions that can and should be made about the divine nature are from *our* side—they are rational distinctions, rather than "real distinctions."

We must take care not to misunderstand Aquinas's account of divine simplicity—it does not mean that there are no distinctions whatsoever in God, nor does it mean that theologians mislead when they predicate distinct attributes of God. The denial that there are "real" distinctions within God is simply the denial that God is composed of things and other things; it is the denial that God is made up of elements more fundamental than God himself. But just as one must be careful not to misunderstand (or caricature) Aquinas's account, neither should one overlook the theological motivation for this doctrine. Aquinas's rationale is clearly stated and reflects much traditional thinking to this point: every composite is (logically, at least) posterior to its constituent parts and is thus dependent upon them. As Alvin Plantinga puts it, "Suppose God has the property of being omnipotent and suppose that property is an object distinct from him, is uncreated by him and exists necessarily. Then in some sense he does depend on that property."[23] Furthermore, every composite has a cause, as discrete and independent things cannot be united unless something unites them. But God, of course, is the Uncaused Cause or First Cause. Furthermore, all composites include potentiality and actuality; they include the possibility of dissolution. But such a possibility is utterly repugnant to the doctrine of God. Muller notes that "if some of the late patristic and medieval expositions of the doctrine class as philosophical and perhaps speculative, the basic concept is not: from Irenaeus to the era of Protestant orthodoxy, the fundamental assumption was merely that God, as ultimate Spirit is not a compounded or composite being."[24]

Aquinas's version of the doctrine of divine simplicity is not without its critics, from within the classical Christian tradition, from modern philosophy of religion, and from so-called "new atheists." Some of the more important criticisms concern the internal coherence of the doctrine. Plantinga, for instance, says that the "substantial problem" with the doctrine of divine simplicity is this: "If God is identical with each of his properties, then each of his properties is identical with each of his properties, so that God

23. Alvin Plantinga, *Does God Have a Nature?* (Milwaukee: Marquette University Press, 1980), p. 34.

24. *PRRD* 3: 276. Muller goes on to point out, "It is also the case that, from the time of the fathers onward, divine simplicity was understood as a support of the doctrine of the Trinity."

has but one property . . . this seems flatly incompatible with the obvious fact that God has several properties."[25] Worse yet is what he calls the "monumental problem": "if God is identical with each of his properties, then, since each of his properties is a property, [then] he is a property—a self-exemplifying property."[26] But surely "no property could have created the world" or become incarnate in it.[27] This leaves us with the conclusion that if God is a property, then God is not personal, so while the doctrine of simplicity "begins in a pious and proper concern for God's sovereignty; it ends up flouting the most fundamental claims of theism,"[28] for "if God is a living, conscious being who knows, wills, and acts—if, in a word, God is a person—then God is not a property or state of affairs or set or proposition or any other abstract object."[29] Other criticisms focus on the compatibility of Aquinas's doctrine of divine simplicity with other major doctrinal claims—some critics charge that the traditional doctrine (or at least Aquinas's formulation of it) is inconsistent with the doctrines of the Trinity and incarnation.[30]

But beyond Aquinas there are other accounts of divine simplicity within the tradition directly inherited by Arminius. Notably, the formulation of John Duns Scotus would have been well known by Arminius.[31] Whereas Aquinas allows for only "rational distinctions" rather than "real distinctions," Scotus, the "Subtle Doctor," carves out conceptual space for yet another distinction.[32] Between "rational distinctions" and "real distinctions," Scotus sees a proper place for "formal distinctions." To understand this distinction, one must see that a "real distinction" is a distinction between independent things. Not merely conceptual or rational distinctions that are made by convention or for convenience, such distinctions point to the real existence of independent things. They can be different things of the same essence (for example, different chairs) or different things of different essences (for example, tables and chairs). Or they can be different *parts* of the same thing (for example, the legs and seat of a

---

25. Plantinga, *Does God Have a Nature?* p. 47.

26. Plantinga, *Does God Have a Nature?* p. 47.

27. Plantinga, *Does God Have a Nature?* p. 47.

28. Plantinga, *Does God Have a Nature?* pp. 53–54.

29. Plantinga, *Does God Have a Nature?* p. 57.

30. E.g., Hughes, *A Complex Theory of a Simple God.*

31. As is pointed out by Muller, *God, Creation, and Providence,* pp. 129–130.

32. Cf. Richard Cross, *Duns Scotus on God* (Aldershot, UK: Ashgate, 2003), pp. 99–114.

chair). In any case, *real separability* is both necessary and sufficient for a real distinction; if two things can exist independently of one another, then they are *really* distinct. Scotus locates his controversial "formal distinction" between real distinctions and merely rational distinctions.

The formal distinction is "such that exists between two (or more) formal aspects of the essence of a thing."[33] For Scotus, two entities are formally distinct if the distinction is genuine (that is, it is within the thing itself and not merely rational or mental)—but not between two different essences or between separable parts or pieces of the same thing. In other words, two entities are formally distinct if (and only if) they are both really identical and genuinely distinct on account of distinction within itself. The key here, once again, is *inseparability*; separation is logically impossible, it is not even logically possible for the entities in question to be separated and still to exist. So two entities can be formally distinct—but not "really" distinct (in the technical sense in play here)—if they are both *really inseparable* and *genuinely distinct on account of distinctions found in themselves* (not artificial or merely "rational"). While illustrations or analogies from mundane life are not prevalent or perfect, we are not entirely without some ability to grasp this: the hardness of a table is genuinely distinct from the flatness of the table but not separable from either the flatness or the table itself; the will is genuinely distinct from the intellect but utterly inconceivable without it.[34] Scotus puts this distinction to work in various ways. Inasmuch as the divine attributes are formally distinct from one another (omnipotence is inseparable from omnibenevolence, though genuinely distinct from it), the divine attributes are formally distinct from the divine essence, and the divine persons are formally distinct from the divine essence. As for the doctrine of the Trinity, the divine persons are formally distinct; they are genuinely distinct (thus avoiding modalism) while yet really inseparable (thus rejecting tritheism), although Scotus will also employ the more traditional language of the divine persons as *really* distinct.

Returning to the theology of Arminius, it is important to understand that he fully endorses the doctrine of divine simplicity:

---

33. Richard A. Muller, *Dictionary of Latin and Greek Theological Terms: Drawn Principally from Protestant Scholastic Theology* (Grand Rapids, MI: Baker, 1985), pp. 93–94. For Duns Scotus's use of this distinction, see *God and Creatures: The Quodlibetal Questions*, trans. with an intro., notes, and glossary by Felix Alluntis and Allan B. Wolter (Princeton: Princeton University Press, 1975). For an expanded description of "formal distinction," see ibid., pp. 505–507.

34. Granting, of course, the proper metaphysical commitments. Cf. *PRRD* 3: 286.

Simplicity is a supereminent mode of the essence of God, by which it is free (*expers*) from all composition and of component parts, whether sensible or intelligible. [Free] from composition, because free from external cause; [free] from component parts, because free from internal cause (Rom. 11:35–36; Hebrews 2:10; Isaiah 40:12, 22). The essence of God therefore does not consist of material, integral, and quantitative parts, neither of matter and form, nor of kind and difference, nor of subject and accident, nor of form and the thing formed . . . nor of individual substance (*supposito*) and nature, nor of potency and act, nor of essence and being. Therefore God is his own essence and his own being.[35]

Arminius clearly endorses the doctrine of simplicity. First of all, note the use of the supereminent mode expressed in the negative way; that is, Arminius defines simplicity primarily by declaring what the divine essence lacks (*expers*). Arminius uses this method of predication for the other supereminent modes as well. Furthermore, he does not take the fairly standard Thomist line on simplicity, for he goes on to say that some things predicated of God "are likewise distinguished by a formal reason."[36] Muller notes that Arminius does not explain the term, nor does he set out its history. But as Muller points out, "Yet he has made a major doctrinal decision and has exchanged his Thomist accent for a Scotist one."[37] As we will see, Arminius's commitment to the doctrine of divine simplicity—and his endorsement of a Scotist account—will have important implications for his overall theology, and especially his doctrine of predestination. Indeed, it is hard to grasp his overall theology without seeing the importance of the doctrine.

## A.2. Divine Infinity

Central and basic to the theology of Arminius is the doctrine of divine infinity: infinity is another "supereminent" mode of God's essence. Arminius appeals to Scripture to establish this doctrine; here Psalm 145:3 and Is.

---

35. *Disp. pub.* IV.11.

36. *Disp. pub.* IV.11.

37. Muller, *God, Creation, and Providence*, p. 130. The relation of Arminius's doctrine of simplicity to the theology of later Remonstrants and other "Arminians" is underexplored. Cf. Simon Episcopius, *Institutiones theologicae privatis lectionibus Amstelodami traditae* IV.ii.7, in *Opera theologica* (Amsterdam: Joannes Blaev, 1650), pp. 286–287.

43:10 both ground the doctrine. Infinity means that the divine essence is "free from all limitation and boundary, whether from something higher or lower, from before or after."[38] Observe once again that the definition consists of a negation—in this case, infinity is simply a negation of all finitude. Of course, Arminius is not a pantheist, so he does think that there are indeed limits to the being of God in some sense. He continues by saying that the divine essence "is terminated inwardly by its own property, according to which it is what it is and nothing else: yet by this no limits are prescribed to its infinity; for by the very circumstance—that it is its own being (esse), subsisting through itself, neither received from another nor in another—it is distinguished from all others, and others are removed from it."[39] In contrast to pantheism, then, the divine being is not mixed with anything. As Muller explains, for Arminius this simply means that "God cannot be less than good, cannot cease to live, cannot become complex or compound, cannot be other than Father, Son, and Spirit. God is and must be God." But this circumscription of divine infinity "does not threaten the concept of divine infinity; rather, it defines and reinforces the concept."[40]

### A.3. Eternity, Immensity, Impassibility, and Immutability

From simplicity and infinity, as well as from the direct biblical witness, Arminius derives the supereminent attributes of eternity, immensity, impassibility, immutability, and incorruptibility. The eternity of the divine essence means that it is free from the limitations of time. He considers and adapts the venerable definition of Boethius (ca. 480–ca. 525): whereas Boethius had defined eternity as the "simultaneous and perfect possession of endless life," Arminius defines it as the "interminable, entire, simultaneous, and perfect possession of essence."[41] He is not denying that eternity belongs to the divine life; he is merely insisting, in a way completely consistent with his understanding of the divine nature,

---

38. *Disp. pub.* IV.12. Arminius here goes on to explain, "[Free from anything] higher, because it has received its being (esse) from no one; [free from anything] lower, because the form, which is itself, is not limited to the capacity of some material that may receive it. [Free from anything] before, because [it is] from no efficient [cause]; [free from anything] after, because it does not exist for the sake of some final [cause] (finis)." Cf. *Disp. pub.* XXVIII.5.

39. *Disp. pub.* IV.12.

40. Muller, *God, Creation, and Providence,* p. 131.

41. *Disp. pub.* IV.14. Cf. *Disp. pub.* XXVIII.6. See also Muller, *God, Creation, and Providence,* p. 134.

that eternity belongs to life through essence rather than the other way around. God is not encompassed or limited by time, for there are no limits of beginning and end. Nor is there any succession of past and future. Rather, God, as a simple being, is not composed of temporal parts but is fully actualized and equally present to all times. This does not mean that God is, strictly speaking, "timeless," nor does it mean that he is "outside of time," which would be to reify time. Nor need it imply that God lacks duration of any kind. Rather, it means that God, as the creator of all, is related to all points of time at once; it means that God is actively present to all points of time.[42] Whatever "duration" we might ascribe to God surely differs from duration as experienced by creatures, and at any rate, it is duration without succession.

Just as God is not composed of temporal parts, neither is he made up of spatial parts. "Immensity is thus a supereminent mode" of the divine essence, which means that it is free from all limits of space and location. From this immensity follows "the omnipresence or ubiquity of the essence of God."[43] Just as divine eternity means that God is present to all points of creaturely time, so also divine immensity (or unmeasurability), as God is inwardly (*ad intra*), becomes omnipresence when considered in his external relations and actions toward creation (*ad extra*); that is, God is present to all points of created space.[44] This does not mean that the incarnate Son, according to his human nature, is at all places simultaneously or everywhere present, for Arminius's acceptance of the Reformed (and catholic) understanding of the communication of attributes (*communicatio idiomatum*) is far too nuanced and sophisticated to allow such a conclusion. In other words, Christ is not omnipresent according to his human nature, but he is nonetheless omnipresent (according to his divinity).

Arminius similarly embraces immutability and impassibility, again tying these doctrines to infinity and simplicity and defining them by what the divine essence lacks—namely, change and suffering.[45] The doctrines of divine immutability and impassibility are often assailed for endorsing

---

42. Cf. *PRRD* 3: 345.

43. *Disp. pub.* IV.15–16.

44. See *Disp. pub.* IV.13–16, 27; VI.10.

45. *Disp. pub.* IV.17–18; *Disp. pub.* XXVIII.8–9. *Impatibilitas*, the term Arminius uses along with *immutabilitas*, was not often employed among the Reformed orthodox. *PRRD* 3: 309–310.

(or at least entailing) the view that God is immobile, inactive, or without genuine affections. Sometimes the classical doctrine of impassibility is taken to entail that God has no affective or relational life; often, it is understood to be the denial of the core Christian conviction that God is love.[46] Many contemporary interpreters of the classical Christian tradition protest, however, that such criticisms are based upon misunderstandings (misunderstandings that are perpetuated by caricatures), and such a view recently has been exposed as the caricature that it is. As Thomas Weinandy points out, the classical doctrine affirms that divine love is completely and unalterably steadfast and perfect: "to say that God is impassible is again to ensure and accentuate his perfect goodness and unalterable love,"—the affirmation of impassibility helps to "safeguard and enhance his perfect and dynamic passion—his all-consuming goodness and ardent love."[47] Similarly, Richard A. Muller says that, for the Reformed orthodox, the doctrine of divine immutability (as traditionally understood) "in no way implies that God is *inactive*."[48] As "pure act" (*actus purus*), the divine essence is the opposite of "inactive." Traditionally, the immutability and impassibility of God do not deny his ability to move, change, display his affections, or carry on genuine relationship with his people. For example, the act of creation itself is a relative change that implies no imperfection in God. God is not the victim of a tumultuous emotional life; he is devoid of all *passiones* (or ill effects), and the suffering of the incarnate Son is to be predicated of the human nature of the Son.

---

46. For Jürgen Moltmann, the doctrine of divine impassibility is a moral outrage: a God who cannot suffer "cannot love either." Jürgen Moltmann, *The Trinity and the Kingdom: The Doctrine of God*, trans. Margaret Kohl (Minneapolis: Fortress Press, 1993), p. 38. For Moltmann, any answer other than "God suffers" to the problem of evil "would be blasphemy," for "there cannot be any other Christian answer to the question of this torment. To speak here of a God who could not suffer would make God a demon. To speak here of a God who could not suffer would make God an annihilating nothingness. To speak here of an indifferent God would be to condemn men to indifference." Idem, *The Crucified God: The Cross of Christ as the Foundation and Criticism of Christian Theology*, trans. R. A. Wilson and John Bowden (Minneapolis: Fortress Press, 1974), p. 274. See similar sentiments in Clark H. Pinnock, "Systematic Theology," in *The Openness of God: A Biblical Challenge to the Traditional Understanding of God* (Downers Grove: InterVarsity Press, 1994), pp. 117–119.

47. Thomas Weinandy, *Does God Suffer?* (Notre Dame: University of Notre Dame Press, 2000), p. 111. For an analysis of the patristic doctrine of impassibility, see David Bentley Hart, "No Shadow of Turning: On Divine Impassibility," *Pro Ecclesia* 11/2 (2002): 184–206; Paul Gavrilyuk, *The Suffering of the Impassible God: The Dialectics of Patristic Thought* (New York: Oxford University Press, 2006). For the Reformed orthodox perspective, see PRRD 3: 308–320.

48. PRRD 3: 309.

These corrections bring us to a place where we can better understand Arminius's conception of immutability and impassibility. Arminius fully endorses these doctrines. When discussing the "repentance of God," especially as reflected in the book of Jonah, Arminius unambiguously warns: "God is immutable, so that no shadow of change falls or can fall on him; the one who feels or speaks otherwise is a blasphemer. Unskilled is the one who says any such things from which the mutability of God can be inferred."[49] But his endorsement of these doctrines does not, of course, mean that he is committed to denying that God has an affective life. Following in the Latin theological tradition, Arminius denies that God's life is devoid of affections. Along with his theological predecessors, he is not committed to any view that makes God out to be a remote abstraction. Rather, he is just as committed to the conviction that biblical affirmations of the love and wrath of God give genuine insight into the character and life of God. His view is fully consistent with the classical understandings of immutability and impassibility: God is constant and incorruptible. He is "always the same, enduring in his eternity."[50] It is not as though God cannot feel emotion but that he is not controlled and corrupted by emotion as humanity is. God is not subject to fluctuating emotions because within the Triune life he is already fully actualized as holy love. He does not love more at certain points than at other points because, as pure act (*actus purus*), he is fully and infinitely loving. The doctrine of divine impassibility does not contradict—nor is it even in tension with—Arminius's basic conviction that holy love is at the center of God's own life. For him it is, rather, completely consistent with, and even an expression of, that core conviction.

### A.4. Unity, Goodness, and Holiness

Arminius also affirms a strong doctrine of divine unity, which is not surprising, given his doctrine of divine simplicity. Here he holds that "the unity of the essence of God is that according to which it is in every possible way so at one in itself, as to be altogether indivisible with regard to number, species, genus, parts, modes, and so on."[51] Arminius is not here denying

---

49. *Ep. ecc.* 60, p. 114: "Deus ita est immutabilis, ut nulla mutationis vel umbra in illum cadat aut cadere possit: blasphemus est qui secus sentit aut loquitur; imperitus qui talia dicit unde Dei mutabilitas concludi possit." Cf. Augustine, *De civitate Dei* VIII.v, in *PL* 41: 230, who declares it is horrible (*nefas*) to attribute mutability to God.

50. *Oratio prima*, in *Opera*, p. 29; *Works* 1: 326.

51. *Disp. pub.* IV.21.

that there are any genuine distinctions within God; he is denying that God is at all subject to division or internal contradiction. As we shall see, this insight becomes important in later controversies.

As divine simplicity is closely related to Arminius's doctrine of divine unity, so also is his account of the holiness of God. As usual, Arminius formulates the doctrine of holiness from the explicit teachings of Scripture, and he notices that the biblical portrayal of holiness "designates a separation."[52] This concept of distinctness, one that is deeply woven into the scriptural account (Genesis 2:3; Exodus 13:2; Joshua 24:19; Is. 6:3; 1 Thessalonians 5:23; 1 Peter 2:2–9), is one that he recognizes to be congruent with the doctrine of divine simplicity. In Aquinas's classic statement of the doctrine of simplicity, he denies that the divine essence enters into any composition with anything that is not God, and thus rejects outright any suggestion of monism, pantheism, or panentheism.[53] Arminius draws a similar conclusion. Just as there is no composition within the life of God, neither does God enter into the composition of other things. Therefore, God is "neither the soul of the world nor the form of the universe."[54] God, as distinct from all else, is holy and wholly other.

This is not to say that divine holiness is strictly a metaphysical rather than "moral" concept for Arminius. Divine holiness is closely related to divine goodness,[55] and for Arminius a proper understanding of the goodness of God is critically important for any adequate theological worldview. God is the supreme or highest good (summum bonum), and is goodness itself (ipsum bonum).[56] The goodness of God is a theological non-negotiable for Arminius; he is deeply convinced that the loss of a proper vision of God's goodness leads straight to heresy.[57] God is absolutely good, reliably good, and necessarily good. In his defense of the necessity of God's goodness, he claims that it would be "the height of blasphemy to say that God

---

52. *Disp. pub.* IV.22.

53. *ST* Ia.iii.8.

54. *Disp. pub.* IV.22.

55. Arminius thinks of divine goodness and holiness in terms of the divine will, but he also sees them in relation to the divine essence, e.g., in *Disp. pub.* IV.23. Indeed, given Arminius's commitment to the doctrine of simplicity, divine goodness and holiness are (at most) only formally distinct from the divine essence and the will of God.

56. *Disp. pub.* IV.23.

57. He specifically mentions Manicheeism in *Exam. Gom.*, pp. 76–77; *Works* 3: 590–591.

is freely good."[58] More concrete expressions of this will be seen in Arminius's statements on divine justice or righteousness *(iustitia)*.

## B. The Divine Life

For Arminius, God is not to be considered merely with reference to the divine essence. One must also think of the *life* of God in order to understand God rightly: "It is much more unbelievable that God is something empty and dead, than that there is no God."[59] These attributes of the divine life are considered under the "second moment of the divine nature."[60] Here, again, the fundamental conviction of the simplicity and aseity of God is central. God does not achieve life, nor does he receive it from another source. Nor does he depend upon anything other than himself for that life. Rather, "He is the life of himself, not having it from his union with another thing . . . he being life itself, and living by the first act, but bestowing life by the second act."[61] "Therefore the life of God is most simple, so that there is no real distinction from his essence."[62] The life that God enjoys is the life that he enjoys eternally and necessarily, with no possible threat of loss of that life or diminution of it. He alone is immortal.[63] This is why God distinguishes himself from all false gods and the idols that tempt his creatures. And this is cause for joy among those who know God rightly: "And since the essence *(essentia)* of God is infinite and most simple, eternal, impassible, immutable, and incorruptible, we ought likewise to consider his life with these modes of being and living; on which we account to him per se immortality, and a most prompt, powerful, indefatigable, and insatiable desire, strength *(robur)*, and joy to act and to enjoy, also in the action and the enjoyment."[64] Arminius considers three divine faculties: as faculties of the divine life the understanding, the will, and the power of God. Unlike the incommunicable, supereminent modes of the divine essence, the faculties of the divine life do have analogies with rational creatures.

---

58. *Apologia*, art. 22, in *Opera*, pp. 166–167; *Works* 2: 33–34.

59. *Disp. priv.* XVI.1.

60. *Disp. pub.* IV.25.

61. *Disp. priv.* XVI.2.

62. *Disp. priv.* XVI.3: "sic ut re ab essentia non distinguatur." Cf. *Disp. pub.* IV.28.

63. *Disp. pub.* IV.28.

64. *Disp. priv.* XVI.5.

### B.1. *Understanding and Omniscience*

Arminius is an intellectualist in the Thomistic tradition; thus, the divine intellect, or understanding, is first in the sense that it has regulative priority over the divine will, which then in turn regulates the divine power.[65] Arminius defines the understanding (*intellectus/intellectio*) of God as "the faculty of his life which is first in nature and order, and by which the living God distinctly understands all and singular things, which, in whatever manner, either have, will have, have had, can have, or might hypothetically have, a being (*entitatem*) of any kind."[66] The intellect is the divine faculty by which God "distinctly understands the order, connection, and relation of all things and each of them between each other."[67] God knows all that exists, and he knows all that could exist. God does not know things as we know them. He does not know things by "appearances," nor does he know them by "similitude." Rather, he knows all things by "his own and sole essence."[68] Arminius is insistent that the mode of divine knowledge is different from ours, and, like other attributes, cannot be understood "univocally" with human modes of knowledge.[69] Whereas humans know things by "discursive" reasoning or by reasoning from one thing to another ("if . . . then"), for Arminius "the mode by which God understands is not by composition and division, not by gradual argumentation (*discursum*), but by simple and infinite intuition, according to the succession of order and not of time."[70] Muller explains that Arminius, following Aquinas here, insists that:

> God's knowledge is neither abstractive nor discursive, compositive or dialectical. God does not know things, in other words, by first apprehending the idea or intelligible species of the individual thing and then applying it to or finding it in the thing—nor does God know by the application of a knowledge of previously apprehended things to other things, newly apprehended. Rather, God knows all things by a simple, infinite, immediate apprehension.[71]

---

65. Muller, *God, Creation, and Providence*, pp. 78, 144; Witt, "Creation, Redemption and Grace," p. 287.

66. *Disp. priv.* XVII.1; *Disp. pub.* IV.30. Cf. Muller, *God, Creation, and Providence*, p. 146.

67. *Disp. priv.* XVII.1.

68. *Disp. priv.* XVII.2. God knows evil things only indirectly (by privation).

69 Witt, "Creation, Redemption and Grace," p. 337.

70. *Disp. priv.* XVII.3. Cf *Disp. pub.* IV.33.

71. Muller, *God, Creation, and Providence*, pp. 147–148.

Beyond this, Arminius is willing to speculate further about the order of the objects of divine knowledge: first, God knows himself "entirely and adequately," and this understanding is, again according to the doctrine of divine simplicity, just his own being (*esse*). Second, God knows "all possible things in the perfection of their own essence." Here he draws further distinctions: he knows what things can exist strictly and solely by his own act, he knows all things (both possible and actual) that can exist from his creatures (of course by his own "conservation, motion, assistance, concurrence, and permission"), and he knows what he can do about the acts of his creatures in a way that is consistent with his own nature and with the creaturely, contingent nature of those actions. Third, "he knows all [actual] entities, even according to the same order as that which has been demonstrated in his knowledge of possible things."[72]

It is evident that with respect to omniscience (considered broadly), Arminius takes a strongly traditional line: God is omniscient, and his knowledge covers the past, the present, and the future. In other words, God possesses foreknowledge (*praescientia*), which Arminius takes to be the dominant assumption throughout Scripture (which is only "fore-" knowledge in the sense that the knowledge extends to what is future "to us"). Arminius writes that God "knows all things possible, whether they be in the capability (*potentia*) of God or of the creature. . . . God can deservedly be said to know things infinite."[73] As Muller puts it, "Granting this infinite self-identical self-knowledge and granting that God is the first cause of all things, God must know all possibility and all actuality (which is to say, actualized possibility) and know these categories exhaustively."[74] God knows all truths—including all

---

72. *Disp. priv.* XVII.4. Cf. *Disp. pub.* IV.34. Given Arminius's commitment to the doctrine of divine simplicity, it is important to bear in mind that these distinctions, while useful, are only conceptual or at most formal. God does not know things discursively because the omniscience of God is "according to that of a most pure act." See *Disp. pub.* IV.39.

73. *Disp. pub.* IV.31: "[God] knows all things possible, whether they be in the capability (*potentia*) of God or of the creature; in active or passive capability; in the capability of operation, imagination, or enunciation: he knows all things that could exist (*existerent posita*) by some hypothesis; he knows things other than himself, those that are necessary and contingent, good and evil, universal and particular, future, present and past, excellent and vile: [he knows] things substantial and accidental of every kind, actions and passions, the modes and circumstances of all things; external words and deeds, internal thoughts, deliberations, counsels, and decrees; and entities of reason, whether complex or non-complex. All these things, being jointly attributed to the understanding of God, seem to bring it about (*id efficere*) that God can deservedly be said to know things infinite (Acts 15:18; Heb. 4:13; Matt. 11:21; Ps. 147:4; Is. 41:22, 23; 44:7; Matt. 10:30; Ps. 135; 1 John 3:20; 1 Samuel 16:7; 1 Kings 8:39; Ps. 94:11; Is. 40:28; Ps. 147:5; 139; 94:9–10; 10:13–14)."

74. Muller, *God, Creation, and Providence*, pp. 146–147.

contingent truths as well as all necessary truths—and God knows them exhaustively. Divine knowledge does not bring necessity to the thing known. As omniscient, God knows necessary things as necessary, and he knows contingent things as contingent. "For as he knows the thing itself and its mode, if the mode of the thing is contingent, he must know it as such, and therefore it remains contingent with respect to the divine knowledge."[75] In his general affirmations of divine omniscience, Arminius is completely consistent not only with the broader patristic and medieval tradition but also with his Reformed predecessors and contemporaries.

Arminius is also in step with the main lines of the Christian tradition in his simultaneous affirmation of foreknowledge and denial of determinism. Although most theologians have recognized a potential tension in holding these two concepts together, many coherent solutions have been proposed over the centuries. Arminius draws upon the distinction, so common among the medieval scholastics, between the necessity of the consequence and the necessity of the consequent.[76] The necessity of the consequence is captured by such statements as "necessarily, if God knows that Tom is eating an apple, then Tom is eating an apple"; while the necessity of the consequent can be seen in such statements as "if God knows that Tom is eating an apple, then, necessarily, Tom is eating an apple." The necessity of the consequent is required for determinism, while the necessity of the consequence is all that is required for foreknowledge. But the necessity of the consequent is not entailed by the necessity of the consequence; thus it is possible to have foreknowledge without determinism.[77] With this distinction, Arminius affirms foreknowledge but rejects determinism. Certainty or infallibility, on the one hand, and necessity, on the other hand, are not the same: "'infallibly' is said with respect to the infinite divine foreknowledge: but 'necessarily,' with respect to God's decree and the divine will."[78] God, by his foreknowledge, thus

---

75. *Disp. priv.* XVII.7. Cf. *Disp. pub.* IV.38.

76. E.g., *Exam. Perk.*, in *Opera*, pp. 704, 708; *Works* 3: 374–375, 381.

77. Although he did not use the same terminology, this conclusion is consistent with Augustine, *De civitate Dei* V.ix.1, in *PL* 41: 149: "In order that we may confess the highest and true God, so we confess his will and highest power and foreknowledge. Therefore let us not fear that we do something not by the will which we think we are doing by the will, because he whose foreknowledge cannot fail foreknew that we would do it." For helpful contemporary discussion of freedom and foreknowledge (in a way consistent with the views of Arminius), see Alvin Plantinga, "On Ockham's Way Out," *Faith and Philosophy* 3 (1986): 235–269.

78. *Exam. Perk.*, in *Opera*, pp. 704–705; *Works* 3: 375. Cf. ibid., in *Opera*, p. 771; *Works* 3: 474.

knows "who by his grace would believe, and who by their own fault would remain in unbelief."[79]

> The certainty of the event is properly from the foreknowledge (*praescientia*) of God; but the necessity from the omnipotent and irresistible action of God: which, indeed, can be the foundation of the foreknowledge of some event; but is not of this [irresistible action], because God has decided to save believers through grace, that is, through gentle and sweet persuasion, agreeing or congruent with their free choice (*arbitrio*); not through omnipotent action or motion, which they are neither willing nor able to resist, nor can be willing to resist. Much less does the condemnation of some people proceed from an inescapable necessity imposed by God.[80]

As Arminius sees things, freedom and determinism are strictly incompatible, but foreknowledge, which neither equates with nor entails necessity, indeed is consistent with genuine freedom.[81]

Where Arminius differs sharply from his Reformed contemporaries is in his advocacy and defense of the doctrine of middle knowledge. The theory of middle knowledge (sometimes called "Molinism" after Luis de Molina) posits three logical moments within the divine knowledge, the first two of which were common to most scholastic accounts. The first is God's *necessary* knowledge, or knowledge of simple intelligence. This is God's "prevolitional knowledge of all necessary truths."[82] Muller defines this as "the uncompounded, unqualified, absolute, indefinite, or unbounded knowledge of God that God has necessarily according to his nature and by which God

---

79. *Exam. Perk.*, in *Opera*, p. 750; *Works* 3: 443.

80. *Exam. Perkins, Opera*, p. 750, *Works* 3: 443.

81. E.g., *Exam. Perk.*, in *Opera*, pp. 713, 769–771; *Works* 3: 388, 473–474. It is clear that Arminius rejects (what is now called) "compatibilism," but the extent to which he departs from his Reformed contemporaries on this issue is not so clear. On the one hand, John Frame conflates determinism with Calvinism and declares that "those Calvinists who place great weight on antiquity and tradition will have to concede . . . that the oldest extracanonical traditions do not favor their position." John Frame, *The Doctrine of God: A Theology of Lordship* (Phillipsburg: P & R, 2002), p. 138 n. 23. But for a very different view, see Willem J. Van Asselt, et al., eds., *Reformed Thought on Freedom: The Concept of Free Choice in Early Modern Reformed Theology*, Texts and Studies in Reformation and Post-Reformation Thought (Grand Rapids, MI: Baker Academic, 2010).

82. Thomas P. Flint, *Divine Providence: The Molinist Account* (Ithaca, NY: Cornell University Press, 1998), p. 41.

perfectly knows himself and the whole range of possibility."[83] It is God's simple knowledge of all that *must be*—it is also God's knowledge of all that *could be*. It logically precedes any act of the divine will; it is logically independent of the divine will. The second moment, God's *free* knowledge, or knowledge of vision, is his knowledge of what *will be*, and it follows and is logically dependent upon the divine will. It is God's "voluntary knowledge, of actual things brought freely into existence by the divine will operating within the range of possibility perfectly known to God."[84] By his necessary knowledge, God knows all possibilities, which is to say that he knows all that *could be*, and by his voluntary or free knowledge he knows all that *will be* due to his active willing.

These two categories are relatively uncontroversial within Reformed scholasticism, but it is the third category of *scientia media* ("middle knowledge") that occasions debate. The Jesuit philosopher Luis de Molina famously posited a *scientia media* "between" God's necessary knowledge and his free knowledge. In the words of William Lane Craig, middle knowledge is "the aspect of divine omniscience that comprises God's knowledge, prior to any determination of the divine will, of which contingent events would occur under any hypothetical set of circumstances."[85] Molina himself says, regarding God's middle knowledge:

> in virtue of the most profound and inscrutable comprehension of each faculty of free choice, he saw in his own essence what each such faculty would do with its innate freedom were it to be placed

---

83. Muller, *Dictionary*, p. 274.

84. Muller, *Dictionary*, p. 274.

85. William Lane Craig, "Middle Knowledge: A Calvinist-Arminian Rapprochement?" in *The Grace of God and the Will of Man*, ed. Clark H. Pinnock (Grand Rapids, MI: Zondervan, 1989), p. 147. The theory of middle knowledge has enjoyed something of a revival of interest and defense, as well as criticism, in recent years. The "grounding objection" is often taken to be the strongest objection to the theory, on which see, e.g., Robert M. Adams, "Middle Knowledge and the Problem of Evil," *American Philosophical Quarterly* 14 (1977): 109–117; idem, "An Anti-Molinist Argument," *Philosophical Perspectives* 5 (1991), pp. 343–353; William Hasker, *God, Time, and Knowledge* (Ithaca, NY: Cornell University Press, 1989), pp. 29–52; Timothy O'Connor, "The Impossibility of Middle Knowledge," *Philosophical Studies* 66 (1992): 139–166; Thomas P. Flint, *Divine Providence*, pp. 121–137; Edward R. Wierenga, *The Nature of God: An Inquiry into the Divine Attributes* (Ithaca, NY: Cornell University Press, 1989), pp. 116–165; Richard Otte, "A Defense of Middle Knowledge," *International Journal for Philosophy of Religion* 21 (1987): 161–189; William Lane Craig, "Middle Knowledge, Truth-Makers, and the 'Grounding Objection,'" *Faith and Philosophy* 18 (2001): 337–352.

in this or that or, indeed, in infinitely many orders of things—even though it would really be able, if it so willed, to do the opposite.[86]

So where God's natural knowledge gives him knowledge of truths that are necessary and independent of the divine will, and his free knowledge gives him knowledge of truths that are contingent and dependent upon God's will, divine middle knowledge comprises those truths that are contingent and independent of the decisions of God's will.[87] Natural knowledge includes knowledge of all that *must be* (in the sense of logical necessity) as well as all that *could be* (in the sense of logical possibility), while free knowledge is God's knowledge of what *will be*. Between these, however, is middle knowledge: it is God's knowledge of all that *would be*. "Thus, whereas by his natural knowledge God knows that, say, Peter when placed under a certain set of circumstances *could* either deny Christ or not deny Christ, being free to do either under identical circumstances, by his middle knowledge God knows what Peter *would* do if placed under those circumstances."[88] The doctrine of middle knowledge was seen as attractive because it promises to reconcile two concerns that are very important to traditionally minded Christian theologians: both the biblically based demand for a strong doctrine of providence and the biblically grounded concern for genuine human responsibility and the freedom entailed by such responsibility.[89] Because God knows precisely how every individual would respond in any set of circumstances, God then actualizes a particular world with a particular set of individuals and set of circumstances in which they make free choices.[90]

---

86. Luis de Molina, *On Divine Foreknowledge (Part IV of the* Concordia), trans. Alfred J. Freddoso (Ithaca, NY: Cornell University Press, 1988), IV.lii.9, p. 168. Cf. the discussion in Alfred J. Freddoso, "Introduction," in Molina, *On Divine Foreknowledge*, pp. 1–81; Craig, "Middle Knowledge," pp. 147–148.

87. Flint, *Divine Providence*, p. 42.

88. Craig, "Middle Knowledge," p. 147. For other brief descriptions of *scientia media*, see Dekker, *Rijker dan Midas*, pp. 78–81; "Was Arminius a Molinist?" 338–341.

89. In addition to the (generally recognized) biblical witness to divine providence, divine omniscience, and human moral responsibility, the biblical *locus classicus* of the doctrine of middle knowledge is 1 Samuel 23.

90. Cf. Craig, "Middle Knowledge," p. 152: "While it is impossible in the composed sense, given God's foreknowledge, for anything to happen differently from the way it will, this sense is irrelevant to contingency and freedom. In the relevant, divided sense we are as perfectly free in our decisions and actions as if God's foreknowledge did not exist. Middle knowledge therefore supplies not only the basis for divine foreknowledge, but also the means for reconciling that foreknowledge with creaturely freedom and contingency."

It is not at all hard to discern Arminius's own views on this matter. As he explains it:

> The scholastics say besides, that one kind of God's knowledge is natural and necessary, another free, and another middle (*mediam*). (1) Natural or necessary knowledge is that by which God understands himself and all things possible. (2) Free knowledge is that by which he knows all other beings. (3) Middle knowledge is that by which he knows that "if this thing happens, that will take place." The first precedes every free act of the divine will; the second follows the free act of God's will; and the last precedes indeed the free act of the divine will, but hypothetically from this act it sees that some particular thing will occur (*futurum*).[91]

Not only did Arminius own the second edition of Molina's *Concordia* (1595), but he also explicitly endorsed the idea of "middle knowledge": although God's necessary (or natural) knowledge is important, "it is necessary for that 'middle' [knowledge] to intervene in things which depend on the liberty of created choice."[92]

If Arminius's endorsement of the doctrine of middle knowledge is clear, so is his disagreement with his Reformed colleagues on this point. As Muller points out, "We finally have a point of difference with Reformed teaching that bears directly on the substance of the later debate."[93] And it is an important point, for Arminius wields this view to support his doctrine of salvation: like Molina, Arminius uses the doctrine to argue that "God has eternally determined to distribute to all mankind the grace necessary for salvation. Grace is, thus, unequally distributed but is sufficient for each individual. According to his *scientia media*, God knows how individuals will accept or resist the assistance of his grace and can destine them either to glory or to reprobation on the grounds of their free choice."[94] One can see how important the Molinist account is for Arminius's account of predestination and salvation in his discussion of the divine decrees. The first three

---

91. *Disp. pub.* IV.43. Cf. *Disp. pub.* IV.36; *Disp. priv.* XVII.11–12. Even when Arminius does not use the phrase *scientia media*, it is implicit throughout his theology and in many passages. E.g., see *Exam. Perk.*, in *Opera*, pp. 752–753; *Works* 3: 446.

92. *Disp. pub.* IV.45; *Disp. priv.* XVIII.12.

93. Muller, *God, Creation, and Providence*, p. 154.

94. Muller, *God, Creation, and Providence*, p. 161.

decrees deal with the divine intention to make Christ the one who mediates salvation, while the fourth decree is based on God's middle knowledge.[95]

As a convinced Protestant, of course, Arminius makes very important changes to Molina's account; he insists, for example, that predestination to justification is by God's foreknowledge of *faith*, not merits. But apart from these serious adaptations, Arminius's view is close to that of Molina and indeed relies upon it.[96] Arminius would not live to see the development of further controversy about the doctrine of middle knowledge, but it should be clear that his theology not only incorporates it but also relies quite heavily upon it. As Dekker puts it, *scientia media* occupies a "central place" in Arminius's doctrine of divine knowledge.[97]

### B.2. The Divine Will

Along with intellect, the divine will is "another faculty of God's life." Arminius notes that the phrase "the will of God" is ambiguous, and he points out that it can be disambiguated in several directions. Its most proper usage is with respect to the faculty of willing, but it is also used often in relation to the act of willing and even the object or action willed.[98] He is primarily interested in the "proper" use of the term, and he works to formulate an account of the will of God that is consistent with what he takes to be true of God more generally. Here Arminius takes leave of the Scotist tendencies that Musculus had already contributed to Reformed theology of divine will.[99] This voluntaristic model became dominant in

---

95. *Dec. sent.*, p. 106; *Works* 1: 653–654. Cf. Muller, *God, Creation, and Providence*, pp. 162–163. For more on the decrees of predestination, see chapter 3 in this volume.

96. Muller, *God, Creation, and Providence*, p. 163, provides an apt summary: "Like Driedo and Molina, Arminius assumes a prior, general divine determination to save the human race and to provide sufficient means to this end—and, again like Molina, he assumes that God elects or rejects on the basis of a foreknowledge of human response to grace. The basic outline is Molinist, then, inasmuch as the divine foreknowledge includes knowledge of the rejection as well as the acceptance of grace."

97. Dekker, *Rijker dan Midas*, p. 99. Cf. Muller, *God, Creation, and Providence*, pp. 155–166; idem, "Was Arminius a Molinist?" 337–352. But contra Roger Olson, *Arminian Theology: Myths and Realities* (Downers Grove: IVP Academic, 2006), pp. 195–197; and Witt, "Creation, Redemption and Grace," pp. 354–370. Some later Remonstrants also embraced the doctrine of middle knowledge. E.g., Episcopius, *Institutiones theologicae* IV.ii.19, in *Opera theologica*, pp. 303–304. See the discussion in Dennis W. Jowers, "Introduction," in *Four Views on Divine Providence*, ed. Dennis W. Jowers (Grand Rapids, MI: Zondervan, 2011), p. 17.

98. *Disp. pub.* IV.47. Cf. *Disp. priv.* XVIII.1.

99. See Muller, *God, Creation, and Providence*, p. 168.

Reformed scholasticism, for which reason Reformed orthodoxy has recently been dubbed "Perfect Will theology."[100] But unlike voluntarists, Arminius does not think that the divine will is somehow prior to the divine understanding; instead, he takes the intellectualist line of Aquinas in arguing that the divine will "follows the divine understanding and is produced from it."[101] In accord with the divine understanding, which is omniscient, and in the simplicity of the divine nature, which is necessarily good, the will is informed by the divine intellect and is always oriented toward goodness. Thus the divine will is always oriented toward a good, because only what is good is a proper or adequate object of the divine will. And the divine will is always oriented toward a *known* good, because the divine mind is never lacking in awareness or understanding.[102] Because God always knows what is good, he is able to will the good. And because God *is* good, he always wills what is good.[103] The primary object of the divine will is the chief good, God's own infinite goodness; the secondary object is created, finite goods.[104]

Arminius is well aware that Scripture seems to speak of God's will and its effects in different ways, and he is willing to recognize the legitimacy of language about distinctions within the will of God. Indeed, he delineates eight types of distinctions in God's will. For example, there is one thing that God wills of necessity, while there are other things that God wills with liberty. "God by a natural necessity wills himself, but freely [he wills] all other things (2 Timothy 2:13; Revelation 4:11)."[105] Or again, God wills some

---

100. J. Martin Bac, *Perfect Will Theology: Divine Agency in Reformed Scholasticism as against Suárez, Episcopius, Descartes, and Spinoza,* Brill's Series in Church History, vol. 42 (Leiden: Brill, 2010), p. 16: "Systematically and historically, Reformed scholasticism is best understood as Perfect Will theology." In this sense, Reformed thought was dominated by the "Scotist framework" (ibid., p. 29). Cf. *PRRD* 3: 407–408 (which Bac also cites).

101. *Disp. pub.* IV.49. "Intellectualism" asserts that the intellect is the faculty that directs the will, but "voluntarism" claims that the will is the nobler of the two faculties. Arminius's "intellectualist" view of the divine life is analogous to his view of the faculties of the human soul. See Richard A. Muller, "The Priority of the Intellect in the Soteriology of Jacob Arminius," *Westminster Theological Journal* 55 (1993): 55–72; Stanglin, *Arminius on Assurance,* pp. 100–102. For an analysis of this issue with respect to Calvin, see Muller, *Unaccommodated Calvin,* pp. 159–173. For basic definitions, see idem, *Dictionary,* pp. 157, 330–331.

102. *Disp. pub.* IV.49.

103. "The will of God is the very essence of God, yet distinguished from it according to the formal reason." *Disp. pub.* IV.50.

104. *Disp. priv.* XIX.3. Cf. Muller, *God, Creation, and Providence,* p. 173.

105. *Disp. pub.* IV.56. Cf. *Disp. priv.* XIX.1.

things as an end, but he wills other things as a means to an end.[106] Arminius also sees a legitimate distinction between the efficacious will of God, on the one hand, and the permissive will of God on the other.[107]

Arminius is cognizant of the biblical passages that speak of God's active judgment upon those who rebel against him, and he is also keenly aware that these passages may be used to argue that God wills that people commit evil actions. Arminius draws a distinction therefore between what God wills *per se* and what God wills *per accidens*. What God wills per se is what is *good*—what he wills "accidentally" are the "evils of punishment, because he would rather have the order of justice preserved in punishment than allow an offending creature to go unpunished."[108]

Aside from a quibble about terminology, Arminius is generally favorable to the ancient distinction between the "antecedent" and "consequent" will of God.[109] By his antecedent will, God wills for all people to be saved (1 Timothy 2:4). But by his consequent will, not everyone will be saved, for some refuse (Matthew 23:37–38).[110] Acknowledging the antecedent will would mean acknowledging that God's will can be resisted, and that God wills something that will never happen. Thus, human choice intervenes, for which reason Reformed theologians generally denied this distinction.[111] According to this distinction, God's antecedent will may be resisted, but his consequent will to save penitent believers and to reject impenitent unbelievers cannot be resisted. Similarly, Arminius draws a distinction between the "peremptory," "absolute," or unconditional will of God and the "conditional" will of God.[112] These distinctions also become very important for Arminius's account of the order of salvation (*ordo salutis*). God's "peremptory will is that which strictly and rigidly obtains: such as the words of the Gospel which contain the last revelation of God, 'The wrath of God abides on the one who does not believe.' 'The one who

---

106. *Disp. pub.* IV.57.

107. *Disp. pub.* IV.58.

108. *Disp. pub.* IV.63.

109. The terminology for this distinction goes back at least to John of Damascus, *De fide orthodoxa* II.xxix, in *PG* 94: 969A. See also the discussion in Muller, *God, Creation, and Providence*, pp. 186–188; Dekker, *Rijker dan Midas*, pp. 122–124.

110. *Disp. pub.* IV.60.

111. E.g., see Du Moulin, *Anatome Arminianismi*, V, pp. 24–37 (ET, pp. 27–41). Cf. *PRRD* 3: 467.

112. *Disp. priv.* XIX.5–6; *Disp. pub.* IV.60–62.

believes will be saved.'"[113] The conditional will of God, on the other hand, can be either tacit (as in the case of the warnings of Scripture that come with an implied "if") or explicit. It is "that by which he wills something with respect to the volition or the action of the creature."[114] Thus, properly understood, Arminius can agree that "the will of God is both correctly and usefully distinguished into that which is antecedent and that which is consequent."[115]

Arminius is willing to allow for these distinctions, but he is exercised to oppose any notion of contradictory wills of God. As the divine nature is simple, so the will of God is the divine essence. And as the divine essence, the will of God itself is "most simple."[116] It is not composed of anything at all, so surely it is not composed of things that contradict one another. This conviction that God does not have contradictory wills, grounded as it is in his doctrines of divine goodness and simplicity, is crucial for Arminius's doctrine of divine action.

This issue comes to bear on another distinction in the divine will that Arminius mentions, which was typical among Reformed theologians. It was common to distinguish between God's secret and revealed will. On the one hand, the secret will (*voluntas arcana*), also known as the will of the decree (*decreti*) or of good pleasure (*beneplaciti*), is the ultimate, effective, absolutely unsearchable will of God that underlies the revealed will. It may be partly revealed, but not completely (see Deuteronomy 29:29). It is what God wills to do himself. On the other hand, the revealed will (*voluntas revelata*), also known as the will of the precept (*praecepti*) or of the sign (*signi*), is the moral will that God has for creatures to fulfill (see Rom. 12:2).[117] Though he mentions this distinction in his public disputation of 1603, he omits this distinction later in his final round of private disputations.[118] Indeed, elsewhere he writes, "The distinction of the will of God into that of his good pleasure and that of the sign cannot bear a rigid examination."[119] He does not outright reject the distinction, but he likely

---

113. *Disp. priv.* XIX.5.

114. *Disp. priv.* XIX.5–6.

115. *Art. non.* II.6, in *Opera*, p. 949; *Works* 2: 707.

116. *Disp. pub.* IV.51.

117. *Disp. pub.* IV.58; Muller, *Dictionary*, pp. 331–333.

118. See *Disp. priv.* XIX.

119. *Art. non.* II.7, in *Opera*, p. 949; *Works* 2: 707.

keeps his distance from it for a couple of reasons. First, he generally thinks there is more revealed in God's decree than do the Reformed.[120] God has certainly not revealed everything, but when it comes to predestination and the *ordo salutis* (order of salvation), Arminius will not be as eager as his critics to appeal to an unfathomable, mysterious divine will, such as the *voluntas arcana* (secret will). Furthermore, when used by his opponents, the distinction implies contradictory wills in God, an implication that Arminius does clearly reject.[121]

This conviction that God's will is not self-contradictory plays an important role in Arminius's debates on predestination. In his response to William Perkins, Arminius writes that "the command of God by which he commands faith and repentance upon those to whom the gospel is announced, can in no way conflict with the decree of God. For no will or volition of God whatsoever can be contrary to any other."[122] Arminius explains why a doctrine of unconditional election entails contradictory wills of God: it has God commanding all people to believe and simultaneously withholding the grace necessary for belief.[123] To put it another way, "do not commit adultery" (the revealed will of God) is an outright contradiction of "commit adultery" (as the decretive, or secret, will of God). Similarly, "repent and believe" contradicts "persist in your rebellion; do not repent and believe." But what is to be said to the objection that God does not directly will or decree such evils, but that God merely withholds the grace that is necessary? Here Arminius compares the doctrine of predestination to the doctrine of providence, and he says that "just as it cannot

---

120. Stanglin, *Arminius on Assurance*, p. 231 n. 161.

121. *Disp. priv.* XIX.cor. 1–3; *Exam. Perk.*, in *Opera*, p. 667; *Works* 3: 318–319.

122. *Exam. Perk.*, in *Opera*, p. 667; *Works* 3: 318.

123. *Exam. Perk.*, in *Opera*, p. 667; *Works* 3: 318–319: "The command by which God commands (*mandatum . . . mandat*) faith for anyone, declares that God wills that the one to whom the command is prescribed should believe. If, now, anyone ascribes some decree to God by which he wills such a one not to believe, then that decree will be contrary to the command. For it cannot happen (*Fieri . . . non potest*) that God simultaneously wills contradictory things, in whatever mode or under whatever distinction the will is considered. But to believe and not to believe—to will that someone should believe, and to will that the same one considered in the same mode should not believe—are contradictory things. But such is the decree by which God is said to have arranged (*statuisse*) to deny his concurrence either of general governance or of special grace, without which he knew that the act of faith could not be fulfilled (*praestari*) by the one whom he exhorts to faith by his command. For he who wills to deny to someone the help necessary to fulfill the act of faith, the same wills that such a one should not believe."

be said that God wills him still to exist to whom he denies the act of his conservation, so also it cannot be said that he wills that act to be performed by anyone, to whom he denies his concurrence and help necessary for the performance of that act."[124] Either way, he concludes, an outright contradiction is entailed.

To be clear, Arminius does not object to the view that there are distinctions within the will of God.[125] Instead, he objects to the notion that there are contradictory wills of God: "He cannot be said to be willing and not willing (*volens et nolens*) the same object—namely, willing and not willing the conversion of one and the same person."[126] While conceptual distinctions may be helpful to gain an understanding, such conceptualizing should not mislead. God, in accordance with his nature as pure and simple goodness, wills what is good. Thus it "is impossible for God, by any mode of willing whatever, to will contrary or contradictory things."[127]

Does the fact that God wills something make it inevitable or necessary? Does divine volition entail determinism? Arminius recognizes the importance of such questions, and he is attuned to the force that they may have when wielded by his opponents. He readily agrees that there is a sense in which God is the cause of all things, but he denies that this removes freedom or replaces contingency with necessity. God "acts through second causes, either with them or in them, [and] he does not take away their own divinely imparted proper mode of acting." Instead, God allows secondary causes to produce their own effects—"necessary things necessarily, contingent things contingently, and free things freely."[128] He "neither wills sin to happen, nor wills it not to happen. For permission is the act of a relaxed will; which relaxing of the will here was fitting in God, because he made man with a free power of choice, that he might test (*exploraret*) his free and voluntary obedience; which he could not have done, if he had placed any insuperable obstacle in man's way."[129]

---

124. *Exam. Perk.*, in *Opera*, pp. 667–668; *Works* 3: 319.

125. *Exam. Perk.*, in *Opera*, p. 668; *Works* 3: 320.

126. *Exam. Perk.*, in *Opera*, p. 668; *Works* 3: 320. Arminius goes on to write, "I wish it to be explained to me how God may will from the heart for that person to believe in Christ, whom he [also] wills to be alien from Christ, and for whom he has decreed to deny the necessary aids (*auxilia*) to faith: for this is not to will the conversion of someone."

127. *Exam. Perk.*, in *Opera*, p. 699; *Works* 3: 366.

128. *Disp. pub.* IV.54.

129. *Exam. Perk.*, in *Opera*, p. 696; *Works* 3: 361.

As noted above, immutability and impassibility do not imply a lack of affections in God. Arminius treats affections as part of the divine will. Although Arminius first treated goodness under God's essence—since God is the highest good and goodness itself—nevertheless he also treats it as the chief affection of God's will. The first or principal (*primitivi*) affections in God are love and goodness.[130] Goodness and love, therefore, enjoy a place of priority in God's will. When exercised toward creation, goodness precedes and is the cause of love.[131] Love is an affection of union in God, whose objects are himself and the creature and its happiness. Adjoined to goodness and love is the divine grace extended freely to creation.[132] Again, these affections do not undermine God's immutability. Divine love and its opposite, hatred, are expressions of the same singular will, but are perceived in relation to human beings who have changed. God always, immutably, loves righteousness and always hates sin; human righteousness and evil are the changing aspects in the divine-human relationship.

To summarize, Arminius holds that God, as pure act, wills what is good. In his wisdom, he wills that there should be free creatures who know him in his goodness. For the benefit of the creature, God creates a world in which it is possible freely and rightly to relate to God; he creates a world where it is possible to obey, enjoy, glorify, and love God.[133]

### B.3. Divine Power

God is not just a being who knows and wills; he also brings his will for the known good to fruition. Consistent with his doctrine of divine simplicity, Arminius denies that there is passive power in God. God is, once again, pure act, and thus his power is an active power. He describes divine power as "a faculty of the life of God, posterior in order to the understanding and the will, by which God can, from the liberty of his own will, operate extrinsically all things whatsoever that he can freely will, and by which he does whatsoever he freely wills."[134] Arminius insists that the "measure of the divine

---

130. *Disp. pub.* IV.66.

131. *Disp. priv.* XX.3. Arminius follows Aquinas, *ST* Ia-IIae.xxvii.1 resp.

132. *Disp. pub.* IV.67, 69; *Disp. priv.* XX.4, 8.

133. Cf. *Exam. Perk.*, in *Opera*, p. 726; *Works* 3: 408.

134. *Disp. pub.* IV.78–79; *Disp. priv.* XXII.1–2. Nor does Arminius show interest in talking about the necessary *ad intra* productions of the divine power.

power is the free will of God,"[135] and his emphasis on the freedom of the divine will has caused some interpreters to conclude that he embraces a kind of nominalist account of the divine will as absolute power (*potentia absoluta*).[136] Muller points back to Isaak Dorner as an example of this misinterpretation.[137] Dorner thinks that Arminius's theology "is still essentially connected with Calvinism," for it "lays a onesided emphasis upon [God's] supreme sovereignty." Indeed, according to Dorner, Arminius's thought "exceeds Calvinism" in its refusal to "consider free divine sovereignty to be bound to any law in God."[138] The implication is that God's power and even knowledge of the good become subject to the arbitrary whims of the divine will.

On closer inspection, however, such a voluntarist reading cannot be sustained by Arminius's own statements, and he is not the "Calvinist" (or even hyper-Calvinist) that Dorner depicts. Muller argues that "Arminius' radical intellectualism places the divine knowledge of the good prior to all acts of divine willing and identifies the human good as derived from the divine good." Muller explains Arminius's view further: "Indeed, the ultimate good of all human beings arises, for Arminius, in the vision of God as the highest good and depends, ontologically, on the participation of the creature in the creative goodness of God: God wills first his own goodness and, second, the goodness of the creature in and through himself." Thus "Arminius's affinity for Thomism stands firmly in the way of a view such as proposed by Dorner."[139] In other words, though the divine will may regulate the divine *potentia ad extra* (power extended outward), the divine will is regulated by the divine intellect. God knows the good, his will is for creation's good, and he will thus act for its good. As Arminius puts it, "God's dominion over the creatures is not so infinite that he can *rightfully* do with them whatever his infinite and absolute power *could* do with them."[140] Furthermore, Arminius never departs

---

135. *Disp. pub.* IV.80.

136. Muller, *Dictionary*, p. 231, defines the *potentia absoluta* as "the omnipotence of God limited only by the law of noncontradiction."

137. Muller, *God, Creation, and Providence*, p. 173.

138. Isaak August Dorner, *History of Protestant Theology Particularly in Germany Viewed according to Its Fundamental Movement*, 2 vols., trans. George Robson and Sophia Taylor (Edinburgh: T & T Clark, 1871), 1: 418.

139. Muller, *God, Creation, and Providence*, p. 173.

140. *Exam. Gom.*, pp. 121–122; *Works* 3: 627. Cf. *Exam. Perk.*, in *Opera*, pp. 692–693; *Works* 3: 356–357.

from his doctrine of divine simplicity, and he insists that "the will of God can only will that which is not opposed to the divine essence (which is the foundation of both his understanding and will)."[141] Since the power and will of God rest upon an intellect that "has the very essence of God for its foundation, and since God can freely will those things alone which are not contrary to his essence and natural will, and which can be comprehended in his understanding as entities and true things, it follows that . . . therefore his capability (*potentia*) also [is] bound by those alone."[142]

The upshot of this is that Arminius's account of divine power allows him to maintain that God freely exercises his power, and that God does so while fully informed by the divine intellect and fully consistent with the divine essence (from which it is only formally distinct). Thus God can do all things that are possible (Luke 1:37; 18:27; Mark 14:36)—where *possible* is understood not only in the sense of merely logical possibility but also as what is in accord with the divine nature.[143] So God cannot do what is logically impossible, nor can he do what is opposed to his nature. For instance, "God cannot make another God, is incapable of being changed (James 1:17); he cannot sin (Ps. 5:5); cannot lie (Numbers 23:19; 2 Tim. 2:13; Philippians 4:19), cannot cause a thing at the same time to be and not to be, to have been and not to have been," and so forth. "When we make such assertions as these, we do not inflict an injury on the capability of God, but we must beware that things unworthy of him are not attributed to his essence, his understanding, and his will."[144] God can do anything that is logically possible for a maximally great and morally perfect being to do. So God is still rightly called "omnipotent" (Rev. 1:8; Ephesians 3:20; Matt. 3:9; 26:53; Rom. 9:19; Phil. 3:21), and his power is infinite.[145]

## B.4. The Righteousness and Justice of God

Arminius sees divine righteousness or justice (*iustitia*) as having some analogy to what are commonly termed *moral virtues*. Considered "universally," this refers to the divine attribute by which he administers the works

---

141. *Disp. priv.* XXII.4.

142. *Disp. pub.* IV.81.

143. *Disp. pub.* IV.81.

144. *Disp. pub.* IV.82.

145. *Disp. pub.* IV.83.

of creation, providence, and redemption. The justice of God, being "one with wisdom, presides over all his actions, decrees and deeds: and according to which God is called just and right *(iustus et rectus)*." In all he says and does, God is "just in all his ways."[146] This is seen in reflection on divine words and deeds.

First, with respect to deeds, we see that justice applies to all that God does, all of which is done for the "communication of the good." Here we see Arminius's consistency with the Thomist account of the *summum bonum* (the highest good). All that God does, whether in creation or salvation, is oriented toward the communication of God's own goodness. This is not merely abstract for Arminius's theology; it is expressed in specific and concrete form in "the prescribing of duty or in legislation, which consists in the request of a deed, and in the promise of a reward and the threat of a punishment."[147] Consequent to the activity of creatures, the justice of God is expressed in "the judgment of deeds, which is retributive, being both communicative of a reward and vindicative."[148] In all of this, as Arminius is at pains to emphasize, the incredible magnanimity of God is to be held as central, and is seen both in distributive and commutative justice.[149]

Second, when considering justice in divine communication, Arminius points out that it is threefold. First of all, the justice of God implies that all that God communicates is utterly truthful. God "always enunciates or declares exactly as the thing is, to which is opposed falsehood."[150] Given divine righteousness, Arminius thinks it impossible that God would communicate anything other than truth. Second, Arminius argues that divine righteousness entails utter "sincerity and simplicity." It is, for Arminius, unthinkable that a perfectly just God is possessed of any hypocrisy or double-speak; when God commands or invites or warns or entreats, he certainly means it and he says it with utter sincerity. Finally, with respect to justice in communication, Arminius emphasizes the fidelity of God; God is "constant in keeping promises ... to which [are] opposed inconstancy and dishonesty."[151]

---

146. *Disp. priv.* XXI.2. Cf. *Disp. pub.* IV.75. For the emphasis on divine justice in Arminius's theology, see Den Boer, *God's Twofold Love*, especially pp. 49–153.

147. *Disp. priv.* XXI.4.

148. *Disp. priv.* XXI.4.

149. *Disp. priv.* XXI.4. On distributive and commutative justice, see *ST* IIa-IIae.lxi.

150. *Disp. priv.* XXI.5.

151. *Disp. priv.* XXI.5.

Along with justice, Arminius emphasizes the congruence or fitting-
ness of divine patience, long-suffering, gentleness, clemency, and readi-
ness to forgive. After discussing the relationship of these qualities to
justice, the conclusion of his reflections includes a question that intimates
the direct relevance of this doctrine to other, more controversial matters:
"Does the justice of God permit him to destine to eternal death a rational
creature who has never sinned? We reply in the negative."[152]

### B.5. *Divine Perfection, Blessedness, and Glory*

In Arminius's disputation on God's nature, he began by considering the
attributes of the divine essence under the supereminent attributes of simplicity and infinity. From these he proceeded to consideration of various
attributes associated with the divine life. To conclude the disputation, he
summed them all up by emphasizing the perfection, blessedness, and glory
of God. "From the simple and infinite combination of all these things,
considered with the mode of supereminence, the perfection of God has its
existence."[153] Arminius is thus clearly a "perfect being theologian"—God
has all attributes or properties that a perfect (or "maximally excellent")
being would have, and God has these in the best possible way or degree.
As Arminius points out, "simplicity and infinity fulfill" God's perfection
(he also argues that the doctrine has a biblical basis in such texts as Matt.
5:48; Gen. 17:1; Exod. 6:3; Ps. 1:10; Acts 17:25; and Js. 1:17).[154] Furthermore, it
is from this perfection that one deduces the blessedness and glory of God.

The blessedness (*beatitas*) of God is God's pure delight in his own perfection. It is both an act of the understanding and an act of the divine will
(again, he is presupposing divine simplicity). God fully and completely
enjoys his own perfection as only he can; it is "fully known by his understanding and supremely loved by his will."[155] It is unique to God alone, and
is thus to be considered an incommunicable attribute. But as God is the
supreme good of all creation, so also the redeemed creature who delights
in God's greatness and goodness finds "repose" in satisfaction in the riches
of God's being, "in which consists the blessedness of the creature."[156]

---

152. *Disp. priv.* XXI.cor.

153. *Disp. pub.* IV.87.

154. *Disp. pub.* IV.87.

155. *Disp. pub.* IV.90.

156. *Disp. pub.* IV.91. Cf. *Disp. priv.* XXIII.5.

As the blessedness of God follows his perfection (which in turn follows a consideration of the attributes of the simple and infinite God), so also the glory of God is "from his perfection."[157] God's eternal glory, when expressed extrinsically or *ad extra*, finds two primary "modes of manifestation" in Scripture: first, by "an effulgence of light and of unusual splendor," or, conversely, by "dense darkness"; and second, by "the production of works which agree with his perfection and excellence."[158] Arminius insists that the simplicity and aseity of God imply that God lacks *nothing* good—thus the external display of the divine glory is not necessary for God. "God is blessed in himself and in the knowledge of his own perfection. He is, therefore, in want of nothing; neither does he require the demonstration of any of his properties by external operations."[159] Drawing an important distinction between divine glory *ad intra* and *ad extra,* Arminius observes: "God does not need (*indigere*) a sinner for the illustration, either external or internal, of his glory; not internal, because he is perfect; not external, although he may will to illustrate his glory outwardly . . . he does not need to illustrate his glory extrinsically, by mercy and justice or wrath, nor by grace, as is here understood. But God can make use of the sinner for the glory of his grace, mercy, wrath, or severity, if he sees fit to do so (*visum fuerit*)."[160] Arminius's extended reflection on divine blessedness and glory shows not only remarkable systematic consistency but also a sharply doxological bent. Thus he concludes discussion of divine perfection and glory with these words:

> but ceasing from any more prolix discussion of this subject, let us with ardent prayers suppliantly beseech the God of glory, that, since he has formed us for his glory, he would deem it worthy more and more to make us the instruments of illustrating his glory among people, through Jesus Christ our Lord, the splendor of his glory, and the express image of his person (*characterem hypostaseos*).[161]

---

157. *Disp. pub.* IV.92.

158. *Disp. pub.* IV.93. Cf. Muller, *God, Creation, and Providence,* p. 207.

159. *Art. non.* II.9, in *Opera,* p. 949; *Works* 2: 707.

160. *Exam. Gom.,* p. 55; *Works* 3: 572.

161. *Disp. pub.* IV.93.

## C. Summary: Simplicity, Infinity, and the Living Love of God

It is clear that Arminius holds to a so-called "classical" doctrine of God. Within the simplicity of the Triune life, God is infinite goodness. Arminius understands this conviction to be grounded in the biblical revelation and articulated in the Christian tradition with the use of scholastic categories. It is utterly bedrock for his theology, and, as we will see, it is particularly important for his doctrines of providence and predestination. Within the simplicity of the divine life, there are no parts or pieces—thus there can be no competing wills within God. Within the perfection of divine aseity, God can lack nothing and can have no need— not even the need for glorification through the display of justice or wrath. It is, for Arminius, literally unthinkable that the God of perfect, simple goodness and holy, unalterable love might create humans in his image for the purpose of destruction. On the contrary, humans can begin to glorify God by understanding that the divine purposes and the divine actions are perfectly in accord with the pure and simple goodness of the divine nature.[162]

## II. Doctrine of the Trinity
### A. Arminius's Commitment to Classical Orthodoxy

The doctrine of the Trinity expresses that God is both fundamentally one and fundamentally relational. Even a cursory reading of Arminius's work on the Trinity shows that he was deeply committed to classical Trinitarian orthodoxy. For instance, the *homoousios* of the Nicene Creed is regulative.[163] In this regard he is right in line with Reformed scholasticism.[164] Again in keeping with his Protestant contemporaries, he devotes significant attention to the biblical basis for the doctrine.

---

162. For a recent exchange over some of these issues, see Thomas H. McCall, "I Believe in Divine Sovereignty," *Trinity Journal* n. s. 29/2 (2008): 205–226; John Piper, "I Believe in God's Self-Sufficiency," *Trinity Journal* n. s. 29/2 (2008): 227–234; Thomas H. McCall, "We Believe in God's Sovereign Goodness," *Trinity Journal* n. s. 29/2 (2008): 235–246.

163. E.g., *Disp. pub.* V.16. *Homoousios* is the word used in the Nicene Creed to claim that the Father and Son are of the "same substance."

164. On the issues of continuity and discontinuity of the Reformed scholastics with the earlier Reformers (and the tradition of patristic and medieval Trinitarian theorizing), see *PRRD* 4: 59–74.

Arminius argues for the distinct personhood of the Father. Recognizing that Scripture sometimes portrays the Triune God as Father in relation to creation or to adoption, he nonetheless insists that Scripture teaches as well that there is a clear biblical witness to the distinction of the Father in relation to the other divine persons. So *person* does not and cannot mean mere representation (as in a mask). Instead, by the use of *person*, Arminius means "an undivided (*individuum*) and incommunicable subsistence (*subsistens*) of a living, intelligent, willing, powerful, and active nature (*naturae*)."[165] This definition of *person* is consistent with that of Aquinas, which he learned from Boethius: "an individual substance of a rational nature."[166] Arminius demonstrates that each of these properties in his own definition is predicated of the Father in Scripture. The Father is a distinct subsistence: "he who is, who was, and who is to come" (Rev. 1:4). The Father has life (*vita*): from Jesus we hear that "the living Father has sent me" (John 6:53–54). The intelligence of the Father is the subject of praise in Scripture, for Paul exults in the "depth of the riches both of the wisdom and knowledge of God" (Rom. 11:33). The Father's will is clearly seen in the words of Jesus that "this is the Father's will" (Jn. 6:39), and the divine power is predicated of God in the Lord's Prayer: "yours . . . is the power" (Matt. 6:13). Thus, Arminius concludes, "the title of 'person' cannot be justly denied to him."[167]

The Father is the one who begets the Son, and Arminius takes this to mean that the Father is "first" in an important sense. He is *not* prior in time, as if the Father first existed and then made or created the Son (and Holy Spirit); this is an operation *ad intra* and thus "from eternity."[168] But the Father is "first" nonetheless; he is first in "order."[169] In what will lead to controversy, Arminius says that the "Father is the fountain (*fons*) and source (*origo*) of the entire divinity, and the first principle and cause of the Son himself, which the word 'Father' signifies."[170] This claim is consistent with the early church's view that the Father is the source of divinity (*fons divinitatis*) within the Trinity. Arminius explains

---

165. *Disp. pub.* V.2.

166. *ST* IIIa.ii.2 resp.: "rationalis naturae individua substantia."

167. *Disp. pub.*V.2.

168. *Disp. pub.* V.6.

169. *Disp. pub.* V.4. Cf. *Disp. pub.* IV.27.

170. *Disp. pub.* V.4.

further that in the eternal act of generation the Father communicates *deity* to the Son; although the divine nature itself does not beget and is only communicated, nonetheless the divine nature is what is communicated to the Son in the act of generation by the Father. The Father is thus seen by the church "fathers" to be the "supreme and preeminent authority."[171]

With respect to the Son, Arminius denies that he is the Son by adoption, or by creation *ex nihilo*, or by being formed from preexisting matter. Rather, he is the Son by the eternal act of generation by the Father. As such, he is "by nature a participant in the entire Paternal divinity."[172] He is a divine *person*, and by *person* Arminius means here exactly what he intended by the attribution of personhood to the Father: the Son is "an undivided and incommunicable subsistence" who is living, intelligent, willing, powerful, and active.[173] He is a *divine* person, and the full divinity of Christ is argued by Arminius in a variety of ways. "With orthodox antiquity," he makes his case from the names of Christ in the New Testament, from the attributes of divinity which Scripture ascribes to him, from the works of Christ in the New Testament which can only be the works of God, and from the use of various Old Testament passages that are "uttered concerning the Father" but then appropriate to the Son as well.[174] The Son is called Lord, he is called Son of God, he is called Word, and he is directly called God in the New Testament (both attributively and subjectively).[175] The attributes of divinity are also attributed directly to him in the New Testament: *immensity, eternity, immutability, omniscience, omnipotence, majesty,* and *glory* are all said in Scripture to belong to him.[176] Similarly, the works of the Son point directly to his divinity; he is the creator of all things, he is the one upon whom the cosmos depends for its preservation, he performs miracles, and he is the Savior.[177] Moreover, a correlation of Old Testament passages that speak of God with those of the New Testament that speak of Jesus shows us that the Son is divine (e.g., Num. 21:5–7; 1

---

171. *Disp. pub.* V.4.

172. *Disp. pub.* V.7: "ut filium natura participem totius divinitatis Paternae."

173. *Disp. pub.* V.8.

174. *Disp. pub.* V.9.

175. *Disp. pub.* V.10.

176. *Disp. pub.* V.11.

177. *Disp. pub.* V.12.

Corinthians 10:9; Psalm 68; Eph. 4:8; Ps. 52:25–26; Heb. 1:10–12; Isaiah 6; Jn. 12:40–41; Is. 8:14; Rom. 9:33; 1 Pet. 2:6).[178]

Arminius also points out that the divine Son is the *second* person of the Holy Trinity. The Son's life is from the Father (Jn. 6:57) and in the Father (Jn. 5:26).[179] He is *eternally* begotten of the Father, but in this generation he receives the divine nature from the Father.[180] Thus there is exactly one divine nature or essence; the Father and the Son are *homoousios* ("of the same substance"). And there is a distinction according to the "mode of existence" *(modum existendi vel subsistendi)*; the Father has his divinity from no one, while the Son has his divinity from the Father.[181]

When he turns his attention to the Holy Spirit, Arminius follows a similar method. Recognizing that the very word *spirit* initially seems to signify something less than personal, and that there is a proper sense in which the Triune God is said to be *spirit*, he nonetheless makes a case for the distinct personhood of the Spirit.[182] He is not a mere quality or property (as are goodness, mercy, and the like): the Spirit is a person proceeding from the Father and the Son and thus third in "order" in the Trinity.[183] Like the Father and the Son, the Spirit has genuinely distinct existence and the full divine essence. He has life, and is thus the author of the life of living creatures. He has understanding, will, and power, and is thus rightly called a person.[184] The Spirit is also said to create, to preserve, to vivify or give life, to instruct in knowledge and virtues, as well as to perform other actions.[185] He is the subject of treatment and even blasphemy, and surely nothing can be blasphemed that is not both divine and a person.[186] Just as the Holy Spirit is a distinct person, so argues Arminius, he is also a fully divine person, and this is demonstrated by the way

---

178. *Disp. pub.* V.13.

179. *Disp. pub.* V.14.

180. *Disp. pub.* V.14.

181. *Disp. pub.* V.16.

182. *Disp. pub.* VI.1–2.

183. *Disp. pub.* VI.4.

184. *Disp. pub.* VI.5.

185. *Disp. pub.* VI.6.

186. *Disp. pub.* VI.6.

that Scripture ascribes infinity, eternity, and immensity to him.[187] The Holy Spirit, Arminius concludes, should be "truly distinguished by the name of God."[188]

Consideration of the Spirit as a distinct and fully divine person leads Arminius to conclude that the Spirit's distinct personhood is to be understood only in relation to the Father and the Son. The Spirit proceeds from the Father; the "Spirit is said to proceed and go forth from, to be given, poured out, and sent forth by the Father, and by whom the Father acts and operates."[189] The Spirit also comes from the Son, for he is the "Spirit of the Son (Galatians 4:6)" and is "given and sent by the Son."[190] Arminius therefore concludes that the Holy Spirit is the third person "in order, but not in time and degree."[191] Thus he is *eternally* divine, and he is always fully divine. Yet he is, in some sense, for Arminius, behind or after the Father and the Son in order and in dignity, which he demonstrates by a quotation from Basil of Caesarea.[192] With respect to the question of the *filioque*, there seems to be a sense in which Arminius endorses the standard Western or Latin view: the Holy Spirit "is a person proceeding from the Father and the Son."[193] But it is less than clear that Arminius intends a full or unreserved endorsement of the standard Latin position, for he explains that by "from the Father and the Son" he means that the Spirit "emanates (*emanat*) from the Father and is sent by the Son, and therefore he is the Spirit proceeding from both, and, according to his person, distinct from both."[194] If "sent by the Son" refers only to the mission of the Spirit *ad extra* (which possibility Arminius leaves open to question), then his view is not exactly the same as the standard Latin position.[195] And when Arminius considers the question

---

187. *Disp. pub.* VI.10.

188. *Disp. pub.* VI.11.

189. *Disp. pub.* VI.8.

190. *Disp. pub.* VI.8.

191. *Disp. pub.* VI.8.

192. *Disp. pub.* VI.12, quoting from Basil of Caesarea's *Adversus Eunomium*.

193. *Disp. pub.* VI.4. *Filioque* ("and the Son") was added to the Western, Latin version of the Nicene-Constantinopolitan Creed, reflecting the view that the Holy Spirit proceeds from both the Father "and the Son."

194. *Disp. pub.* VI.3.

195. Thomas Aquinas is representative of the Latin tradition in carefully distinguishing the missions from the processions, and in denying that the former are eternal. E.g., see *ST* Ia.xliii.1–3.

of the *filioque* directly, he says that he does not know. Concerning this "breathing" (*spiratio*), he writes, "whether it is from the Father and the Son, as the Latins say, or from the Father through the Son, as the Greeks prefer, I do not interpose a judgment; because I confess that this matter far exceeds my capacity."[196] He concludes with a word of caution: "if on any subject we ought to speak and think with sobriety, in my opinion, it must be on this."[197]

Arminius admits that the doctrine of the Trinity is deeply mysterious, especially when we are thinking of the internal union and the relation of origin and procession, but he is convinced that the traditionally orthodox doctrine is both biblically based and, by the deliverances of revelation, indeed reasonable. Furthermore, it is reason for praise (especially when we consider the "economy and dispensation" of salvation): "the contemplation is one of admirable sweetness, and produces in the heart of believers the most exuberant fruits of faith, hope, charity, assurance (*fiduciae*), fear, and obedience, to the praise of God the Creator, of the Son the Redeemer, and of the Holy Spirit the Sanctifier."[198]

## B. The Αὐτόθεος Controversy

Arminius's commitment to Trinitarian orthodoxy did not insulate him from controversy, however. For beyond the controversies of the Reformed with the anti-Trinitarians, there was intramural controversy within the ranks of the Reformed. The issue concerned the affirmation of the Son as αὐτόθεος (God from himself)—should an orthodox theologian affirm that the Son is God from himself and has the attribute of aseity? Or is the Son only divine derivatively—does only the Father have aseity? Does the doctrine of the eternal generation of the Son mean that the personal property of the Son is obtained only in relation to the Father, or does it mean that the divinity itself is communicated by the Father? Is the Son *the Son* only in relation to the Father, or is the Son *divine* because of the Father?

In the dispute with his colleague Trelcatius, Arminius stepped into an ongoing debate over this issue, one that had been brewing since the time of the early Reformers. For instance, as Muller explains it, Calvin

---

196. *Epistola*, in *Opera*, p. 938; *Works* 2: 691.

197. *Epistola*, in *Opera*, p. 938; *Works* 2: 691.

198. *Disp. pub.* VI.12.

attributed aseity, or self-existence, to the Son, inasmuch as he shares the full essence of divinity. Eternal generation from the Father grants sonship, not divinity.[199] Muller points out, however, that this view "is not echoed by all of the early orthodox Reformed theologians: as Amyraut noted, there was no debate among the orthodox over the distinct personal identity of the Son, but there was discussion over whether he stood in utterly equal majesty and dignity with the Father."[200] Some (for example, Ursinus) held that the Son has his being and essence from the Father, while others (for example, Polanus and Bucanus) "virtually duplicate Calvin's argument."[201]

Within Reformed circles, the view that the Son is *personally* (but not *essentially*) generated by the Father takes the ascendancy, along with the full affirmation of the Son's aseity.[202] Arminius noted the ambiguity (within the Reformed tradition) and took the minority position. As shown above, he insists that the orthodox doctrine of the Trinity is biblically based and is necessary for a properly Christian understanding of God. And as we have seen, he insists that the Son was eternally begotten; there was no time when the Son was not.[203] Yet he understands the generation of the Son to refer to his divine nature, which he insists is communicated from the Father to the Son. The proper distinction between the Father and the Son amounts to this: the Father has the divine nature from no one, whereas the Son has it "communicated to him by the Father."[204] The nature itself neither begets nor is begotten, but the divine nature is communicated by a

---

199. *PRRD* 4: 324–326: "Calvin consistently agreed with traditional orthodoxy that the person of the Son subsists in relation to the Father by generation, but he also insists that, considered according to his full divinity, the Son shares the divine attribute of self-existence, or *aseitas*. After all, the essence is undivided in the three persons, so that each of the persons contains in and of himself the full essence of the Godhead. . . . Specifically, Calvin defines the generation of the Son from the Father as an origination of sonship, not of divinity. . . . Calvin's view, like that of many of the later Reformed, follows out the line of the Western, Augustinian, trinitarian model, as defined by the Fourth Lateran Council, rather than the Greek model." Cf. Muller, "Christological Problem," 145–163.

200. *PRRD* 4: 326.

201. *PRRD* 4: 326.

202. E.g., William Perkins, *A Golden Chaine: Or, the Description of Theologie,* in *The Workes of that Famous and Worthy Minister of Christ . . . Mr. William Perkins,* 3 vols. (London: John Legatt, 1631–1635), 1: 14 col. 2C-D. Cf. *PRRD* 4: 327–328.

203. E.g., *Disp. pub.* V.15.

204. *Disp. pub.* V.16.

person.[205] The Son possesses the entire divinity, and he possesses it via the Father rather than of himself.

On this final point, Arminius readily admits that there are theologians who are of a different opinion from his, and he recognizes that "our church does not consider such persons as holding wrong views concerning the Trinity."[206] He summarizes the opposing view as this: "because the essence of the Father and of the Son is one, and because it has its origin from no one, therefore, in this respect, the Son is correctly denominated αὐτόθεος, that is, God from himself (a se)."[207] Yet for Arminius, the Son is not, strictly speaking, an essence, but instead has his essence by a certain mode of being. So as the Son is God, he has the divine essence, and he has it wholly and completely. But as he is the Son, Arminius argues, he has this divine essence as the Son; that is, he has it from the Father.[208] He mounts several arguments for this conclusion. First, he is convinced that patristic theology (both Latin and Greek) holds that the Son is generated from the Father with respect to the divine essence.[209] Thus he concludes that "according to the sentiment of the ancient church, the Son, even as he is God, is from the Father . . . [who is] the first principle (principium) of the Son and of the Holy Spirit . . . [and thus] the first principle of the entire deity."[210] More important, he sees it as the direct implication of any orthodox Trinitarian theology; he is convinced that attribution of αὐτόθεος to the Son will strengthen the hands of anti-Trinitarians of various stripes (tritheists and Sabellians alike)—because (according to standard Latin Trinitarian formulations) the divine persons are distinguished only by their internal relations of opposition. As he sees the matter, if the Father and Son do not share the same essence, then the charge of polytheism is undeniable. On the other hand, if they do not possess the divine essence in really distinct ways, then Sabellian modalism looms. So they must have the (numerically) same divine essence, but they must possess it in different ways. And this is, argues Arminius, exactly his position: both Father and Son are fully divine, which is to say that they share the same essence,

---

205. *Disp. pub.* V.5.

206. *Epistola,* in *Opera,* p. 939; *Works* 2: 692.

207. *Epistola,* in *Opera,* p. 939; *Works,* 2: 692.

208. *Epistola,* in *Opera,* p. 939; *Works* 2: 693.

209. E.g., *Epistola,* in *Opera,* pp. 940–941; *Works* 2: 693–695.

210. *Epistola,* in *Opera,* p. 941; *Works* 2: 696.

but the Father has it from no one (and is thus αὐτόθεος) while the Son has it from the Father.

In summary, Arminius will allow for a proper usage of the term αὐτόθεος for the Son: "the Son of God is rightly called αὐτόθεος, as this word is received for that which is God himself, truly God (*ipse Deus, vere Deus*)."[211] In other words, taken as a simple affirmation that the Son is truly God or fully God, the term itself is vague and open to mischievous interpretation, but not inherently problematic. With the ambiguity, though, comes potential trouble, and Arminius insists that if the term is taken to mean that the Son has an essence that is not communicated by the Father it is "dangerous (*periculose*)."[212] Thus the Son is "wrongly designated" αὐτόθεος "so far as it signifies that he has an essence" held in common with the Father but not coming from the Father.[213] Therefore he concludes that orthodox Christians should deny that the Son is *God from himself* and instead should affirm that the divine essence is given to the Son by the Father and thus the Son owes both his existence (as a person) and his essence (as divine) to the Father.

The αὐτόθεος controversy, which began in 1605, plagued Arminius for the rest of his life. The mere fact that he disagreed with Calvin's position did not make his own view untenable in the context of continental Reformed theology; indeed, as Muller notes, "the radical statement of the Son's aseity found in Calvin's trinitarian polemic is not echoed by all of the early orthodox Reformed theologians."[214] On the other hand, Arminius's view of the matter appears to be outside the mainstream Latin tradition. As Muller summarizes it:

> In the traditional Western model, as argued by Peter Lombard and ratified in the Fourth Lateran Council, the divine essence neither generates nor is generated; rather the person of the Father generates the person of the Son—with the result that the Son, considered as to his sonship, is generated, but considered as to his essence is not. Or, to put the point another way, there is no essential difference between the Father and the Son, the only difference being the relation of

---

211. *Art. non.* III.3, in *Opera*, p. 949; *Works* 2: 708.

212. *Art. non.* III.4, in *Opera*, p. 949; *Works* 2: 708.

213. *Art. non.* III.3, in *Opera*, p. 949; *Works* 2: 708.

214. *PRRD* 4: 326.

opposition, namely, the begottenness of the Son. The Son, there-fore, has all of the attributes of the divine essence, including aseity.[215]

Furthermore, and more troubling, there was an apparent inconsistency between, on the one hand, Arminius's repeated and forceful insistence that the Son is "by nature a participant in the entire divinity" of his Father and, on the other hand, the (at least implicit) denial of the attribute of divine aseity to the Son. Arminius worries that the attribution of aseity to the Son (with respect to his deity) would entail multiple gods, but how is it possible to have the "entire divinity" while lacking the attribute of aseity? It is clear that Arminius intends nothing short of a defense of the full di-vinity of the Son, but it is just as clear (from resultant history) that the theology of many later Arminians tended toward subordinationism.[216]

## III. Doctrine of Creation

The doctrine of creation is not as fully developed in the theology of Arminius (when compared to other loci), but it is important nonetheless. Muller points out that it is "apparent not only that Arminius' doctrine of creation, like his doctrine of God, is profoundly indebted to the scholas-tic tradition, particularly the tradition of Thomism, but also that his doc-trine of creation is one of the fundamental pivots of his theological system."[217] Creation and providence are the two primary actions of God ad extra.[218] Creation is "an external act of God, by which he produced all

---

215. PRRD 4: 88.

216. What Arminius seemed to suggest in various passages Episcopius stated emphatically and repeatedly. E.g., Episcopius, Institutiones theologicae IV.ii.32–33, in Opera theologica, pp. 332–338, here IV.ii.32, p. 334: "Unde consequitur, Patrem sic esse primum, ut etiam sum-mus sit, tum ordine, tum dignitate, tum potestate." In these pages, Episcopius also empha-sized "subordination" more than Arminius did. See also the discussion in Stephen Hampton, Anti-Arminians: The Anglican Reformed Tradition from Charles II to George I (Oxford: Oxford University Press, 2008), pp. 162–191. In our estimation, Arminius should not be understood to be promoting heterodox theology on this point. He inherited a theolog-ical problem, and he wrestled with it but did not resolve it. Some later Arminians resolved it in the wrong direction (from the perspective of a commitment to classical orthodoxy), but such views should neither be mistaken for Arminius's own position nor imputed to him. At most, Arminius is guilty of failing satisfactorily to resolve an implicit inconsistency within his doctrine of the Trinity.

217. Muller, God, Creation, and Providence, p. 211. For Muller's analysis of Arminius's doctrine of creation, see ibid., pp. 211–234.

218. Oratio prima, in Opera, pp. 30–31; Works 1: 329.

things out of nothing, for himself, by his Word and Spirit."[219] It is a Trinitarian action; as the works of God are always undivided, so the act of creation also flows from the Triune goodness and holy love of God. It is an act of utter freedom, it is for the purpose of communicating God's own goodness, and it is therefore God's first act of grace. God's creation consists first of purely spiritual, invisible, incorporeal creatures; second, of purely corporeal creatures; and third, of creatures made of body and spirit, of which humanity is an example.[220] The goal of the act of creation is the good of creation, and especially of humanity.[221] God created humanity to "know, love, and worship his Creator, that he might live blessed with him in eternity."[222]

Arminius holds fast to the traditional line in his commitment to the doctrine of creation out of nothing, and in doing so he seeks to emphasize the sovereign transcendence of God. Creation is not the fashioning of pre-existent matter into created forms; neither form nor matter preexisted the act of creation.[223] Arminius denies that the world is eternal: "the world was neither created from all eternity, nor could it be so created."[224] Muller notes that "the notion of the eternity of the world is, thus, deemed to be an error and, beyond that, an impossibility."[225] Arminius is exercised to uphold the sovereignty, transcendence, and freedom of God at this point: the creation was "freely produced, not necessarily."[226] For the "Lord omnipotent did not create the world by a natural necessity, but by the freedom of his will."[227]

Just as Arminius works to uphold proper conceptions of the transcendence of God and the contingency of creation, so also he labors to show that creation is an expression of the goodness of God and indeed shares in that goodness. "For creation is a communication of the good according to its proper inner nature."[228] It is the first external action of God's goodness

219. *Disp. priv.* XXIV.3.

220. *Disp. priv.* XXIV.11–12.

221. *Disp. priv.* XXIV.9.

222. *Disp. priv.* XXVI.10.

223. *Disp. priv.* XXIV.5–7.

224. *Disp. priv.* XXIV, cor i.

225. Muller, *God, Creation, and Providence,* p. 223.

226. *Disp. priv.* XXIV.7.

227. *Disp. priv.* XXIV.10.

228. *Dec. sent.,* p. 80; *Works* 1: 626.

and grace.[229] As the "perfect act of God" by which God displays the divine wisdom, goodness, and omnipotence, it cannot be subordinate to other divine actions.[230] Here Arminius follows the Thomist account of creation as being integral to the divine purpose and plan. As Muller explains, "very much like Aquinas . . . Arminius so holds the identity of being with goodness that he can assert both that all things have their *esse* by participation in the divine *esse* and that all existent things are good by reason of their participation in the goodness of God."[231]

Arminius's doctrine of the contingency of creation in light of God's necessary goodness is not fully developed, but the basic outline seems plain enough.[232] What he holds, it would seem, is a view of the divine will according to which it is free from all external constraint or coercion—and indeed is free from any constraint or coercion with respect to the external act of creation. Thus creation is not inevitable or necessary for God. At the same time, however, the free will of God is one that always works in accord with the divine wisdom and goodness. There is no reason to conclude that creation is necessary for God, for divine action in complete accordance with divine wisdom and goodness does not entail that there is only one course of action open to God.[233] But whatever is done by the will of God is perfectly consistent with his sheer goodness—indeed, how could it be otherwise, when the divine power is only formally distinct from the divine goodness and love?

As we will see in the next chapter, such a formulation of the doctrine of creation, when linked so tightly with Arminius's doctrine of God, becomes very important for Arminius's doctrine of predestination. "God's first action toward some object, whatever it may be, cannot be its casting away or

---

229. *Dec. sent.*, p. 78; *Works* 1: 625.

230. *Dec. sent.*, p. 81; *Works* 1: 627.

231. Muller, *God, Creation, and Providence*, p. 214. Cf. Witt, "Creation, Redemption and Grace," p. 311.

232. Muller, *God, Creation, and Providence*, pp. 224, 232, notes that Arminius's doctrine of creation is faced with a tension, and one that is familiar to traditional formulations of the doctrine: according to Arminius, creation is the result of the radically free act of God and thus is contingent; but it is also the expression and result of the divine goodness that is necessary. Muller further notes that his doctrine is not developed enough to find its way out of the problem.

233. For a proposal that parallels that of Arminius in many respects, see Thomas P. Flint, "The Problem of Divine Freedom," *American Philosophical Quarterly* 20 (1983): 255–264; *Divine Providence*, pp. 51–59.

reprobation to eternal misery. Because God is the highest good, therefore his first volition, by which he is engaged with some object, is the communication of good."[234] Muller is right when he points out that "creation is so placed at the center and foundation of Arminius' theology that the work of salvation can no longer be construed as a restriction of the universal purpose implemented by God in the creative act: there must be a universal will for the whole behind the universal call to salvation rather than an original intention to create for destruction as well as for eternal fellowship."[235] He goes on to say that Arminius's system could be called a "theology of creation."[236] Because of God's love of his own justice and his love for the creature, he has freely—not of necessity—obliged himself to creation and set limits for his own actions. As an act of grace, God has created beings with freedom who have the capacity to love but also to resist God's antecedent will. Creation is a voluntary, gracious, self-limiting act of God in perfect accord with the greatness and goodness of his infinite nature.

---

234. *Exam. Gom.*, p. 76; *Works* 3: 590: "Prima Dei in aliquod obiectum qualecumque id sit actio, non potest esse eius abiectio seu reprobatio ad aeternam miseriam. Quia Deus est summum bonum, itaque prima eius qua circa aliquod obiectum versatur volitio est communicatio boni."

235. Muller, *God, Creation, and Providence*, p. 234.

236. Muller, *God, Creation, and Providence*, p. 268. Cf. idem, "God, Predestination, and the Integrity of the Created Order: A Note on Patterns in Arminius' Theology," in *Later Calvinism: International Perspectives*, ed. W. Fred Graham, Sixteenth Century Essays and Studies, vol. 22 (Kirksville: Truman State University Press, 1994), pp. 431–446.

# 3

## *Providence and Predestination*

*The dogma of predestination and its opposite, reproba-*
*tion, is taught and emphasized in the Scriptures, for*
*which reason it is also necessary. But it must be seen*
*which and what kind of predestination it is that is*
*treated in the Scriptures as necessary, and which is called*
*the foundation of our salvation.*

—JACOB ARMINIUS, 1602

SOMETIMES ARMINIUS HAS been popularly portrayed as rejecting the doctrine of predestination. Of course, no early modern theologian who accepted the authority of the Bible completely rejected predestination, for this doctrine is assumed throughout Scripture. Arminius is no exception to this rule. The question has to do with how divine election is to be understood. "Arminianism" has often been reduced to an "anti-Calvinist" view of predestination. Arminius did have much to say in opposition to various Reformed versions of predestination. His doctrine of predestination, however, can be understood rightly only within the larger context of his account of divine nature and action in general and his understanding of providence in particular, of which predestination is a species.

## *I. Divine Providence*
### A. Providence in General

In *Declaration of Sentiments*, Arminius presents the following description of divine providence:

> [Providence is] a solicitous, continued, and universally present supervision of God over the whole world in general, and all creatures in particular, without any exception, in order to preserve and to

direct (*te besorghen, ende te beleyden*) them in their own essence, qualities, actions, and passions, such as befits him and is suitable to them, to the praise of his name and the salvation of believers.[1]

Divine providence is oriented toward the good of creatures. It is "general" in the sense that it extends to all of creation, but it is meticulous as well in its particularity.

For Arminius, *preservation* and *governance* are two central elements of the doctrine of providence. First, he insists that we should think about providence as the divine action of preserving what God has created. Providence is closely related to creation (as we will see, this is vitally important for Arminius), but it is to be distinguished from creation. In step with the mainstream of Protestant scholasticism, Arminius leaves no room for any hint of occasionalism.[2]

Arminius shares considerable common ground with his fellow scholastic theologians on the broader point of preservation. Without God's continued activity in preserving creation, the created order would pass out of existence, and it would do so immediately. God does not re-create *ex nihilo* moment by moment, nor is he continuously creating. Nonetheless, creation would pass from existence into nothingness if it were not for the continual divine work of sustaining the universe. Creatures, as Arminius puts it, "are always closer to nothingness than to their Creator, from whom they differ by infinite gaps, but by only finite properties are they distinct from nothingness, their primeval womb, since they can fall back into it again."[3] Moreover, for Arminius, the divine work of sustenance is particular, for God upholds both the creation in general and of "each of the creatures with its actions and passions."[4] God's providence does not override created nature, but he sustains all creatures by upholding them as *what* they are created to be with "their own essence, qualities, actions, and passions, such as befits him and is suitable to them."[5] The cosmos (as a

---

1. *Dec. sent.*, p. 111; *Works* 1: 657. Cf. *Disp. priv.* XXVIII.7.

2. For a good overview of the key tenets of occasionalism, see Alfred J. Freddoso, "Medieval Aristotelianism and the Case against Secondary Causation in Nature," in Thomas V. Morris, ed., *Divine and Human Action: Essays in the Metaphysics of Theism* (Ithaca, NY: Cornell University Press, 1988), pp. 74–118.

3. *Oratio prima*, in *Opera*, p. 29; *Works* 1: 327. Cf. Augustine, *De civitate Dei* VIII.xi, in *PL* 41: 236: "In comparison with him who truly is because he is immutable, those things which are made mutable have no being (*non sint*)."

4. *Disp. priv.* XXVIII.5.

5. *Dec. sent.*, p. 111; *Works* 1: 657.

whole) exists because of God's initial creating and ongoing preserving activity, and individual creatures themselves continue to exist—according to their own essences, and with their discrete powers and abilities—because God holds them in being.

The second major locus of Arminius's doctrine of providence concerns the divine government of all creation. Neither the free will nor the actions of rational creatures are beyond divine providence.[6] Indeed, divine providence "sustains, regulates, steers, and governs all things." For Arminius, "nothing happens by chance or accidentally."[7] The "principal acts" of divine government "are motion, assistance, concurrence, and permission." The first three of these relate to whatever is good (in either a metaphysical or a moral sense), while the last category is particularly concerned with evil actions.[8]

Of special significance at this point is Arminius's account of divine concurrence (*concursus*). Concurrence, typically considered to be a vital element of the doctrine of providence, is meant to give an account of divine activity in relation to the contingent agency of finite creatures. In other words, as traditional theology confessed, God is sovereign over the many causes, some principal and others secondary, that may come together to produce an effect.[9] Not only does God sustain or preserve his creatures in existence, but he also gives them abilities and powers, and in this sense can be said to "concur" with their activity.[10] Arminius says that divine concurrence "is necessary to produce every act, since nothing whatever can have any entity except from the first and chief being."[11] But whereas some scholastic theologians take concurrence to mean that God infuses divine power into a creaturely action itself, Arminius disagrees.[12] "The concurrence of God is not his immediate influx into a second or inferior cause, but it is an action of God immediately flowing into the effect of the creature, so that the same

---

6. *Dec. sent.*, p. 111; *Works* 1: 658.

7. *Dec. sent.*, p. 111; *Works* 1: 657: "by gheval, of fortuyne." This phrase is unique in Arminius. In Dutch and in Latin translation (*casu aut fortuito*), these two terms may bear a negative and positive connotation, respectively. Thus, the meaning is that nothing bad or good happens by mere chance.

8. *Disp. priv.* XXVIII.7.

9. E.g., Augustine, *De civitate Dei* VII.xxx, in *PL* 41: 220: "[God] knows and ordains not only principal but also subsequent causes."

10. Cf. Muller, *Dictionary*, pp. 76–77. Cf. Witt, "Creation, Redemption and Grace," p. 415.

11. *Disp. pub.* X.9.

12. See Muller, *God, Creation, and Providence*, pp. 254–255.

effect in one and the same entire action may be produced simultaneously by God and the creature."[13] For Arminius, divine concurrence does not mean that God is *doing* the actions of the creatures, nor does Arminius take the view that the only divine action is to sustain the power of the creaturely agent. No creature acts in complete independence of God; without God's preserving activity they would pass from existence, and without God's concurrence they would be unable to do anything at all. At the same time that he preserves, God also gives creatures the ability to perform actions and concurs with their effects. As Muller summarizes it, for Arminius "the divine *concursus* is, thus, necessary not only to the existence of the cause and of the effect but also to the existence of the causal activity, but the divine involvement is such that the secondary cause is determinative of its own action and, therefore, free."[14]

## B. Providence and Evil

Arminius also includes the category of "permission" within his account of God's providential governance, and this is especially important in his discussion of the problem of evil. Arminius recognizes the gravity of the challenge before him. Scripture points to the wholehearted affirmation that God is altogether good and holy—there is no shadow of anything less than perfect goodness and holiness in him. Scripture also demands a robust view of divine omniscience and "unbounded power" (Ps. 147:5; Mark 10:18; Rom. 1:20; Rev. 4:8). But these affirmations surely seem to be at odds with the obvious fact that sin is in the world.[15]

Arminius sees several options for dealing with this challenge, and he rejects some outright. First, he opposes all views that would deny the presence and power of evil in the world.[16] Evil is not an illusion. Second, he rejects any tendency to deny or even to downgrade the providence of God. People who hold such a view recognize that evil in fact has occurred, they see it as inconsistent with divine providence, and they conclude that it is better "to set up an idle God negligent of mundane affairs, especially of those in which a rational creature's freedom of choice intervenes, than

---

13. *Disp. pub.* X.9.

14. Muller, *God, Creation, and Providence*, p. 255.

15. *Disp. pub.* IX.2.

16. *Disp. pub.* IX.1.

to deprive him of the honor of his goodness, wisdom, and power."[17] Rejecting a view that approximates what would later come to be known as "Deism," Arminius argued that "it is not necessary to adopt either of these methods; and that it is possible to preserve in God without disparagement these three ornaments of supreme majesty, as well as his providence."[18] Arminius was also opposed to the view of the "Manichees," who, in their attempt to remove evil from God's sovereign providence, affirmed that there is an ultimate or eternal evil power standing on equal (or near equal) footing with God.[19] Finally, he is resolutely and forcefully opposed to any view that would entail the conclusion that God is the author of sin. If this were true, then "sin" would cease to be sin, and God would no longer be the *summum bonum*. Those who teach that God "absolutely determined"—without "foresight of sin"—to "declare his own glory through punitive justice and mercy, in the salvation of some people and the condemnation of others" imply this conclusion, as do those who hold that God's action is ordered toward demonstrating his own glory through the damnation of some people "which neither can be done, nor has been done, without the entrance of sin into the world."[20] Such a conclusion is also implied by those teaching that "God has either denied to man, or has withdrawn from man, before he sinned, grace necessary and sufficient to avoid sin," and it is entailed by the view that "humanity was not able to do otherwise than commit sin by a necessity of the consequent."[21] Such necessity removes all liberty, and with no liberty there can be no responsibility—and thus no sin.[22] Arminius specifically criticized Calvin's view that "the reprobate cannot evade the necessity of sinning, especially since this kind of necessity is injected through the ordination of God."[23]

Arminius clearly is not pleased with these three options, but what does he propose in their place? His solution includes both divine involvement

---

17. *Disp. pub.* IX.1.

18. *Disp. pub.* IX.1.

19. *Disp. pub.* IX.2.

20. *Art. non.* X.2, in *Opera*, pp. 954– 955; *Works* 2: 715.

21. *Art. non.* X.4–5, in *Opera*, p. 955; *Works* 2: 715–716. On degrees of necessity and contingency in Arminius, see Dekker, *Rijker dan Midas*, pp. 55–60.

22. *Art. non.* X.5, in *Opera*, p. 955; *Works* 2: 716.

23. *Art. non.* X.6, in *Opera*, p. 955; *Works* 2: 716.

and human freedom. He suggests that there is a sense in which God can be said to "permit" sin. Arminius does not mean by this that God approves of sin, or that God is somehow pleased with it. God does not "permit" sin in the sense that he approves it as proper or appropriate. For Arminius, however, God does indeed permit sinful activities in this sense: rather than making such actions impossible, he allows them to occur. Thus he argues against William Perkins that it will not do simply to observe an event and conclude that it is God's will, for all that can be concluded from any particular evil action is "either [that he willed this] or that he was unwilling to hinder the event which he foresaw was about to take place." Arminius's rationale is clear: "Otherwise the distinction between God's action and permission is taken away. For some things happen because God *does* them, but others because he *allows* them to be done, according to Augustine and the truth of the matter itself."[24] Permission, according to Arminius, "is a middle act between willing and not-willing, namely of a relaxed (*remissae*) will."[25] Whether we are talking of sins of ignorance, infirmity, malice, or negligence, and whether these are by commission or omission, they are nonetheless permitted by God in the sense that he allows them to proceed, not in the sense that they find his approval.[26]

In all of these sins, however, there are two general reasons for ascribing this permission to divine providence. The first is a feature of what would later be called the *free will defense*; it is the "liberty of the will, of which God made the rational creature a partaker," and without which humans would no longer be rational and morally responsible creatures.[27] The second such cause or reason that God permits certain sins is that such sins may be the occasion of a greater display of the glorious splendor of God's perfections, so that "the praise of the divine goodness, mercy, patience, wisdom, justice, and power, may shine out far more brightly and be more clearly made known." Here Arminius follows Augustine's opinion that "God judged that it was the province of his most omnipotent goodness rather to produce good from evils, than

---

24. *Exam. Perk.*, in *Opera*, p. 637; *Works* 3: 271.

25. *Exam. Perk.*, in *Opera*, p. 645; *Works* 3: 284. Arminius is hardly idiosyncratic at this point; cf. Stump, *Aquinas*, pp. 389–426.

26. E.g., *Exam. Perk.*, in *Opera*, pp. 720–726; *Works* 3: 399–408.

27. *Exam. Perk.*, in *Opera*, p. 726; *Works* 3: 408. Cf. Witt, "Creation, Redemption and Grace," pp. 472–473.

not to allow evils to be."[28] Recalling Arminius's clear distinctions between divine glory *ad intra* and *ad extra,* this does not mean that there must be sin in order for God to be glorious (or maximally glorious). Nor does the affirmation that God can bring goodness from evil amount to an endorsement of a *felix culpa* motif, of which Arminius seems quite leery.[29] Furthermore, sin does not somehow contribute to the aesthetic beauty of the universe as a whole. "The entrance of sin into the world has nothing to do (*non pertinet*) with the beauty of the universe."[30] Instead, as he puts it, evil is the "occasion" for the display of the divine perfections.[31] Arminius's affirmation that the omnipotent wisdom of the simple divine nature can bring good from evil does mean, however, that some sinful actions are permitted by God both in accordance with his decision to make free and rational creatures and with his ability to bring "light from darkness." Arminius's own view is seen quite clearly in his endorsement of Augustine: "The good God would never permit evil, if he could not by his omnipotence produce good out of evil."[32]

Why does God make creatures who are capable of sinning? Why does God make a world in which sin is even possible? His answer follows well-worn scholastic paths: only God is absolutely necessary and necessarily good; due to our finitude as creatures (more precisely, as rational creatures), we do not exist necessarily or as perfect beings.[33] This does not mean that sin is necessary or inevitable, but it does mean that, since humanity is only contingently good, we could move away from the *summum bonum* and, in an Augustinian sense, toward non-being. In other words, while actual sin is not necessary for human creatures, the possibility of sinning is inherent to creaturely existence.[34] As human

---

28. *Exam. Perk.,* in *Opera,* p. 726; *Works* 3: 408. Cf. ibid., in *Opera,* p. 645; *Works* 3: 286.

29. With respect to the traditional saying, *O felix culpa* . . . ("O happy fault which merited such and so great a redeemer"), Arminius remarks, in *Exam. Perk.,* in *Opera,* pp. 646–647; *Works* 3: 287: "It easily appears that the 'fault' cannot be called 'happy' except by catachrestical hyperbole, which . . . must be removed proportionally far from a solid investigation of the truth."

30. *Art. non.* V.5, in *Opera,* p. 951; *Works* 2: 710.

31. *Exam. Perk.,* in *Opera,* p. 753; *Works* 3: 447.

32. *Exam. Perk.,* in *Opera,* p. 753; *Works* 3: 447.

33. *Apologia,* art. 6, in *Opera,* 143; *Works* 1: 759–760; *Disp. pub.* IX.4.

34. Cf. *Exam. Perk.,* in *Opera,* 644; *Works* 3: 283.

creatures who were endowed with freedom and responsibility, it was within humanity's reach to reject God—and this is, alas, what happened.

Arminius makes obvious what he means by human freedom: it is the choice to do some action A or to refrain from doing A. "Divine providence does not determine a free will to one part of a contradiction or contrareity, that is, by a determination preceding the actual volition itself."[35] In other words, when Arminius speaks of "freedom," he means what is now sometimes termed *libertarian freedom*.[36] Freedom, according to this view, is a real choice between genuine alternatives, unconstrained by necessity, and therefore strictly incompatible with determinism. God is able to determine human wills,[37] but doing so would remove free choice and would violate the kind of relationship that God desires to have with creation.[38]

When considering the entrance of sin into the world, Arminius believed that "Adam was able to continue in the good and not to sin (*potuit . . . non peccare*)."[39] When Adam sinned, he did so "freely and voluntarily, without any necessity, either internal or external."[40] When God permitted the first sin, it could "happen or not happen."[41] Adam's fall was not the inevitable result of an eternal decree that made it impossible not to sin. Nor did God so desert the first human as to make sin inevitable. Nor, for that matter, did even the divine "permission" make it impossible for him to remain

---

35. *Art. non.* VIII.3, in *Opera*, p. 954; *Works* 3: 714.

36. Alvin Plantinga, *God, Freedom and Evil* (Grand Rapids, MI: Eerdmans, 1974), p. 29, offers a helpful summative characterization of this position: "If a person is free with respect to a given action, then he is free to perform that action and free to refrain from performing it; no antecedent conditions and/or causal laws determine that he will perform the action, or that he won't. It is within his power, at the time in question, to take or perform the action and within his power to refrain from it."

37. *Apologia*, art. 5, in *Opera*, 142; *Works* 1: 755.

38. As we shall see, Arminius repeatedly points out that his view is common in patristic theology. E.g., see Origen, *De principiis* I.pref.5, in *PG* 11: 118B–C, who places this notion of human freedom and responsibility as one of the articles of the rule of faith, that is, a necessary, central teaching of the church handed down from the apostles. For another example, see Novatian, *De Trinitate* I, in *PL* 3: 887B–888A: "When [God] gave him all these things for his service, he willed [humanity] alone to be free . . . so that [humanity] might receive either merited rewards or due punishments as the result of his actions, recognizing these actions as his own, because he willed to act by the movement of his mind in the one or the other direction."

39. *Art. non.* XI.1, in *Opera*, p. 955; *Works* 2: 716.

40. *Art. non.* XI.2, in *Opera*, p. 955; *Works* 2: 716.

41. *Collatio*, in *Opera*, p. 571; *Works* 3: 179.

upright.[42] When Adam sinned, he did so by the violation of his own God-given freedom. God did not make Adam sin; he did not cause Adam to sin; he did not make sin inevitable for Adam. God was not responsible for sin—Adam was!

Yet, notwithstanding his emphasis on human free choice, Arminius was also convinced that even the beginning of human sin falls within the providence of God. God preserves and sustains the first human sinners, and divine concurrence enables them to have the power to eat the forbidden fruit.[43] Similarly, Arminius maintains that God is providentially active throughout the progress of sin. This can be seen in several ways: God directs sin toward particular objects (and away from others); God places limits on the extent of sin and its effects; and God brings an end to sin in either punishment or remission through grace.[44]

Arminius believes, as much as his Reformed contemporaries, that God is providentially active in all that happens in creation. Arminius affirms, again, as much as his Reformed colleagues, both that God is prescient of evil actions and that God works through those actions to bring "light out of darkness." So what is the difference between them? Arminius does not make the connection explicit at this point, yet it is not hard to see that his doctrine of divine middle knowledge is at work here. Muller explains the difference between Arminius and his Reformed colleagues at this point.

> Whereas the Reformed insist upon the almost paradoxical point that an eternal and all-powerful God can in fact predetermine that some events will occur as a result of contingent or free acts of creatures and can therefore foreknow such events according to his *scientia libera seu visionis*, Arminius follows Suárez in placing the divine foreknowledge or *scientia media* prior to the divine intervention, with the result that God can and does offer inducements to his creatures on the basis of his knowledge of their disposition toward or against certain acts.[45]

---

42. *Art. non.* XI.3–4, in *Opera*, p. 955; *Works* 2: 716.

43. *Epistola*, in *Opera*, p. 942; *Works* 2: 697.

44. *Epistola*, in *Opera*, p. 942; *Works* 2: 697. Cf. *Disp. pub.* IX–X. On Arminius's view of divine providence, especially with regard to sin, see John Mark Hicks, "Classic Arminianism and Open Theism: A Substantial Difference in Their Theologies of Providence," *Trinity Journal* n. s. 33 (2012): 3–18.

45. Muller, *God, Creation, and Providence*, pp. 260–261.

Working from the doctrine of middle knowledge, with its divine knowledge of all possible choices and actions of creatures prior to the divine decision, Arminius is thus able to insist upon a robust doctrine of divine providence. It is one in which the particulars of life are within the overall divine plan—but without divine determinism and its implications for God's involvement with (or "authorship" of) sin. As Arminius puts it, "A thing does not happen because it has been foreknown or predicted, but it is foreknown or predicted because it is about to be."[46]

Acts 2:23 (cf. 4:23) says that Jesus Christ was "handed over to" his killers "by God's determined purpose and foreknowledge." This text is often appealed to by those theologians searching for a biblical basis for a deterministic doctrine of providence.[47] Arminius's conversation partners did so as well, and Arminius responded to Perkins by arguing that the passage does not say that "God willed that the Jews should slay Christ"; it cannot serve as a "proof text" for divine determinism.[48] The text does not say or imply that God made it impossible for it not to occur; nor does the text make any claim about the basis of God's plan and nature of his foreknowledge. It does speak plainly of a "plan" or "set purpose" and foreknowledge. Thus any interpretation that would not allow for a plan and foreknowledge could not be a proper one. But beyond this, nothing more can be concluded, for the text neither says nor implies that God makes this mode of death inevitable. Arminius's account of foreknowledge (including "middle knowledge") allows for such a plan, for through his middle knowledge God can use the freely chosen (thus undetermined) evil actions of the conspirators for his broader purposes.

To summarize, Arminius believes that sin is the result of the abuse of creaturely freedom of choice. Sin was not inevitable for creation. It was not forced upon human creatures by some independent evil force—this

---

46. *Disp. priv.* XXVIII.14. But cf. Evert Dekker, "Jacobus Arminius and His Logic: Analysis of a Letter," *Journal of Theological Studies* 44 (1993): 118–142, in which he argues that Arminius's system is unwittingly deterministic. Dekker's argument rests upon his analysis of a letter from Arminius to Johannes Uytenbogaert. Even if we grant Dekker's argument, it is clear that Arminius has either changed or has clarified his views by the time of his engagement with Gomarus. See, e.g., Arminius, *Exam. Gom.*, pp. 25–32; *Works* 3: 547–553.

47. Willem J. van Asselt, J. Martin Bac, and Roelf T. te Velde argue that determinism should not be taken as the standard position of the Reformed orthodox in *Reformed Thought on Freedom*.

48. *Exam Perk.*, in *Opera*, p. 696; *Works* 3: 362.

would be the rejection of Christianity for Manicheeism. It was not forced upon humans by God—this would result in the blasphemous conclusion that God is the original sinner. Sin is the result of the abuse of the precious gift of freedom that God graciously bestowed upon humanity. Arminius recognizes that, with respect to sinful actions, one may affirm that God permits creatures to perform actions and that God grants the ability actually to do them, but the responsibility for what those actions are, and for how they are performed, lies squarely on the creaturely agent.[49] And just as importantly, Arminius also believes that God is providentially active in a world marred by sin. Because God is good, he exercises his omnipotence to bring good from evil.

## C. The Theological Grounding of the Doctrine of Providence

Arminius's doctrine of divine providence, like his doctrine of predestination, will almost invariably (and perhaps inevitably) be misunderstood if taken in isolation from his broader theological project. Notably, one must understand that it is grounded in his basically Thomist doctrine of creation. As he says very pointedly, "The providence of God is subordinate to creation."[50] This means that divine action in providence must be understood in direct relation to God's purposes in the act of creation. What God works to accomplish by his providence cannot be thought to contradict what he initiated in creation; to do so would destroy the unity of the divine purpose and action. God's work in creation is grounded in his sovereignty; it is a free act. It is God's free act whereby he created free creatures in his image. Arminius writes, "It is, therefore, necessary that [providence] should not impinge against creation; which it would do, were it to inhibit the use of free choice (*Liberi arbitrii*) in man, or should deny to man its necessary concurrence or should direct man to another end, or to destruction, than to that which is agreeable to the condition and state in which he was created."[51] Arminius's doctrine of creation is grounded in the *summum bonum*, and he insists that God creates to spread and share his goodness. Accordingly, nothing in divine providence could possibly be oriented toward different ends. It is, therefore, almost unthinkable and nearly blasphemous

---

49. *Disp. pub.* X.9.

50. *Art. non.* VIII.1, in *Opera*, p. 953; *Works* 2: 714.

51. *Art. non.* VIII.1, in *Opera*, p. 953; *Works* 2: 714.

for Arminius that God would so providentially order and govern the universe that it would, by divine design, result in ultimate destruction and ruin (for all or any creatures). Suppose that "the providence of God should so rule and govern man that he should necessarily become corrupt, in order that God might manifest his own glory, both of justice and mercy, through the sin of man, according to his eternal counsel."[52] This concept would be in utter contradiction to Arminius's doctrine of creation: creation would be from benevolence and for goodness, but providence would be for evil and from something markedly different from divine goodness. Simply put, if God's creative action is to share and extend goodness, but God's providential action is to make evil inevitable, then providence is opposed to creation in ways that are stark and sinister.

But Arminius's ultimate concern is not with the doctrine of creation itself, nor is it simply to secure the coherence of creation and providence for the sake of theological tidiness. His ultimate concern—and this can hardly be overemphasized—is with theology proper, that is, the doctrine of God. His doctrine of providence is grounded in, and thus "subordinate to," his doctrine of creation. But his doctrine of creation itself is based upon the doctrine of God, and this is what Arminius thinks is ultimately at stake. And here is where Arminius emphasizes both the sovereignty and the goodness of God. With respect to sovereignty, Arminius "argues a virtually unlimited rule of God over the creation, his list of 'lawful and proper' commands implies no weakening in the doctrine of providence."[53] God is omnipotent, and his authority over creation is ultimate. But recalling our previous discussion of divine power, Arminius denies that omnipotence should be understood as in any way arbitrary or otherwise inconsistent with the perfect goodness of God. As Muller says, "Arminius equally adamantly denies that there can be an arbitrary exercise of absolute power on God's part. The rule of God is limited by the character of the creative act, specifically by the mode of God's communication of the goodness of being to creatures."[54] The "character of the creative act," as Muller puts it, is, in turn, grounded in the utter goodness of God's own being. Since God is the "*summum bonum*, he does nothing but what is good."[55]

---

52. *Art. non.* VIII.1, in *Opera*, p. 953; *Works* 2: 714.

53. Muller, *God, Creation, and Providence*, p. 237.

54. Muller, *God, Creation, and Providence*, p. 237.

55. *Disp. priv.* XXX.5.

This means, of course, that God does nothing evil, "and therefore he can be called neither the efficient cause of sin, nor the deficient cause, since he has employed whatever things were sufficient and necessary to avoid this sin."[56] Neither a robust sense of divine power and government nor a foundational belief in divine goodness should be surrendered. Both are vital to a proper understanding of divine providence.[57]

To summarize, the divine perfections are displayed in providence.[58] This is because God's actions in providence are consistent with his purposes in creation. God's work of creation is the extension of his goodness. And this goodness itself is based in the character and essence of God, who in the simplicity of the divine nature *is* omnipotent holy love.

## II. Predestination
### A. The Context

The doctrine that God predestines individuals to either eternal life or death was a shared belief among Protestants. But various questions about this predestination became controversial. The issue of human free choice, especially with regard to salvation, was frequently and hotly debated. What is the basis of God's predestination of individuals? Is it God's sovereign, deterministic choice alone, or does humanity, created with free will, have a say?

Another common question had to do with the order of God's decrees (*ordo decretorum*). One must understand that the early scholastic Protestant theology to which Arminius contributed considered God's specific decrees concerning predestination as part of the larger decrees concerning providence. Theologians appealed to a variety of biblical texts as a basis for examining and employing the language of "divine decrees" (see, for example, Job 14:5; Ps. 148:6; Is. 46:10; Jer. 4:28; 18:6; Acts 15:18 [variant];

---

56. *Disp. priv.* XXX.5.

57. Arminius is unwilling to surrender either one, but his comments about what someone *should do* if he were to become convinced that one or the other must be released show us his deeper commitment to the holy love of God: "There will be a lesser sin (*minus peccabitur*) in withdrawing an act from the divine efficiency as it is an act, than if sin is attributed to God's efficiency as it is a sin. For it is preferable to deprive God of any act which belongs to him, rather than to attribute to him an evil act which does not belong to him; because a graver injury is charged upon God if he is called the cause of sin, than if he is exhibited as an idle (*otiosus*) spectator of an act." *Exam. Perk.*, in *Opera*, p. 734; *Works* 3: 419.

58. E.g., *Disp. priv.* XXVIII.11.

Eph. 1:4–5; Rev. 13:8). From these passages arise four assumptions that are common to Arminius and his Reformed contemporaries:

1.  God's decree is one, yet manifold, dealing with all sorts of matters. The general decree about anything concerning the created order is called God's providence; the special decree about election and salvation in particular is God's predestination.[59]
2.  God does nothing without having a purpose and plan.
3.  The decree is eternal; its order (an assumed property) is not chronological, but logical. As with divine providence, so also with regard to the specific decree of God concerning predestination, there is a plan and a logical order to that plan. Competing ideas about the order of the decrees will be examined below.[60]
4.  A distinction is preserved between the eternal decree and its execution in time. The decree to *elect* or *reprobate* (that is, generally, to predestine) is enacted in time by various means leading to *salvation* or *condemnation*, respectively.

Any eternal decree of God concerning creation must be actualized in time. For the Reformed, though, this distinction also entails distinct causes. The decrees of election and reprobation are founded in God's will alone, but salvation and condemnation in time are based on Christ's work and human sin, respectively. Arminius admits the distinction between the decree and its execution in time, but he does not acknowledge such a vast distinction between their causes, and therefore he believes that the distinction is not enough to salvage Franciscus Gomarus's supralapsarian version of predestination.[61] As will be seen below, Arminius brings Christ back as the foundation of election (not just salvation) and impenitent unbelief as the cause of reprobation.

---

59. Because of the potential ambiguity and sometimes inconsistent usage of terms, even in Arminius's time, theologians were often careful to define terms such as *predestination*. E.g., see Johannes Kuchlinus, *Theses theologicae de divina praedestinatione*, M. Gerardus Vossius respondens (Leiden: Joannes Patius, 1600), theses 2–6.

60. On these assumptions, and for the various orders of decrees that follow in this chapter, see *Dec. sent.*, pp. 63–70, 96–100, 104–106; *Works* 1: 614–618, 645–647, 653–654; *Disp. pub.* XV; and Louis Berkhof, *Systematic Theology*, 2 vols. (Grand Rapids, MI: Eerdmans, 1938), 1: 82–112. Cf. the succinct definition of *ordo decretorum Dei* in Muller, *Dictionary*, p. 215. See also the Appendix p. 140 for a comparison of different systems.

61. See *Exam. Gom.*, p. 78; *Works* 3: 591–592.

## B. Contra Supralapsarianism

Arminius expends great energy opposing supralapsarianism. He sees it as a species of a more common genus of predestination (rather than something *sui generis*), and he says that, among the different options, its advocates "climb the highest."[62] As we will see, his objections to it are drawn from historical, biblical, systematic, and pastoral theological concerns.

### B.1. Summary of Supralapsarianism

*Supralapsarianism* (from *supra lapsum*, before or above the fall) denotes a view of predestination that places God's decree to elect logically before the decree to permit the fall. The object of predestination, therefore, is considered as pure, not fallen, and in most accounts, not even yet created. The word *supralapsarian* was not yet in use in Arminius's day, but the view denoted by this term was precisely articulated by many of Arminius's opponents (including each of his faculty colleagues at Leiden University). Thus, as Nichols added the word *supralapsarian* in his English translation of *Declaration of Sentiments*, we also use this term as an accurate label for the view Arminius most stringently opposed.

As Arminius summarizes it, supralapsarianism holds the following:

> God, by an eternal and immutable decree has preordained (*verordineert*), from among people (whom he did not consider as being then created, much less as being fallen) certain individuals to everlasting life, and others to eternal destruction, without any regard whatever to righteousness or sin, to obedience or disobedience, but purely of his own good pleasure (*alleen om dattet hem belieft heeft*), to demonstrate the glory of his justice and mercy.[63]

Having thus predestined certain individuals to eternal life and blessedness—and others to eternal condemnation and misery—God then decrees the creation. Following this (in a strictly *logical* order of decrees), God decrees the fall. Subsequently, God decrees the work of Christ as a provision for the salvation of those predestined to salvation, and he then decrees that those for whom Christ died will be drawn to the salvation provided. (For the order of decrees, see the Appendix p. 140.) As Arminius summarizes this scheme,

---

62. *Dec. sent.*, p. 63; *Works* 1: 614: "Dan de gener die allerhoochste climmen."

63. *Dec. sent.*, pp. 63–64; *Works* 1: 614.

"From this decree of divine election and reprobation, and from this administration of the means which pertain to the execution of both of them, it follows that the elect are necessarily saved, it being impossible (*niet moghen*) for them to be lost; and that the reprobate are necessarily condemned, it being impossible for them to be saved."[64] As Arminius further points out, many of the proponents of this doctrine consider it "to be the foundation of Christianity, salvation, and its certainty"; he also points out that many such proponents consider anything less to deprive God of "the glory of his grace, and then merit of salvation is attributed to the free will of man and to his own powers and strength."[65] In other words, the primary motive of supralapsarianism is to preserve God's absolutely sovereign decision over all human affairs and sin.

### B.2. Arminius's Objections: A Preview

Arminius intensifies his concerns about the doctrine of predestination in his critique of supralapsarianism. First, he says, supralapsarianism is not the foundation of Christianity, nor is it the foundation of salvation, nor is it the foundation of the certainty or assurance of salvation. The assurance or certainty of salvation, as Arminius sees things, is dependent upon this decree, "The believer will be saved; I am a believer, therefore I will be saved"—but supralapsarianism embraces neither of these premises.[66] Thus Arminius concludes that "the doctrine of this predestination is not necessary to salvation, either as an object of knowledge, belief, hope, or performance."[67]

### B.3. The Supralapsarian Option and the Christian Tradition

Arminius advances historical-theological arguments against the supralapsarian position. First, he points out that neither supralapsarianism nor anything remotely like it was "admitted, decreed, or approved" by any of the major ecumenical councils of the patristic era. Neither Nicaea (325) nor Constantinople (381) affirms or demands anything close to the supralapsarian

---

64. *Dec. sent.*, pp. 68–69; *Works* 1: 617.

65. *Dec. sent.*, p. 69; *Works* 1: 617.

66. *Dec. sent.*, p. 71; *Works* 1: 619.

67. *Dec. sent.*, p. 72; *Works* 1: 620: "Waer uyt ick dan vorder besluyte, dat de leere deser Predestinatie niet noodich is ter salicheyt bekendt te worden, noch als die ghelooft, ghehoopt ofte ghedaen moet wesen." The summary below follows the outline in *Dec. sent.*, and material from other works of Arminius supplements his critique. For a briefer summary of Arminius's criticisms of supralapsarianism, see Bangs, *Arminius*, pp. 308–312.

view in or with their condemnations of various forms of theological error. The same is true for the later ecumenical councils (Arminius mentions Ephesus, Chalcedon, Constantinople II, and Constantinople III).[68]

More pertinent than the ecumenical councils that codified the doctrines of the Trinity and of Christ, nothing remotely approaching the supralapsarian view is demanded by the very councils and synods that dealt with and unambiguously condemned various forms of Pelagianism and "semi-Pelagianism." None of the councils that rejected Pelagianism (and semi-Pelagianism) came anywhere close to an affirmation of supralapsarianism. Moreover, Arminius argues, the stark absence of anything like supralapsarianism is not only to be observed in the formal statements of the important synods and councils that dealt with related issues, it is also absent from the major patristic theologians themselves. Arminius challenges his opponents to find anyone in the first six hundred years of the Christian faith who "ever brought this doctrine forward or gave it their approval," and he concludes that "neither was it professed and approved by a single individual of those who showed themselves to be the principal and keenest defenders of grace, against Pelagius."[69]

In his own day, Arminius argues that his non-Reformed contemporaries declare themselves against the supralapsarian view. Both the Lutherans and the Anabaptists, as well as the Roman Catholics, hold this to be an "erroneous" doctrine.[70] Referencing the debate between the "Philippists" and the "Gnesio-Lutherans," he makes the case that Melanchthon held this doctrine of predestination to be indistinguishable from Stoic fatalism.[71] He notes that Niels Hemmingsen (and "all the Danish churches") are obviously opposed to supralapsarianism, for when Hemmingsen was faced with the questions, "Do the elect believe?" or, "Are believers the elect?" he insisted that the former option was not substantially different from the "doctrine of the Manichees and Stoics," while the latter option is "in obvious agreement with Moses and the Prophets, with Christ and his apostles."[72]

---

68. *Dec. sent.*, p. 73; *Works* 1: 620.

69. *Dec. sent.*, p. 74; *Works* 1: 621.

70. *Dec. sent.*, p. 94; *Works* 1: 640–641.

71. *Dec. sent.*, p. 94; *Works* 1: 642. Melanchthon famously referred to Calvin as Zeno. See Barbara Pitkin, "The Protestant Zeno: Calvin and the Development of Melanchthon's Anthropology," *Journal of Religion* 84/3 (2004): 345–378.

72. *Dec. sent.*, p. 95; *Works* 1: 643.

In fact, Arminius points out, the supralapsarian account "does not conform or correspond with" the "Harmony of the Confessions of the Reformed and Protestant Churches."[73] With respect to his own (immediate) tradition's confessional documents, Arminius insists that it is "very properly" a question of doubt whether supralapsarianism is demanded by either the Belgic Confession or the Heidelberg Catechism. Not only does Arminius conclude that there is nothing in the confessional statements of his own tradition to *demand* supralapsarianism, he also thinks that the coherence of the supralapsarian view with those statements is dubious at best.[74] Indeed, he worries that a commitment to supralapsarianism would be practically detrimental to the future of the Reformed Churches; for many people had threatened to leave the Reformed Church "unless they be fully assured that the Church holds no opinion of this description," and "there is likewise no point of doctrine which the Papists, Anabaptists, and Lutherans oppose more and use as an occasion to blacken these [our] Churches and make [our] whole doctrine a stench."[75] In fact, some of them viewed this doctrine not only as error but also as a kind of blasphemy, worse than which cannot be conceived, for "of all the blasphemies against God which can be conceived and expressed, there is none so foul as not to be deduced by fair consequence from this opinion of our doctors."[76]

### B.4. Supralapsarianism and the Doctrine of God

As important as these historical observations are for Arminius, however, it is distinctly theological concerns that are at the heart of his rejection of the supralapsarian doctrine. The view that God created humans so that he could save some and condemn others by his unconditional decree is seen by him to be utterly inconsistent with any adequately Christian understanding of the nature and character of God. Arminius says that the view of

---

73. *Dec. sent.*, pp. 74–75; *Works* 1: 621–622. The *Harmony of Confessions*, compiled by Jean-François Salvard and published in 1581, was a compilation from eleven different Lutheran and Reformed confessions and was intended to promote ecumenism among Reformed Protestants. See Jill Raitt, "Harmony of Confessions," in *The Oxford Encyclopedia of the Reformation*, ed. Hans J. Hillerbrand, 2: 211–212.

74. *Dec. sent.*, pp. 75–76; *Works* 1: 622–623.

75. *Dec. sent.*, p. 95; *Works* 1: 643: "Daer en is gheen punct der leered at de Papisten, Wederdoopers, Lutherische meer bestrijden, ende als een occasie ghebruycken, om dese kercken swart ende de geheele leere stinckende te maken." This last phrase alludes to a common statement in the Old Testament. E.g., see Gen. 34:30.

76 *Dec. sent.*, p. 95; *Works* 1: 643.

his opponents is especially repugnant to divine wisdom, divine justice, and divine goodness. It "contends against the wisdom of God," first, because it represents God as decreeing something for "a particular end which neither is good nor can be good."[77] According to the doctrine under consideration, God created human beings in the image of God (*imago Dei*) for the purpose of eternal perdition. So unless Christians are to commit themselves to the incredible proposition that eternal perdition is somehow *good*, the supralapsarian position entails that God decreed something for evil. And this, Arminius concludes, simply is not consistent with the wisdom of God. Second, Arminius takes the opposing view to be inconsistent with divine wisdom because it presents God as creating humans for condemnation so that "the glory of his mercy and justice" might be demonstrated. The problem with such a move, as Arminius sees things, is this: according to the supralapsarian view, God "cannot demonstrate this glory except by an act that is contrary at once to his mercy and his justice."[78] In other words, to demonstrate his justice and mercy, God would have to do something that is neither just nor merciful.

So far, Arminius is only asserting that the justice of God is compromised by the doctrine under consideration. But he mounts a set of arguments to this assertion as well. Arminius here considers two dimensions of divine justice. The first is God's steadfast love of righteousness and hatred of sin, and here Arminius thinks that supralapsarianism's notion that God has unconditionally decreed the salvation of some sinners without consideration of their belief or obedience entails the conclusion that God loves such persons "more than his own justice."[79] While some modern readers might simply shrug at such a complaint, given Arminius's own doctrine of divine simplicity, such a notion is simply absurd—as if God could love anything more than his own righteousness, which is his own goodness, which is goodness itself and his own being.

Arminius raises an additional concern related to the justice of God. Whatever one might say about God's justice in relation to the saved, there is another problem with respect to the damned. The problem is simply stated: according to supralapsarianism, God "wishes to subject the creature to misery (which cannot possibly have any existence except as the

---

77. *Dec. sent.*, p. 77; *Works* 1: 623.

78. *Dec. sent.*, p. 77; *Works* 1: 623.

79. *Dec. sent.*, p. 78; *Works* 1: 624.

punishment of sin), although, at the same time, he does not see the creature as a sinner, and therefore as not liable to either wrath or to punishment."[80] This conclusion follows quickly and directly, Arminius is convinced, from any doctrine which teaches that God's decree to condemn sinners precedes their own sin (or even God's decree that they commit sin). If God decrees their miserable damnation before they actually sin, much less before he even decrees that they *will* sin, then surely their miserable punishment and condemnation from God precede the actions that merit such punishment. That is, the supralapsarian scheme has God reprobating people for no just cause. Surely, concludes Arminius, this is opposed to any acceptable notion of justice.

Nor will Arminius let his opponents rest with a quick and easy appeal to the inscrutable freedom of the divine sovereign will (*voluntas arcana*). For according to the doctrine of divine simplicity, there can be no divine action that is not completely consistent with the divine nature, nor can there be any possibility of competing or contradictory attributes within the divine nature. Given divine simplicity, "it cannot happen that God should at the same time will contradictory things."[81] Recall Arminius's belief that to say that God is *freely* good is the height of blasphemy.[82] Against Perkins, Arminius denies that "it is universally true that whatever is just, is just by this, because God wills it"; rather, "there are many things which God wills because they are just."[83] This does not mean that there is no place for divine command theory in his thought, for "it is truly part of our duty, in the laws divinely imposed upon us, not so much to see whether what he commands be just in itself, but simply to obey because God prescribes and commands."[84] But Arminius will have nothing to do with either a raw, nominalist theory of divine command or a theory of natural law that conceives of standards of goodness and righteousness as independent of God. On the contrary, "This duty of ours rests upon this foundation, that God

---

80. *Dec. sent.*, p. 78; *Works* 1: 624: "Teghens de tweede strijdt dese leere van Predestinatie: want sy stelt dat Godt sijne Creature wilt ellende toevoeghen, die niet anders als strafe der sonden can zijn, daer hy nochtans die Creatuere niet aen en siet als sondich, ende oversulcx niet als torn ofte strafwaerdich."

81. *Exam. Perk.*, in *Opera*, p. 667; *Works* 3: 318.

82. *Apologia*, art. 22 (2), in *Opera*, pp. 166–167; *Works* 2: 33–35.

83. *Exam. Perk.*, in *Opera*, p. 693; *Works* 3: 357.

84. *Exam. Perk.*, in *Opera*, p. 693; *Works* 3: 358.

cannot prescribe what is unjust, because he is justice, wisdom, and omnipotence itself."[85] Working from this doctrine of divine simplicity, he
insists that to attribute something to the liberty of the divine will that
would "impinge upon his justice" is to make a theological mistake of cata-
strophic proportions.[86]

As has been demonstrated, the goodness of God is a core conviction for
Arminius. "Will not the judge of all the earth do right (Exod. 32:33)?"[87] He
places consideration of divine goodness within the context of his commitment to the doctrine of divine simplicity, and it informs his understanding
of such attributes as divine mercy. Thus "it must be understood that mercy
is not an essential property of God, as distinguished from his goodness,
but is comprehended in goodness itself as its source (*matrice*), and proceeds from goodness; indeed, is goodness itself, displaying itself toward a
sinful and miserable creature."[88] As we have seen, Arminius's account of
divine goodness includes the view that God communicates God's own
goodness (so far as it is "fitting and proper"). But according to the doctrine
being criticized by Arminius, God "wills the greatest evil (*quaet*) to his
creatures, and from eternity he has preordained that evil for them, or predetermined to impart it to them, even before he predetermined to bestow
upon the creatures any good." For "this doctrine" holds that God willed to
damn creatures to eternal torment *before God decreed to create them*. So, the
divine will to create—which should be the first "sending out (*uytganck*) of
God's goodness"—according to this scheme, actually *follows* his will to
condemn human people to hell.[89] But God does not desire the death of the
sinner (Ezek. 18:23; 33:11); how much more, then, does God not desire the
"death of the non-wicked, indeed, of the creature not yet in existence?"[90]

Arminius's concerns are obvious. God is the *summum bonum*, and
"because God is the highest good (*summum bonum*), therefore his first
volition, when engaged about any object, is the communication of good.
If it holds otherwise, [then] God is the highest evil (*summum malum*) (may

---

85. *Exam. Perk.*, in *Opera*, p. 693; *Works* 3: 358.

86. *Exam. Perk.*, in *Opera*, p. 683; *Works* 3: 342–343.

87. *Exam. Perk.*, in *Opera*, p. 635; *Works* 3: 268.

88. *Exam. Perk.*, in *Opera*, p. 642; *Works* 3: 279.

89. *Dec. sent.*, p. 78; *Works* 1: 625.

90. *Exam. Gom.*, p. 104; *Works* 3: 613.

blasphemy be far from this saying)."[91] In other words, God's first action toward any creature cannot be its reprobation. But according to supralapsarianism, creation is the means for reprobation (*via reprobationis*): it is *God* who makes creatures for the express purpose of their eternal condemnation. Such a doctrine, Arminius exclaims, is even worse than Manicheeism; for where the Manicheans at least had two gods, one of whom was perfectly good, this doctrine attributes something less than perfect goodness to the omnipotent Sovereign.[92] Arminius thus concludes "how vastly different are such statements as these from the goodness of God, by which he does good not only to the unworthy, but also to the evil and those worthy of punishment—which trait we are charged to imitate in our heavenly Father."[93]

According to supralapsarianism, once such creatures are sinners (by divine determination), God then calls the reprobate to believe. But, Arminius asks, to believe in *what*—in a gospel that was never intended for them? Such a doctrine "imputes hypocrisy to God, as if, in his exhortation to faith addressed to such, he requires them to believe in Christ, whom, however, he has not set forth as a Savior to them."[94] For Arminius, this is worse than merely saying that God created humans in order to condemn them, for not only does God create humans in order that they may be damned, but he also deals with "some of his creatures by hypocrisy and by fraud, and with wonderful art leading them into sin, in order that the poor wretches might seem to perish by their own fault."[95] Such people "are commanded to believe a lie"—that the gospel is for them—"and because they do not believe the lie they are more heavily punished."[96] It is utterly inconceivable that the God of perfect goodness could engage in such hypocrisy.[97]

Arminius argues that a view such as Perkins's entails that "sin coheres necessarily with God's decree, indeed, it also depends on it, so that humanity is not able not to sin (*non possit non peccare*). . . . Therefore it follows, since

---

91. *Exam. Gom.*, p. 76; *Works* 3: 590.

92. *Exam. Gom.*, p. 76; *Works* 3: 590.

93. *Dec. sent.*, p. 78; *Works* 1: 625: "Voorwaer dit selfde verschilt veel vande goedicheydt Godes, deur welcke hy niet alleen den onweerdighen, maer oock den quaden ende strafweerdighen goet doet, t'welcke wy belast worden in onsen Hemelschen Vader nae te volghen."

94. *Exam. Perk.*, in *Opera*, p. 663; *Works* 3: 313. Cf. *Exam. Gom.*, pp. 76–77; *Works* 3: 590–591.

95. *Exam. Gom.*, p. 92; *Works* 3: 603.

96. *Exam. Gom.*, p. 102; *Works* 3: 611.

97. *Dec. sent.*, pp. 86–87; *Works*, 1: 631; *Exam. Perk.*, in *Opera*, p. 663; *Works* 3: 313.

God has ordained people to sin, but has absolutely decreed to punish sin in many, God has simply ordained most people to the fire of hell."[98] As Arminius sees things, supralapsarianism is inconsistent with the goodness of God on many levels: from creation to redemption, it compromises the perfection of the simple divine nature.

Arminius argues that supralapsarianism entails the conclusions that "God is the author of sin . . . that God truly sins, indeed, that God alone sins."[99] God must be the author of sin, because God makes creatures for whom sin is inevitable. God must himself truly be a sinner, because he is the immediate cause of their sin (it most certainly does not—and cannot—arise within them). On this view, God is the only agent who can perform such actions voluntarily or freely; thus he must be the only sinner.[100] And what could be further from the goodness of God than this consequence, one which the church has been concerned to avoid since its earliest days?[101] Even if the proponents of supralapsarianism deny that God is the author of sin, if it is a fair consequence, then this undermines the doctrine. As Arminius says, "If the consequence of a doctrine is false, then that [doctrine] must also be false."[102] Thus he concludes in this case, "Far be it from us to attribute [such things] to a good God."[103]

Arminius's strong words throughout his critique are for the cause of God. Nothing less than the glory of God is at stake: "Come, O God, and vindicate your glory from tongues speaking perverse things about you; indeed, correct their minds, that they may consecrate their tongues to you, and may hereafter rightly proclaim true things, and things worthy of you, in accordance with your word."[104]

---

98. *Exam. Perk.*, in *Opera*, p. 690; *Works* 3: 352.

99. *Exam. Gom.*, p. 157; *Works* 3: 657. Cf. *Exam. Perk.*, in *Opera*, p. 694; *Works* 3: 359; *Dec. sent.*, p. 85; *Works* 1: 630.

100. *Exam. Perk.*, in *Opera*, p. 694; *Works* 3: 359; cf. *Exam. Gom.*, p. 157; *Works* 3: 657.

101. As an example of this concern in early Christian theology, Irenaeus wrote a letter on the topic "that God is not the maker of evil." Eusebius, *Historia ecclesiastica* V.xx.1, in *PG* 20: 484A. See also Den Boer, *God's Twofold Love*, pp. 294–320, for a survey of this theological debate in the Middle Ages and the sixteenth century.

102. *Dec. sent.*, p. 61; *Works* 1: 609. Cf. *Cap. VII Rom.*, in *Opera*, p. 825; *Works* 2: 490.

103. *Exam. Gom.*, p. 102; *Works* 3: 611.

104. *Exam. Gom.*, p. 92; *Works* 3: 603: "Adesto Deus, et vindica gloriam tuam a linguis perversa de te loquentium; imo potius corrige mentem illorum, ut linguas suas tibi consecrent, et vera teque digna posthac iuxta tuum verbum recte pronuntient." Cf. *Dec. sent.*, pp. 83–85; *Works* 1: 629–630.

### B.5. *Supralapsarianism, Human Nature, Creation, Sin, and the Gospel*

Arminius thinks that the supralapsarian scheme is inconsistent with an adequate theological anthropology. First of all, it is seen by Arminius to be inconsistent with the freedom of the will. His complaint centers on the concern that this doctrine "binds and determines the will precisely to one thing, either to do this or to do the other."[105] Cast in modern terms, he presupposes that freedom and determinism are incompatible; he is a libertarian or incompatibilist with respect to human freedom. Arminius is concerned about this matter, and he thinks that any doctrine that entails "injury" to the innocent (not yet fallen) human person at the hands of God clearly is not acceptable. But what is interesting to note is that even here—in his discussion of human freedom—he is also very concerned about the directly *theological* implications of determinism. In other words, he is worried about what such a view would say about God. If, on the one hand, God were to create humans with freedom but also to determine the will, God could be charged with lack of thought or consideration (*onbedachtsaem*). But if, on the other hand, God were to hinder the use of liberty after God had formed human persons, God might be charged with being mutable or variable (*veranderlijck*). Either way, concludes Arminius, God might be blameworthy. But surely this is not the case, as he exclaims, "Let this be far from us!"[106]

Furthermore, Arminius notes that the doctrine under scrutiny destroys an adequate understanding of the inclination and capacity for salvation with which humans were bestowed. As he explains it, "Since by this predestination it has been preordained (*verordineert*) that a great part of humanity will lack this salvation and will inherit eternal condemnation—and since this predetermination took place even before the decree had passed for creating humanity—such persons are deprived of something, for the desire of which they have been endowed by God with a natural inclination (*genegentheydt*)." The real problem here is again strictly theological, for this great privation that they suffer is not due to any "preceding sin and merit, but only through this predestination of God."[107] In other words, it would be

---

105. *Dec. sent.*, p. 79; *Works* 1: 626.

106. *Dec. sent.*, pp. 79–80; *Works* 1: 626.

107. *Dec. sent.*, p. 80; *Works* 3: 626. That God gave humanity the desire for himself is acknowledged throughout the Christian tradition. E.g., Augustine, *Confessionum libri tredecim*, I.i.1, in *PL* 32: 661, speaks of the restlessness of the unregenerate heart finding its rest in God. Even Calvin acknowledges that the *sensus divinitatis*, common to all people, is "beyond dispute." John Calvin, *Institutio Christianae religionis* (1559), in *Ioannis Calvini opera quae supersunt omnia*, ed. G. Baum, E. Cunitz, and E. Reuss, vol. 2 (Brunswick: C. A. Schwetschke and Son, 1863–1900), I.iii.1, 3.

*God* who first decreed that they would be damned, and only then decreed that they should be created with the inclination and longing for salvation. Again, Arminius insists, it would be God who is responsible both for their condition and for their longing for redemption from it, a longing that cannot possibly be met. And this, concludes Arminius, simply is not consistent with a Christian view of God and the creation of humanity.

As Arminius sees things, the *imago Dei* (image of God) consists (at least in part) of the capacity to serve God in righteousness and holiness. The "end of creation in a state of righteousness is this, that rational creatures may know, love, worship God their creator, and live blessed with him forever."[108] Exaggerations of human insignificance (*parvitas*) run the risk of doing "injury to God's creation."[109] The doctrine of the *imago Dei* not only entails the conclusion that humans are "qualified and empowered" to know God, but it also obliges humanity to know, love, worship, and serve him. Yet according to the doctrine of predestination under consideration, "it was preordained that man would be defective and would sin—that is, that he would not know, would not love, would not worship, and would not serve God; and that he should not perform that which, by this nature of God, he was well-qualified, empowered, and obliged to fulfill."[110] Arminius understands this doctrine to be nonsense on stilts, for it amounts to the following assertion: "God has created humanity in his image, in holiness and righteousness; but, nevertheless, he preordained and decreed that humanity should become unholy and unrighteous, that is, be conformed to the image of Satan."[111] Arminius is convinced that to be a human person made in God's image is by definition to be made to know, love, enjoy, and glorify God; but according to supralapsarianism, some people instead were made for sin and hell.[112]

Arminius believes that supralapsarianism is opposed in other ways to the doctrine of creation. In his response to Gomarus, he emphasizes, first of all, that it is absurd to decree to predestine specific individuals before

---

108. *Exam. Gom.*, p. 90; *Works* 3: 601.

109. *Exam. Perk.*, in *Opera*, p. 636; *Works* 3: 271.

110. *Dec. sent.*, p. 79; *Works* 1: 625: "ende dese Predestinatie daer tusschen comende, jae voorcomende, heeft verordineert dat de Mensche soude ghebreeckelijck worden ende sondighen, dat is, dat hy Godt niet en kenne, niet en beminne, niet en eere, noch en diene; ende also niet en doe t'ghene hy nae desen aert Godes bequaem, machtich ende schuldich was te volbrenghen."

111. *Dec. sent.*, p. 79; *Works* 1: 625.

112. *Exam. Perk.*, in *Opera*, p. 690; *Works* 1: 352.

they are even considered as created. God cannot demonstrate his love and good pleasure toward a non-entity (*non ens*); neither can he will salvation and blessing for a non-entity.[113]

Later, in *Declaration of Sentiments*, Arminius's main point about creation is that it cannot be a means of reprobation. Arminius follows a long tradition in seeing creation as the "communication of good according to the intrinsic property of its nature."[114] As noted above, the goal of creation is that humans "may know, love, worship God their creator, and live blessed with him forever."[115] Thus, creation is a work of divine love, a "perfect action of God" that is "proper" to God (*opus proprium Dei*), and as such cannot be an "act of hatred" or "means of reprobation."[116] The problem with supralapsarianism is immediately obvious to Arminius, and it is every bit as serious as it is glaring. According to the doctrine of predestination under consideration, the reprobate (the "greater part of humanity") have been created *in order that they might be evil and be damned.* The intention of the Creator would be to condemn, and the end or *telos* of creation would be eternal perdition.[117] "In that case," concludes Arminius, "creation would not have been a communication of any good, but a preparation for the greatest evil both according to the purpose of the Creator and the sending forth (*uytgangh*) of the matter."[118] And does not our Lord say as much, asks Arminius, when he says that "it would have been good for that man, if he had never been born" (Matt. 26:24)?[119]

Arminius also mounts an argument that supralapsarianism is inconsistent with Christian hamartiology. Sin is, as Arminius puts it, the "meritorious cause" of condemnation. But on the scheme under consideration,

---

113. *Exam. Gom.*, pp. 66–67; *Works* 3: 581–582. Cf. *Collatio*, in *Opera*, p. 644; *Works* 3: 282; *Art. non.* V.2, in *Opera*, p. 951; *Works* 2: 710. On Arminius's understanding of *ens* and *non ens*, see Dekker, *Rijker dan Midas*, pp. 71–74.

114. *Dec. sent.*, p. 80; *Works* 1: 626; *Exam. Gom.*, p. 88; *Works* 3: 600.

115. *Exam. Gom.*, p. 90; *Works* 3: 601.

116. *Exam. Gom.*, pp. 87–90; *Works* 3: 599–602.

117. Arminius put this as a syllogism:

1. Creation is the communication of good (definition);
2. Creation intended as a means of reprobation is not a communication of good;
3. "Therefore, creation which is effected with that intention is not creation, and for that reason true creation is not a way of reprobation." ("Ergo creatio quae fit cum ista intentione non est creatio, et propterea creatio vera non est via reprobationis.") *Exam. Gom.*, p. 88; *Works* 3: 600.

118. *Dec. sent.*, pp. 80–81; *Works* 1: 626–627.

119. *Dec. sent.*, p. 81; *Works* 1: 627.

reprobation to condemnation actually precedes sin, and thus supralapsarianism inverts the order of sin and damnation. Whereas classical Christian hamartiology thinks in terms of reprobation for sin, the supralapsarian view reverses the order and entails that sinful dispositions and actions occur as a result of the decree of reprobation. More fundamental, however, is the basic Christian view that sin is disobedience and rebellion. Neither of these terms, argues Arminius, is remotely appropriate to the sin of the reprobate person "who by a preceding divine decree is placed under an unavoidable necessity of sinning."[120] What seems to be at stake here for Arminius is the core conviction that sin must be understood as that which God does not want. Sin is, in classical terms, contrary to nature, contrary to reason, and, most fundamentally, contrary to God.[121] Sin is whatever is opposed to the divine law; it is whatever is set in rebellion against the divine will; and it is whatever is contrary to the nature or character of God. But any system of theology that holds that the sins of the reprobate are made necessary by God entails the conclusion that the reprobate sin *in accordance with* the will of God. If God's decree makes sin inevitable for a person, then the sinful actions of that person must be said to be done in obedience to the divine decree. But that outcome, concludes Arminius, destroys any acceptable understanding of sin as what is against God's will and ways.

Sin is the transgression of God's law; the prototypical expressions of sin are voluntary and willful transgressions of God's law. But if one is determined or "ordained" to sin by some other entity, then that sin is inevitable. This means that sin is necessary for a person. For Arminius, this is a problem for supralapsarianism: freedom and necessity are opposed, so if sin is inevitable for someone, then we are left to conclude that such a person "cannot sin." Why not? "For sin," declares Arminius, "is voluntary, and God's decree concerning sin introduces the necessity of sinning."[122] If an act of sin is the act of going against God, then someone who does something that God has made inevitable for them surely does not go against God. Thus Arminius concludes that supralapsarianism leaves us with the unfortunate conclusion that sin is not really sin; consequently, such a doctrine of predestination wreaks havoc on the doctrine of sin.

---

120. *Dec. sent.*, p. 83; *Works* 1: 628.

121. Even the sinfulness of the devil is against nature. See *Exam. Gom.*, p. 84; *Works* 3: 597: "For the devil is so not by nature and God's creation, but by his own vice and fault."

122. *Exam. Perk.*, in *Opera*, p. 691; *Works* 3: 354.

Just what is the relation between God's glory and human sin? Arminius knows that to sin is to "fall short" of God's glory (Rom. 3:23), and he insists that it is opposed to divine glory.[123] He is also convinced that God "has always set before himself as the supreme and ultimate end the manifestation of his own perfection, that is, his own glory."[124] So in all of his actions, God's own glory is of paramount importance. This includes, of course, all of God's dealings with evil and sinners. But sin is not precisely a vehicle or a means of God's glory. Surely it is not the necessary or only or primary vehicle or means of God's glory; as noted in chapter 2, God is perfectly blessed and self-sufficient within his own life.[125] Instead, "Sin is therefore, in that respect, not per se the means (*medium*) of illustrating the divine glory, but only the occasion; an occasion not given for this very end, nor by its own nature fitted for it, but seized by God, and applied to this purpose with wondrous art and laudable diversion of use."[126] In other words, though sin is utterly opposed to the glory of God, yet it is not outside or beyond the range of God's foreknowledge and providential action, for God brings "light from darkness."

Arminius does not stop here. He continues his critique in *Declaration of Sentiments* by suggesting that the supralapsarian doctrine of predestination goes "against the nature of God's grace."[127] Contrary to some modern misunderstandings of the issue, the basic disagreement of Arminius with his Reformed contemporaries does not concern the fact that Arminius holds to the doctrine of prevenient grace. To see the real heart of the disagreement, we must look elsewhere.[128]

---

123. E.g., *Exam. Perk.*, in *Opera*, p. 697; *Works* 3: 364.

124. *Exam. Perk.*, in *Opera*, p. 640; *Works* 3: 276.

125. *Exam. Gom.*, p. 55; *Works* 3: 572: "It follows from here that God does not need the sinner for the illustration, either external or internal, of his glory." Cf. *Exam. Perk.*, in *Opera*, p. 697; *Works* 3: 364: "God did not need the wrongdoing of humanity for the illustration of his own glory."

126. *Exam. Perk.*, in *Opera*, pp. 645–646; *Works* 3: 285.

127. *Dec. sent.*, p. 83; *Works* 1: 628: "soo is dese Predestinatie de nature vande ghenade Godes te weder."

128. Cf. *Exam. Perk.*, in *Opera*, p. 769; *Works* 3: 472. Perkins objects that "from the necessity of fivefold grace" (which includes prevenient grace) there is no "sufficient grace" because "no one of the five graces is alone sufficient to salvation." But this amounts only to a criticism of Arminius's understanding of it in relation to the other distinctions in the doctrine of grace; Perkins does not object to the doctrine of prevenient grace itself. Given the historical affirmations of the doctrine, to deny all versions or uses of the doctrine itself would be awkward for supralapsarians, who claim continuity with the Augustinian doctrine of grace. For the Augustinian background of prevenient grace, see chapter 4 of this volume.

Even though the proponents of the supralapsarian account might tout it as the highest expression of the "doctrines of grace," Arminius argues that it undercuts and threatens to destroy a proper understanding of grace. First of all, Arminius argues that grace is meant to restore *nature*. As sin is contrary to nature, so also is saving grace given for the restoration of created nature, which is itself from the beginning a gratuitous gift of God. Grace is not given to destroy what is truly natural, including free will; rather, it is offered to "give it a right direction, to correct its depravity, and to allow man to follow and to perform his own movement (*beweginghe*)."[129] Writing to Franciscus Junius, he puts it succinctly: "When I say 'grace,' I do not exclude nature."[130] Arminius here draws upon, and echoes, a long tradition of teaching regarding the relation of nature and grace. But whatever one makes of this tradition, this much is clear—Arminius thinks that grace is given to restore and perfect nature, and he is convinced that the supralapsarian scheme actually would threaten to destroy nature.

Arminius also presents several directly exegetical reasons for holding that the supralapsarian view is opposed to an adequate conception of grace. Here he notes that Scripture depicts God's grace as something that is capable of being resisted; Acts 7:51 says, "You always resist the Holy Spirit." Likewise, grace can be "received in vain" (2 Corinthians 6:1). From these passages and others (Heb. 12:15; Matt. 23:37; Luke 7:30), Arminius concludes that "it is possible for humanity to avoid yielding assent to it, and to refuse all cooperation with it."[131] The supralapsarian view, however, holds that grace "has a certain irresistible force and operation."[132] Arminius's conclusion is swift: if some view of predestination holds to the irresistible operation of grace, while Scripture teaches that grace indeed can be—and is—resisted, then so much the worse for that view of predestination.

Arminius further argues that the proponents of supralapsarianism confuse *sufficient* grace, which is the grace necessary for salvation, with *efficacious* grace, which, in Reformed thought, is irresistible. Conflating them helps the supralapsarian cause, because the denial of irresistible grace would amount to the same thing as the rejection of any necessary

---

129. *Dec. sent.*, p. 83; *Works* 1: 628–629.

130. *Collatio*, in *Opera*, p. 567; *Works* 3: 172.

131. *Dec. sent.*, p. 83; *Works* 1: 629.

132. *Dec. sent.*, p. 83; *Works* 1: 629.

operation of grace (of which Arminians are sometimes accused). Arminius argues that they should not be conflated, and he also turns the tables on the supralapsarian position. For if one denies sufficient grace for all, which the supralapsarians do by collapsing it into efficacious grace, then those who do not have such grace could not be responsible for their rejection of it. After all, if it was not sufficient for them then it was not available to them, and if it was not available to them then they could not have rejected it. Arminius thus concludes that "if sufficient grace be taken away, they are justly excused who do not believe and are not converted, because without that they could neither believe nor be converted."[133]

What of the worry, raised by Arminius's critics, that his theology undercuts the sheer gratuity of grace? Is it true that God "owes" grace to no one, and that, as Junius claims, because "it is grace, therefore [it is] not owed"?[134] And does Arminius's view entail the conclusion that God "owes" grace? Once again, Arminius cannot conceive of a God whose actions are not fully in accord with the divine nature (which is, in simplicity, justice and goodness itself). He says that:

> God owes grace to no one simply and absolutely, but can make himself a debtor to grace by a twofold mode: by promise, and by the requirement (*postulatione*) of an act. By promise, when he has promised that he will bestow it, whether under a condition or without a condition. By the requirement of an act, when he requires such an act from humanity as is not performable without his grace; for then he is bound to its bestowal: otherwise he "reaps where he has not sown."[135]

In other words, God has freely obliged himself to the bestowal of grace.

Furthermore, for supralapsarians, God may give grace to some reprobate persons only to remove it again. But Arminius argues that this is simply antithetical to a proper understanding of grace, for "grace conduces to the good of those persons to whom it is offered and by whom it is received."[136]

---

133. *Exam. Perk.*, in *Opera*, p. 666; *Works*, 3: 316.

134. *Collatio*, in *Opera*, p. 617; *Works* 3: 246.

135. *Collatio*, in *Opera*, pp. 617–618; *Works* 3: 246. Cf. *Exam. Perk.*, in *Opera*, p. 644; *Works*, 3: 283–284.

136. *Dec. sent.*, pp. 83–84; *Works* 1: 629.

To him, the contrast is glaring: one view maintains that God gives grace so that condemnation might be greater, while the other view holds that grace is intended for the good of those persons to whom it is offered and by whom it is received. The superiority of the latter is something that Arminius takes to be obvious enough to warrant no further argument.

Arminius is also troubled about supralapsarianism's implications for Christology. This doctrine, he says, "is detrimental to the honor of Jesus Christ the Savior." First, it moves Christ from the center of the doctrine of predestination (cf. Eph. 1:1–11). It also affirms that some human creatures are predestined to be saved *prior* to the decree that Christ would be the Savior, effectively removing Christ from the foundation of election. Finally, it puts Christ in the position of "only a subordinate cause of the preordained salvation, and thus only a minister and instrument to appropriate that salvation."[137]

Arminius highlights other Christological problems as well. He argues that Scripture teaches quite clearly that Christ paid the ransom ($\lambda\acute{v}\tau\rho o\nu$) for the sins of the whole world (Jn. 1:29; 3:16; 6:51; Rom. 14:15; 2 Cor. 5:19–21; 1 Tim. 4:10; Heb. 2:9; 2 Peter 2:1; 1 Jn. 2:2; 4:14).[138] To his Reformed contemporaries who, following Augustine, argued that "all" and "everyone" can refer to "all of a group" or "everyone who is part of the elect," Arminius responds that while universalizing language *can* mean "all" in a such a sense, the exegetical question is not whether it *can* be so used—the question is, rather, if indeed it *is* being so used. And Arminius thinks that it is not so used, as such expressions as "especially those who believe" indicate.[139] Meanwhile, he finds the arguments for "definite" or "limited" atonement (as the view will come to be labeled) from Scripture to be far from conclusive; yes, the Bible says that Jesus prayed for the elect (and "his sheep"), but this does not entail that Jesus did not give himself for others as well—and at any rate, Jesus also prays for those who are not among the elect.[140] His critics argue that his view implies that all people are saved (and that this is

---

137. *Dec. sent.*, p. 85; *Works* 1: 630: "want sy ontkendt dat Christus zy de verdienende oorsaecke die ons de verlorene salicheyt hebbe verworven, stellende hem alleen eene ghesubordineerde oorsaecke van de te vooren gheordonneerde salicheyt, ende also alleen een dienaer ende instrument om de salicheydt toe te eyghenen." Cf. *Exam. Perk.*, in *Opera*, pp. 657–658; *Works* 3: 304.

138. E.g., *Exam. Perk.*, in *Opera*, pp. 674, 735; *Works* 3: 328–329, 420–421.

139. *Exam. Perk.*, in *Opera*, p. 674; *Works* 3: 329.

140. *Exam. Perk.*, in *Opera*, p. 672; *Works* 3: 326.

contrary to biblical teaching); to this, Arminius responds that they are confusing satisfaction for sins with the remission of sins. For "satisfaction precedes, as consisting in the death and obedience of Christ, but remission of sins consists in the application of satisfaction through faith in Christ."[141] He is convinced that all who hold that conversion and justification are distinct from the atoning work of Christ (however dependent they are upon that work) must admit that there indeed is a distinction between satisfaction for sins and remission of sins. In addition, the very notion of "sufficiency" is important here; while all parties agree that the work of Christ is "sufficient for all, but efficient only for the elect," Arminius argues that the common Reformed views of this issue collapse at just this point. For they affirm that the work of Christ is sufficient for all—by which they mean that it would have been sufficient if God had intended it to be—while also rendering pointless the very affirmation: "For if the λύτρον [ransom] has not been offered and paid (*solutum*) for all, then truly it is not a λύτρον, much less sufficient (*sufficiens*) for all. For a λύτρον is that which has been offered and paid. Therefore, the death of Christ might be said to be sufficient for redeeming the sins of all people, if God had willed him to die for all: but the λύτρον cannot be called sufficient, unless it has actually been paid for all."[142]

If he thinks that the doctrine under consideration is inconsistent with an adequate account of the divine nature and attributes, a healthy doctrine of creation, a robust understanding of sin, a biblical account of grace, and a proper Christological basis, and thus obscures the glory of God, then it is no wonder that Arminius also thinks that supralapsarianism produces an inadequate doctrine of salvation and is "a perversion of the gospel of Christ."[143]

> The gospel says, "For God so loved the world, that he gave his only-begotten Son, that whoever believes in him should have eternal life" (Jn. 3:16). But this doctrine says "that God so loved all those whom he had precisely elected to eternal life, that he gave his Son to them alone, and by an irresistible force he infused (*onwederstandelijcke cracht instortet*) faith in him." To say this in a few words: The gospel says . . . "Believe, and you will live." But this doctrine says,

---

141. *Exam. Perk.*, in *Opera*, p. 637; *Works* 3: 423–424.

142. *Exam. Perk.*, in *Opera*, p. 671; *Works* 3: 325.

143. *Dec. sent.*, p. 87; *Works* 1: 632.

"Since it is my will to give you life, it is therefore my will to give you faith."[144]

This is, concludes Arminius, "a real and most manifest inversion of the gospel."[145] Even worse, further reflection leads to the conclusion that "to many to whom the gospel is announced, God, by the absolute decree of reprobation, neither wills that Christ should be of advantage (*prodesse*), nor is willing to grant remission of sins. Therefore they are commanded to believe a lie, and because they do not believe the lie they are more heavily punished; which be it far from us (*absit*) to attribute to a good God."[146] To Arminius, this is anything but good news (that is, gospel).

The sheer number and depth of Arminius's concerns about supralapsarianism indicate the degree to which a whole theological system may be affected by these controversies, as well as the extent to which Arminius differed from some of his contemporaries. These concerns come together for Arminius in such a way as to lead him to the conclusion that supralapsarianism is nothing other than the subversion of the "foundation of religion in general, and of the Christian religion in particular."[147] At the most basic (theistic) level, Arminius argues, the "twofold love of God" (*tweederley liefde Godes / duplex Dei amor*) is foundational, a point he emphasized throughout his writings.[148] Vital to any proper understanding of God is an understanding of God's love, and to understand divine love rightly is to see the proper distinctions.[149] As noted in our previous chapter, according to Arminius, God's will tends toward himself and his creation; since his will is loving, his love also tends toward himself and his creation. Thus, the first

---

144. *Dec. sent.*, p. 88; *Works* 1: 633. Cf. *Exam. Perk.*, *Works* 3: 309–317.

145. *Dec. sent.*, p. 88; *Works* 1: 633.

146. *Exam. Gom.*, p. 102; *Works* 3: 611.

147. *Dec. sent.*, p. 90; *Works* 1: 634: "stoot dese leere om verre het fundament der Religie int gemeen, ende ooc der Christelijcke Religie int besonder."

148. *Disp. pub.* IV.67; XII.4; XVII.4; *Disp. priv.* XX.4–5; *Art. non.* II.3–5, in *Opera*, p. 949; *Works* 2: 707; *Dec. sent.*, pp. 90–94, 110; *Works* 1: 634–638, 656; and from his final conference in The Hague (August 1609), reported by Hommius, in P. J. Wijminga, *Festus Hommius* (Leiden: D. Donner, 1899), Bijlage G, pp. xii, xiv. On *duplex Dei amor*, see Stanglin, *Arminius on Assurance*, pp. 89–91, 219–231. Cf. Den Boer, *God's Twofold Love*, pp. 154–166. On the relation of this concept to assurance of salvation, see chapter 4 of this volume.

149. Recall our discussion of divine simplicity, particularly the "formal distinction," in chapter 2.

aspect of his love is the love of righteousness or love of justice. This is God's love for righteousness itself—which is, given Arminius's doctrine of divine simplicity, exactly the same thing as God's love for himself. It is this love (which is essential to God) that gives rise to his hatred of sin (which is, properly understood, a contingent expression of God's holy love).[150] This love finds expression toward sinful humanity in this way: it is not God's will and pleasure to bestow eternal life on any except those who are rightly related to God. The second aspect of the *duplex amor* (twofold love) is this: God's love for the creature. This is expressed in the divine will to give eternal life to all who respond rightly to God's gracious initiative.

Remembering Arminius's doctrine of divine simplicity, one should note that these are not two separate loves, nor are they in any way contradictory to or even in tension with one another (recall the formal distinction). The love for the creature—which, in the current discussion, is focused upon God's love for the sinful human creature—is an expression of the love for righteousness. It is not one that is necessary or, strictly speaking, essential to God (God need not have created at all). There is "in every direction abundant scope for the emanations" of it,[151] but any expressions of it will always be in complete accord with the love of righteousness. The consequence is that "God condemns no one, except on account of sin."[152] To reprobate or condemn apart from sin would undermine God's love of righteousness and the creature. To ignore sin would also be inconsistent with the love of righteousness, and to love the creature more than the love of justice (himself) would be impossible.

Arminius insists that supralapsarianism skews a proper understanding of the *duplex amor*. It does so in two ways: first, by holding that God wills (absolutely) to save certain humans without any consideration of their response to him and his grace, without any regard to their (God-enabled) faith and holiness. This would mean that the love of God toward sinners—at least those sinners who are elect—supersedes his love for righteousness. On the other hand, according to supralapsarianism, God wills absolutely to condemn certain persons without any regard to their disobedience and rebellion. This would entail nothing less than the conclusion that God hates creatures "without any need or cause derived from his love

---

150. *Dec. sent.*, p. 90; *Works* 1: 634.

151. *Dec. sent.*, p. 90; *Works* 1: 634–635.

152. *Dec. sent.*, p. 90; *Works* 1: 635.

of righteousness and his hatred against sin" (for, according to supralapsarianism, the decree to reprobate precedes the decree of the fall).[153] This would imply that God has contradictory wills and that God's "loves" are not consistent with one another. It would mean the loss of an adequate doctrine of divine simplicity, and it would mean as well that the foundational Christian understanding of the love of God is compromised.

Arminius thinks that the problems intensify when it comes to the work of Christ. A proper understanding of Christ's work must also be built upon the foundational *duplex amor*. And, he argues, the supralapsarian position will not allow for such an understanding. Any adequate understanding of Christ's work and this twofold love is said by Arminius to include the following elements. First, after the fall, the love of righteousness is declared in Christ alone, for "it was his will that sin should not be expiated in any other way than by the blood and death of his Son."[154] Second, this love of righteousness is manifested each day in the proclamation of the gospel, in which God "declares it to be his will to grant a communion of Christ and his benefits" only to those who are converted and believe in Christ. God's love for creatures, now understood as miserable sinners, is the love "by which he gave Christ his Son for them, and constituted him as a Savior" to all who respond positively to divine grace.[155] The love of sinners is, when appropriately related to the love of righteousness, the love that calls forth obedience and holiness.

When considering his account of the *duplex amor* and the work of Christ for sinners in relation to supralapsarianism, Arminius revisits and sharpens the criticisms. He complains that, because the supralapsarian position has God decreeing unconditional election and salvation *prior* to the work of Christ to satisfy the love of righteousness, it again threatens to subordinate God's love of justice to his love of sinners. Moreover, by teaching that "it is the will of God absolutely to condemn certain sinners without any consideration of their impenitence (*onboetveerdicheyt*), when

---

153. *Dec. sent.*, p. 91; *Works* 1: 635.

154. *Dec. sent.*, pp. 91–92; *Works* 1: 636.

155. *Dec. sent.*, p. 92; *Works* 1: 636: "Ende ten tweeden, die hy daghelijcx betoont inde vercondinghe des Evangelij, daer hy verclaert niemant te willen gunnen de gemeenschap Christi ende zijner weldaden, ten zy dat hy sich van sonde bekeere ende in Christum geloove. De liefde tot de elendige sondaers, daerop de Christelijcke religie rustet, is voor eerst de liefde deur welcke hy Christum zijnen Sone voor hen ghegheven ende tot eenen Salichmaecker ghestelt heeft den ghenen die hem ghehoorsamen."

at the same time a most plenary and complete sacrifice had been rendered, in Christ Jesus, to God's love of righteousness and to his hatred of sin," supralapsarianism holds that the ultimate and only thing standing between miserable sinners and their salvation is the inscrutable divine will. And this, argues Arminius, is nothing short of a denial of the love of God for miserable sinners.[156]

After an extended refutation of Gomarus's version of predestination, Arminius (at the height of polemic) concludes that supralapsarianism is inspired by Satan and is a doctrine quite compatible with the kingdom of darkness. At the same time, though, Arminius does not impugn the sincere motives of supralapsarians, affirming his belief that God in his goodness pardons those who teach false doctrine out of ignorance.[157]

## C. Other Reformed Options

Most of Arminius's attention (especially in the *Declaration of Sentiments*) on predestination is occupied with the first, supralapsarian, position, in part due to the fact that his debate partners at Leiden were supralapsarians. But he also deals with two other positions (second and third), albeit briefly. As Arminius sees things, these views hold in common the conviction that God determined within himself to create a portion of the human race to share in his glory and grace, while "passing by" the majority of humans, and then punishing these latter persons with death and damnation. Predestination, then, is understood to be the means by which God knows which (and how many) persons are to be saved. God first elects sinners to salvation, and then decrees the means to that end (the work of Christ on their behalf, and the work of the Holy Spirit to regenerate, sanctify, and preserve). As for the reprobate, their condemnation is "before all things and causes which are in the things themselves or arise out of them, that is, without notice of any sin."[158] The major difference between these two views and the supralapsarianism with which Arminius engages at length is this: such views do not set out "the creation or the fall as a mediate cause preordained by God for the execution of the preceding decree of

---

156. *Dec. sent.*, p. 92; *Works* 1: 637.

157. *Exam. Gom.*, p. 158; *Works* 3: 658.

158. *Dec. sent.*, pp. 98–99; *Works* 1: 646. For a brief analysis of these two predestinarian options, see Dekker, *Rijker dan Midas*, pp. 224–225.

predestination."[159] In other words, particularly with the third view, the decree to elect is subsequent to the fall. For this reason, it was later called *infralapsarianism* (from *infra lapsum*, below or after the fall) (see Appendix p. 140 for the infralapsarian order). The primary difference between supra- and infralapsarianism is whether the decree of election is considered before or after the fall, respectively. Another way of expressing this distinction is the identification of the "lump/mass of clay" from which God saves (see Rom. 9:21). Is it a *fallible* or an already *fallen* mass that God considers as objects of predestination? The motivation for infralapsarianism, claiming that God reprobates out of an already fallen mass (in contradistinction to supralapsarianism), is the concern to avoid the implication that God is the author of sin.

Despite their efforts, however, Arminius sees this very implication as the Achilles' heel of these versions. Any view that holds to the necessity of the fall, sin, and condemnation, in order that God might be able to work some other plan for some other people, makes both the fall and sin a means to the end of God's glory. Even worse, Arminius reasons, if it is God who decrees that it will be impossible to avoid sin and damnation, then two unwelcome results follow: sinners are not morally responsible for their sinful actions, and God is responsible for such sin. Any denial of the moral responsibility of sinners is seen by Arminius as impossible to square with Scripture, and any affirmation of the notion that God is the author of sin is understood by him (and most other Reformed theologians) to be anathema. He is convinced that these are the entailments of the infralapsarian views (despite the protestations of infralapsarian theologians to the contrary). Thus Arminius concludes that not only do these alternative systems fail to avoid the conclusion that God is the author of sin, but they also fall into "a patent and absurd self-contradiction" in their insistent denials.[160] Appeals to divine "permission" are seen here to be mere subterfuge by Arminius, for while he is not at all opposed to the concept of divine permission, he is exercised to combat the notion that "permission" can meaningfully be reduced to something like "God makes

---

159. *Dec. sent.*, p. 100; *Works* 1: 647. One version holds that the decree unconditionally to save and to damn certain individuals precedes the fall but still uses the language of "passing over" or "passing by." The other version holds that the decree to save and damn comes after the decrees of creation and fall, and is thus infralapsarian.

160. *Dec. sent.*, p. 102; *Works* 1: 648.

sin inevitable and then 'allows' or 'permits' creatures to do what is impossible for them to refrain from doing." In other words, Arminius sees this particular use of the language of "permission" as an attempt to obscure the real issue, and he dismisses it as misleading and unhelpful.[161] Finally, as he did with supralapsarianism, Arminius criticizes these versions of unconditional election which hold that sin is necessary for the display of the glory of God (which itself is considered necessary).[162]

In summary, we can see that Arminius mounts objections to unconditional predestination from a range of perspectives. Most of his energy is directed against supralapsarianism, and he begins by arguing from the tradition: no major creeds or councils ever commend it or anything like it, no major patristic theologians (at least before Augustine) endorse it (or any of its cousins), no important confession of the Reformed Churches demands it, and many major Protestant theologians actively reject it. Arminius then turns to "systematic" theological argumentation, and here he makes the case that it is repugnant to the doctrine of God (divine wisdom, justice, goodness, and love); that it is at odds with any acceptable theological anthropology; that it is opposed to adequate doctrines of creation and fall, sin, and grace; that it undermines the centrality of Christ's redeeming work; and that it inverts the order of the gospel. All in all, he says, it succeeds only in besmirching the glory of God and in robbing Christians of the joy of assurance. When he turns his attention to other schemes, he argues that while they are aware of the problems associated with making God the author of sin, they do not finally succeed in avoiding the implication. Even worse, they threaten to imply that God's glory is somehow dependent upon creation and sin. These "milder" versions of predestination cannot escape

---

161. *Dec. sent.*, pp. 102–103; *Works* 1: 651–652.

162. *Dec. sent.*, p. 103; *Works* 1: 652: "t'welc niet en can gheschieden, ten zy dat sonde, ende deur de sonde elende, ofte ten minsten verdienste van elende inde werelt come, ende also wort de sonde oock nootsaeckelick inghevoert, uyt de nootsaeckelijckheyt vande verclaeringhe, dusdaniger eerlijckheyt Godes. Wanneer nu de val Adams wort gestalt nootsaeckelijck ende oversulcx een middel om uyt te voeren een voorich decreet van Predestinatie, zoo wordt te ghelijcke de scheppinghe selfs ghestelt als een middel, dienstich tot uytvoeringhe van het selfde decreet, want de val en can de scheppinghe niet volghen nootsaeckelick, dan deur een decreet van Predestinatie, welcke niet tusschen de scheppinghe ende den val can werden ghestelt, maer dat beyde te ghelijcke voorgaet, ordonnerende de scheppinghe tot den val, ende beyde te ghelijcke tot uytvoeringe van een decreet, om rechtveerdicheyt int straffen der sonde, ende barmherticheyt, int vergheven der selve te betoonen; andersins soude het geene nae de scheppinghe nootsaeckelijc moest volghen, van God inde scheppinghe niet voorghenomen zijn, twelck onmoghelijck is."

the problems entailed in the assertion that God creates people who will
have no opportunity whatsoever for fellowship with him.

## D. Arminius on Romans 9

Even before the Reformation, Romans 9 became the *locus classicus* for the
doctrine of individual, unconditional predestination. Arminius admits
that, for some time, Romans 9 "always seemed to me enveloped in the
densest shade, and most difficult of explanation."[163] After much study,
however, he finds a clearer understanding of it. The scope of Romans 9,
he says, is the same as that of the epistle as a whole. This is the message
that "the gospel, not the law, is the power of God to salvation, not to the
one who works, but to the one who believes; because in the gospel is made
manifest the righteousness (*iustitia*) of God, by which salvation is obtained
through faith apprehended in Christ."[164] Arminius argues that the ninth
chapter defends this basic message against the objections of the Jews,
"who were endeavoring with all their might to overthrow it."[165] As Arminius sees it, here is the problem being addressed by Paul: "The Jews" are
claiming that God's word has failed if Paul is correct. For "if righteousness
and salvation consist in faith in Christ whom Paul preaches," and,
"because most of the Jews do not believe in Christ," then "it follows that a
great part of the Jews have been rejected from the covenant."[166] But, of
course, Paul denies that God's word has failed (Rom. 9:6). The difference
between Arminius and Theodore Beza (whom Arminius takes as his interlocutor here) is clear to Arminius. Beza's view entails this answer to the
problem: "God, indeed, by the word of promise invites all Jews, and calls
them to communion in the covenant; but yet by his eternal decree and
purpose he has determined to make only some from among the Jews actually partakers of it, the rest being passed by (*praeteritis*) and left in their
former state."[167] His own interpretation, on the other hand, answers the
question by denying that the word of God has failed because "God, by
his very word and expression of promise, signified that he would reckon

---

163. *Cap. IX Rom.*, in *Opera*, p. 778; *Works* 3: 485.

164. *Cap. IX Rom.*, in *Opera*, p. 778; *Works* 3: 485–486.

165. *Cap. IX Rom.*, in *Opera*, p. 778; *Works* 3: 486.

166. *Cap. IX Rom.*, in *Opera*, p. 779; *Works* 3: 486–487.

167. *Cap. IX Rom.*, in *Opera*, p. 780; *Works* 3: 488.

(*censere*) as his sons those only of the Jews who would pursue righteous-ness and salvation from faith; but that he would hold as foreign those who would pursue the same from the law" (see Rom. 9:30–32).[168]

The crucial issue, then, is the attempt to earn salvation through the works of the law rather than acceptance of salvation by faith in Christ. Arminius is convinced that the answer to this problem is clear indeed, and he takes it as important in the interpretation of this passage. Salvation is through faith in Christ rather than by attempts to earn it through keeping the law, and Armin-ius understands Esau and Jacob in a correspondingly typological way. Nei-ther should be considered "in themselves, but as types."[169] More specifically, Esau (and Ishmael, too) is a "type" of the "children of the flesh"; Esau typifies those who seek to earn salvation through the law. Jacob, on the other hand, typifies the "children of promise" who respond in faith to God's provision of salvation in Christ.[170] This typology thus signifies "first, that the purpose (*propositum*) of God is according to election; then, that that purpose depends on him who calls, and not on works. . . . [This] is a sign that that purpose does not depend on works, but on him who calls; that is, that God loves those who seek righteousness and salvation by faith in Christ; but hates those who seek for the same from the works of the law."[171]

In consideration of the statement "no one resists his will" (see Rom. 9:19), Arminius denies that there could be any contradictory wills within God.[172] His reason for this position is very deeply rooted: the doctrine of divine simplicity removes any such possibility. He takes Paul's denial of injustice within God in this way: when Paul exclaims "May it never be (*Absit*)!" (Rom. 9:14), he intends that "it ought by no means to enter into our thought that there is any injustice in God, who, in himself just (*in se iustus*), indeed, existing as justice itself, does nothing, and, indeed, can do nothing except what is most thoroughly in agreement with that nature of his."[173] God "has mercy on whom he will have mercy" (Rom. 9:15), and "the charge of injustice is removed from God merely by the word 'mercy' here employed; which, since it presupposes misery, and therefore sin," means that

---

168. *Cap. IX Rom.*, in *Opera*, p. 780; *Works* 3: 488.

169. *Cap. IX Rom.*, in *Opera*, p. 781; *Works* 3: 490.

170. *Cap. IX Rom.*, in *Opera*, pp. 780–785; *Works* 3: 489–495.

171. *Cap. IX Rom.*, in *Opera*, p. 784; *Works* 3: 495.

172. *Cap. IX Rom.*, in *Opera*, pp. 791–792; *Works* 3: 505–506.

173. *Cap. IX Rom.*, in *Opera*, p. 787; *Works* 3: 499.

the injustice and blame fall upon humanity.[174] In other words, God's will to save penitent believers and condemn impenitent unbelievers will not change and cannot be resisted.[175] Arminius thus concludes that while Beza's position indeed does remain open to the charge of divine injustice, on his own interpretation of the text "it follows that God can in no way be convicted of injustice."[176] Jacob and Esau are to be understood typologically, and, on a proper understanding of the passage, it should be clear that God's word has not failed and that God is not unjust. On the contrary, the God of justice, wisdom, and goodness has elected to provide salvation to all who receive salvation by accepting Christ and his benefits in faith.

## E. Conclusion: Arminius's Own Views on Predestination

Arminius's major treatises that deal with predestination give much more attention to what he opposes than to what he proposes. Nevertheless, much of what Arminius thought about predestination should be clear from the previous discussion of his criticisms. He insisted that God is omniscient and sovereign, and the unmitigated goodness of the simple divine nature is absolutely foundational. But he was also deeply convinced of the reality of human sin and depravity. Thus he was convinced that divine grace is both necessary and available.

A concluding summary of his position shows that he holds a view that could fairly be called "conditional predestination." He lists the order of decrees as follows (see Appendix p. 140 for Arminius's order in comparison with that of supralapsarianism and infralapsarianism).[177] First, already assuming the creation of humanity and the permission of sin, God absolutely

---

174. *Cap. IX Rom.*, in *Opera*, p. 787; *Works* 3: 500.

175. This is an example of how God's antecedent will can be resisted, but his consequent will cannot. In addition, this is an early appearance of the corporate predestination theme that will remain important in Arminius's later formulations of the doctrine. Cf. Dekker, *Rijker dan Midas*, p. 185.

176. *Cap. IX Rom.*, in *Opera*, p. 788; *Works* 3: 501.

177. For other secondary accounts of Arminius's own views on predestination, see Bangs, *Arminius*, pp. 350–355; Stanglin, *Arminius on Assurance*, pp. 83–93, 229–230; Dekker, *Rijker dan Midas*, pp. 178–231; Richard A. Muller, "Grace, Election, and Contingent Choice: Arminius' Gambit and the Reformed Response," in *The Grace of God and the Bondage of the Will*, ed. Thomas Schreiner and Bruce Ware, 2 vols. (Grand Rapids, MI: Baker, 1995), 2: 254–259; Witt, "Creation, Redemption and Grace," pp. 684–724; Clarke, *Ground of Election*, pp. 148–164. Arthur Skevington Wood, "The Declaration of Sentiments: The Theological Testament of Arminius," *Evangelical Quarterly* 65 (April 1993): 111–129.

decrees that Jesus Christ will be the Mediator, Redeemer, Savior, Priest, and King for the salvation of sinful humanity. By his death and victorious resurrection, Christ might destroy sin, and by his obedience, he might obtain salvation and offer it to humanity. This will of God for the salvation of all people corresponds to God's antecedent will, expressed in 1 Tim. 2:4. The second absolute decree is to receive in gracious favor all who repent and believe, trusting in Christ for their salvation, and thus to bring them home in persevering faith to the end, "but to leave in sin and under wrath all impenitent persons and unbelievers, and to condemn them as aliens from Christ."[178] With this decree, Arminius has in mind a class of people— either penitent believers or impenitent unbelievers—not individuals. This second decree is what Dekker calls "properties-predestination" (*eigenschappen predestinatie*).[179] It is a decree of corporate salvation and condemnation with reference to the properties of belief and unbelief in general. These first two decrees are absolute and, in themselves, are not dependent or contingent on anything external to them. The third decree is God's decision to grant, in accordance with his wisdom and justice, the means of grace that are necessary for repentance and faith.

The fourth decree is that by which God "decreed to save and condemn certain specific persons," and here is where we see the sharpest point of departure from his Reformed colleagues (including the infralapsarians). The foundation for this decree is "in the foreknowledge of God, by which he knew from eternity which persons . . . through his prevenient grace would (*souden*) believe and through subsequent grace would persevere, and also who would not believe and persevere."[180] This decree is based on God's consequent will to save those individuals, known by way of divine middle knowledge, who would actually accept his grace.[181] Interestingly, in these four positive decrees, Arminius never uses the words *predestine*, *elect*, or *reprobate*. Since he seems more willing to use these words when

---

178. *Dec. sent.*, p. 104; *Works* 1: 653.

179. Dekker, *Rijker dan Midas*, pp. 183–185, 227.

180. *Dec. sent.*, p. 106; *Works* 1: 653–654.

181. Bangs, *Arminius*, p. 354, calls this fourth decree "speculative," and, in its specification of certain individuals, thinks that "Arminius threw over his whole case." Bangs, however, does not address the solution provided by middle knowledge. Moreover, if the fourth decree is speculative (and not practical), then the whole *ordo decretorum*, to which Arminius here contributes, is perhaps equally speculative. Such a strategy, though, was helpful in articulating his alternative vision.

describing the other options, this language perhaps reflects his tendency to collapse Reformed theology's hard and fast distinction between the decree (to elect or reprobate based on God's will) and its execution in time (to save because of Christ or condemn because of sin).[182]

Here we see, in brief and clear form, Arminius's doctrine of conditional election: persons are elected on the condition of being in Christ by grace through faith, "according to the foreknowledge of God" (Rom. 8:29; 1 Pet. 1:2). "Faith is a 'condition' of election for the same reason that faith is a condition of justification."[183] Those who believe in Christ are predestined to salvation; their faith is, in a logical sense, prior to predestination.[184] Conversely, God's love of righteousness and hatred of sin and unbelief, which govern his will to condemn impenitent unbelievers, are the impulsive cause of reprobation.[185] As Arminius sees things, however, for unconditional election there is no condition whatsoever on the human side to effect being chosen by God. Faith is a means of election, not a cause. One way of putting this fundamental difference between Arminius's account and that of his opponents is to ask the question: "Do we believe because we are elect (Reformed opponents), or are we elect because we believe (Arminian)?"[186]

Arminius's doctrine of predestination is named "Arminian" only in the sense that he taught it—not in the sense that it originated with him. Arminius's affirmation of conditional election is in line with the great majority of the early Christian tradition, in which many theologians have affirmed that divine predestination is based on what God foreknows about a person.[187] For example, Irenaeus writes, "Therefore God foreknowing

---

182. On the occasional ambiguity of this language, though, cf. Stanglin, "Arminius *avant la lettre*," 66–68.

183. Witt, "Creation, Redemption and Grace," p. 707.

184. *Exam. Gom.*, p. 137; *Works* 3: 640.

185. *Exam. Gom.*, pp. 105–106; *Works* 3: 614.

186. *Dec. sent.*, p. 95; *Opera*, p. 115; *Works* 1: 642–643.

187. There are, of course, important differences as well. Where both Arminius and many theological predecessors agree on the conditionality of predestination (based on foreknowledge), Arminius makes it clear (in ways that some of these predecessors do not) that it is foreknowledge of faith rather than works or merits. See the discussion in Thomas H. McCall and Keith D. Stanglin, "S. M. Baugh and the Meaning of Foreknowledge: Another Look," *Trinity Journal* n. s. 26 (2005): 24 n. 26, and James Jorgenson, "Predestination According to Divine Foreknowledge in Patristic Tradition," in *Salvation in Christ: A Lutheran-Orthodox Dialogue*, eds. John Meyendorff and Robert Tobias (Minneapolis: Fortress Press, 1992), pp. 159–169; on the issue of "faith and works" in salvation in patristic theology, see Thomas C. Oden, *The Justification Reader* (Grand Rapids, MI: Eerdmans, 2002).

(*praesciens*) all things, prepared apt habitations for both [groups of people]: to those who seek after the light of incorruptibility, and return to it, he is kindly giving this light which they desire."[188] Origen, in his comments on predestination from Rom. 8:29, insists that "what is future depends on the choice of the doer."[189] Similarly, John Chrysostom maintains that God's predestination of Jacob and Esau "is of foreknowledge."[190] This thread of corporate election and conditional individual predestination also runs through the subsequent history of the Western Church and was debated and formulated more precisely in the late medieval period—all of which paved the way for the debates of the sixteenth and seventeenth centuries.[191]

Arminius argues that this doctrine of predestination enjoys several benefits that are not available to the doctrines of his Reformed opponents. Indeed, his arguments in favor of his view correspond exactly to the twenty reasons he gave in opposition to supralapsarianism. Contrary to supralapsarianism, this predestination "is the foundation (*fundament*) of Christianity, of salvation, and of the certainty of salvation."[192] He maintains that this doctrine is consistent with the teachings of the creeds and councils, that it has been the majority view among orthodox Christians of various confessions, that it "agrees with the Harmony of all Confessions which has been published by the Protestant churches," and it "likewise agrees with the Dutch Confession and Catechism."[193] It is consistent with gospel ministry, as well as with robust spiritual formation and the pursuit of holiness that is possible for those who enjoy Christian assurance. It is consistent with a proper understanding of the (middle) knowledge, wisdom, justice, and goodness of God. It agrees with

---

188. Irenaeus, *Adversus haereses* IV.xxxix.4, in *PG* 7: 1111B.

189. Origen, *In Epistolam ad Romanos* VII.vii, in *PG* 14: 1123C.

190. John Chrysostom, *In Epistolam ad Romanos homiliae* XVI.vi, in *PG* 60: 557.

191. E.g., see Heiko A. Oberman, *The Harvest of Medieval Theology: Gabriel Biel and Late Medieval Nominalism* (1963; reprint, Grand Rapids, MI: Baker, 2000), pp. 185–248; James Halverson, "Franciscan Theology and Predestinarian Pluralism in Late-Medieval Thought," *Speculum* 70/1 (1995): 1–26.

192. *Dec. sent.*, p. 106; *Works* 1: 654. Arminius emphasized this point about predestination in several passages. *Disp. priv.* XL.9; *Ep. ecc.* 88, p. 160; *Epistola*, in *Opera*, p. 943; *Works* 2: 698; *Art. non.* XV.6, in *Opera*, p. 957; *Works* 2: 719; *Apologia*, art. 4, in *Opera*, p. 139; *Works* 1: 748; *Exam. Gom.*, pp. 34–35, 149; *Works* 3: 554, 650. For a discussion of this *fundamentum* language, see Stanglin, *Arminius on Assurance*, pp. 89–93, 227–235.

193. *Dec. sent.*, p. 107; *Works* 1: 654: "5. Comt overeen met de tsamenstemminghe aller confessien byde protesterende Kercken gemaeckt. 6. Comt zeer wel over een met de Nederlantsche Confessie ende Catechismo."

defensible doctrines of creation and the fall, and with biblical accounts of sin and grace. It sees creation and preservation as a work of divine love, and thus a "perfect and appropriate work of God."[194] Arminius's view understands that sin "really is disobedience"—there is no secret obedience to a hidden will of God alongside disobedience to a known commandment from God—and thus "the meritorious cause of condemnation."[195] It "harmonizes with the nature of grace" by "reconciling it most completely to the righteousness of God and to the nature and liberty of the human will."[196] Indeed, the goal of predestination is the praise of God's grace.[197] Arminius's view "conduces most conspicuously to the glory of God—his justice and his mercy. It also represents God as the cause of all good and of our salvation, and humanity as the cause of sin and his own damnation." It promotes a biblical doctrine of salvation by driving away the twin dangers of security and despair.[198] Elsewhere, Arminius mentions the great use of this doctrine of predestination: "It serves to establish the glory of God's grace, to comfort afflicted consciences, and to upset the impious and drive away their security."[199] His doctrine of predestination is motivated by a plethora of such practical outcomes.

Perhaps most important, Arminius is convinced that his view of predestination rightly exalts Jesus Christ. Arminius refers to Christ as the foundation of election, not merely a means for election.[200] This point is based on the fact that, in the *ordo decretorum*, everything subsequent to the decree to predestine constitutes the means of election and reprobation. Thus, the means of predestination are described in Supralapsarian decrees 2 through 5, Infralapsarian decrees 4 and 5, and Arminian decrees 5 and 6 (as enumerated in the Appendix p. 140). For supra- and infralapsarianism, Christ is part of the means of election, and is the foundation of salvation (in time), not (eternal) election.[201] For Arminius, though, Christ is the foundation of

---

194. *Dec. sent.*, pp. 108–109; *Works* 3: 654–655.

195. *Dec. sent.*, p. 109; *Works* 3: 655.

196. *Dec. sent.*, p. 109; *Works* 3: 655.

197. *Disp. pub.* XV.9.

198. *Dec. sent.*, pp. 109–110; *Works* 1: 655.

199. *Disp. pub.* XV.14.

200. *Disp. pub.* XV.5; *Dec. sent.*, p. 109; *Works* 1: 655.

201. This view is made explicit against the Arminians in the *Canons of the Synod of Dort*, I. art. vii, in Philip Schaff, ed., *The Creeds of Christendom, with a History and Critical Notes*, 3 vols., 6th ed. (1931; reprint, Grand Rapids, MI: Baker, 1998), 3: 553. Cf. Du Moulin, *Anatome Arminianismi*, XXV, pp. 177–185 (ET, pp. 199–209).

election and salvation. "We place Christ as the foundation of this predestination. . . . For the love with which God loves people absolutely for salvation, and according to which he absolutely intends to give them eternal life, does not exist except in Jesus Christ his dear Son."[202] Unlike the other Reformed options, for Arminius, Christ's work of redemption comes logically prior to the decree of election. Being in Christ, therefore, is the conditional basis for election and salvation. In fact, if God can will election and salvation without respect to Christ, then Christ's work is unnecessary.[203]

In sum, Arminius's view is the "ground (*grondvest*) of the Christian religion, because in it the twofold love of God for righteousness and humanity may be joined together and conveniently attached to each other."[204]

The extent of sin, the operation of grace, and the means of salvation will be discussed in the next chapter. For now, it is worth reiterating the consistently *theological*—rather than "anthropocentric"—orientation of Arminius's account of providence and predestination. Rather than elevate "free will," which he only mentions to retain human responsibility for sin and to preserve grace as a genuine gift, he stresses God's concurrence in all things, elevates God's character and love, and emphatically insists upon the necessity and primacy of divine grace. Even the prelapsarian humans, though endowed with "such a portion of knowledge, holiness, and power, as enabled them to understand, esteem, consider, will, and to fulfill the true good," could not actually do good "except through the assistance of God's grace."[205] As a sinner, a man, "of and from himself, cannot think, will, or do the good that is truly good; but it is necessary that he be reborn and renewed by God in Christ through his Holy Spirit in intellect, affection or will, and in all his powers (*crachten*), that he may rightly understand, think, will, and fulfill the true good."[206] And even then, Arminius insists, this is only possible by the "continued aids of divine grace."[207]

---

202. *Disp. priv.* XL.4.

203. *Exam. Perk.*, in *Opera*, pp. 653, 657–658; *Works* 3: 296, 303–304; *Dec. sent.*, pp. 85–86; *Works* 1: 630–631.

204. *Dec. sent.*, p. 110; *Works* 1: 656.

205. *Dec. sent.*, p. 112; *Works* 1: 659: "ghevoele ick dat de mensche inden eersten stant zijner scheppinghe, is gheweest begaeft met sodanighe kennisse, heylicheyt ende cracht dat hy het waere goet heeft connen verstaen, bedencken, willen ende volbrenghen, sulcx als hem bevolen was, weverstaende, met bystant der ghenade Godes."

206. *Dec. sent.*, pp. 112–113; *Works* 1: 659–660.

207. *Dec. sent.*, p. 113; *Works* 1: 660.

# Appendix: Order of God's Decrees
## (Ordo decretorum Dei)

Supralapsarian *ordo decretorum*: God decrees to

1. Predestine; that is, elect some individuals (though not yet considered as created or fallen) to eternal life with God and reprobate others;
2. Create (in some versions, this decree comes before predestination);
3. Ordain or permit the fall, with ensuing guilt, corruption, and total inability;
4. Appoint Christ as foundation of salvation to redeem the elect;
5. Provide the means of salvation: Holy Spirit to save, regenerate, and preserve the redeemed.

Infralapsarian *ordo decretorum*: God decrees to

1. Create;
2. Permit the fall, with ensuing guilt, corruption, and total inability;
3. Predestine; that is, elect some created and fallen individuals to eternal life with God, and reprobate, or pass by, the rest of the sinners;
4. Appoint Christ as foundation of salvation to redeem the elect;
5. Provide the means of salvation: Holy Spirit to save, regenerate, and preserve the redeemed.

Arminian *ordo decretorum*: God decrees to

1. Create;
2. Permit the fall;
3. Appoint Christ as foundation of election to redeem;
4. Save, in Christ, (the class of) penitent believers, and condemn unbelievers;
5. Provide means [grace] for repentance and faith;
6. Save or condemn single, specific individuals foreknown to believe or not believe.[208]

---

208. Arminian decrees 3 through 6 above correspond to the four decrees in *Dec. sent*. The first two above are assumed in Arminius's discussion. When he enumerates the decrees in *Dec. sent*., Arminius never uses the words *predestine, elect,* or *reprobate* in his order of decrees.

# 4

## Sin and Salvation

*Unto what end has God restored the fallen to the state of integrity, reconciled sinners to himself, accepted enemies into grace? . . . So that we might be sharers in eternal salvation and utter praises to him forever.*

—JACOB ARMINIUS, 1603

THE DOCTRINE OF salvation was the central theological concern of the European Reformation. The condition of fallen humanity and what must be done to redeem human nature, the reconciliation of divine grace and human freedom, the ground of justification, the role of good works and merit, and the assurance of one's salvation—all of these soteriological issues were hotly debated in the early modern Western Church. Moreover, one cannot isolate these soteriological questions from other doctrinal *loci* that affect and are affected by them. A thorough account of salvation assumes a certain doctrine of God and humanity. A fundamental shift in one doctrine will have repercussions throughout the system. Like his Protestant contemporaries, Arminius gave soteriology a central place in his teaching, but not without reference to his own views of God and humanity. Arminius's doctrine of salvation was, in many ways, consistent with typical Protestant Reformed theology. For instance, his teaching on divine grace was foundational to his theology. But his distinctive views on God, creation, and predestination, which we have already surveyed, had, as Arminius acknowledged, "much in common" with soteriological topics and affected his understanding of the nature of grace, the role of faith and assurance in salvation, and the life of sanctification.[1]

---

1. Cf. *Dec. sent.*, p. 111; *Works* 1: 657.

## *I. Sin*

Before exploring Arminius's doctrine of salvation, it is necessary to describe the fallen condition from which humanity needs to be saved. What was human nature like before the fall, and how did sin change this condition?

## A. The First Sin

It is important to distinguish between, on the one hand, the first sin committed by the primordial couple and, on the other hand, the lasting effects of that sin on the couple and their posterity, known especially in the Western Church as "original sin."

Arminius analyzes the nature and causes of the first sin most clearly in one private and two public disputations.[2] He describes the first sin of humanity's first parents as disobedience and offense against the "legal covenant" that God had made with humanity, resulting in a fall from the original "state of integrity."[3] This so-called legal covenant (*legale foedus*) or covenant of works (*foedus operum*) became typical in Reformed covenant, or federal, theology as a description of the prelapsarian economy of either attaining salvation by means of perfect fulfillment of God's law or meriting condemnation by disobedience. This covenant of works is opposed to the evangelical covenant of grace (*foedus gratiae*), the first announcement of which (*protoevangelium*) immediately follows the first sin (Gen. 3:15).[4]

---

2. *Disp. pub.* VII and XXXI; *Disp. priv.* XXX. Cf. the discussions of the first sin in John Mark Hicks, "The Theology of Grace in the Thought of Jacobus Arminius and Philip van Limborch: A Study in the Development of Seventeenth-Century Dutch Arminianism" (Ph.D. diss., Westminster Theological Seminary, 1985), pp. 29–32; Mark A. Ellis, *Simon Episcopius' Doctrine of Original Sin*, American University Studies, Series 7: Theology and Religion, vol. 240 (New York: Peter Lang, 2006), pp. 69–72.

3. *Disp. pub.* VII.2; XXXI.1, 3. Arminius discusses this covenant in *Disp. priv.* XXIX.

4. Arminius participated in and contributed to the development of covenant theology. On the covenant theology of Arminius and Arminianism, see Raymond A. Blacketer, "Arminius' Concept of Covenant in Its Historical Context," *Nederlands archief voor kerkgeschiedenis* 80 (2000): 193–220; and Richard A. Muller, "The Federal Motif in Seventeenth Century Arminian Theology," *Nederlands archief voor kerkgeschiedenis* 62 (1982): 102–122. The literature on the nature and development of Reformed covenant theology is vast. See the works and bibliographies of Peter A. Lillback, *The Binding of God: Calvin's Role in the Development of Covenant Theology*, Texts and Studies in Reformation and Post-Reformation Theology (Grand Rapids, MI: Baker Academic, 2001); and Willem J. van Asselt, *The Federal Theology of Johannes Cocceius (1603–1669)* (Leiden: Brill, 2001). For a popular-level treatment of Reformed covenant theology, see Michael S. Horton, *God of Promise: Introducing Covenant Theology* (Grand Rapids, MI: Baker Books, 2006).

There were many factors that brought about this first breach of the legal covenant. Chiefly, it was caused by the free will and desire of humanity through the persuasion of Satan in the form of the serpent.[5] By virtue of being created in the image of God and endued with righteousness and holiness, humanity "had both the obligation and the ability to resist (*resistere debuit . . . potuit*)" the actual causes of sin.[6] At least in the prelapsarian state, "ought" implies "can." Arminius is making the point that God is in no way the cause of this sin, either as "efficient" or "deficient" cause. That is, he neither caused this sin directly, nor through indirect means; neither did he withdraw anything necessary for humanity to avoid this sin.[7] Rather, God permitted sin by not impeding the freedom of the human will to transgress.[8] He therefore has no culpability in it. Arminius's primary critique of the Reformed theology typical of his day is that it implies that God is the author of sin. In that context, his disputation uses strong language to distance God from any causal role in the fall of humanity. To suggest otherwise, he writes, would be the "highest blasphemy" (*summa blasphemia*).[9]

God may test people, but not for the purpose of working evil through them.[10] God's only role in their sinful actions (in addition to sustaining them and "concurring" by granting ability to them) was that of permitting humanity to exercise free will and power.[11] The question of why God permitted this sin is complex and puzzling, one that has burdened Christian thought in general and Arminius in particular. Arminius hesitates to speculate on this matter, but is content to reply, following Tertullian and Augustine, that God's gift of freedom was intended for the enjoyment of the creature, and the omnipotent Creator must be able to bring some good from the permitted evil.[12] Yet this sin has no proper end or goal directed toward the good.[13]

---

5. *Disp. pub.* VII.3.

6. *Disp. pub.* VII.7. Arminius says the same thing in *Apologia*, art. 23, in *Opera*, p. 168; *Works* 2: 37.

7. *Disp. pub.* VII.8; XXXI.5; *Disp. priv.* XXX.5.

8. *Disp. pub.* VII.9. Cf. Bangs, *Arminius*, p. 220.

9. *Disp. pub.* XXXI.5. He elsewhere calls it the "most grave" of all blasphemies. See *Exam. Gom.*, p. 154; *Works* 3: 654.

10. See *Apologia*, art. 23, in *Opera*, p. 168; *Works* 2: 36–37.

11. *Disp. pub.* VII.9.

12. *Disp. pub.* VII.10.

13. *Disp. pub.* VII.13; XXXI.14; *Disp. priv.* XXX.9.

The key theme in Arminius's disputations on the first sin is his establishing the contingency of this act. When Arminius conducted the oral disputation of 1604 on this topic (*Disp. pub.* VII, cited in this section) in the presence of his faculty colleagues, he underscored the contingency of the fall more than is evident in the written theses alone.[14] Yet, even in the printed theses of this and other disputations, his emphasis is clear that the first sin was committed freely, apart from any internal or external compulsion.[15] He writes, "Therefore it stands unshaken that the man fell by his own free will, not by any necessity."[16] Free will by itself, apart from any coercion, is capable of evil and accounts for its origin. Put in an Augustinian way, humanity before the fall was "able not to sin" (*posse non peccare*).

Establishing the contingency of this act is crucial for Arminius, given the necessity that he detects in his opponents' discussions of the first sin. It is true that early Reformed scholasticism was moving away from the more deterministic models of providence articulated by John Calvin and Theodore Beza.[17] Reformed theologians such as Franciscus Junius acknowledged that since God ordains the evil only as a remote cause, then God should not be considered the author of evil.[18] Despite such distinctions and denials, however, Arminius felt that the doctrine of Calvin and Beza, and of anyone else who followed their opinion, entails that the first sin was made necessary by God's decree,[19] thereby rendering God the true author of sin. In response to Junius, Arminius writes, "From the opinion of Calvin and Beza, God is established necessarily as the author of sin. Therefore it must be repudiated. . . . He who ordains that humanity falls and sins, he is the author of sin."[20] He found this to be the unavoidable implication of the doctrine of unconditional predestination, in which the fall functions as

---

14. *Ep. ecc.* 70; *Works* 1: 150 n.

15. *Disp. pub.* VII.4; XXXI.7–10; *Disp. priv.* XXX.4.

16. *Disp. pub.* XXXI.10: "Stat igitur inconcussum, hominem sua voluntate libera, non ulla necessitate lapsum esse."

17. See Muller, *God, Creation, and Providence,* p. 40; idem, "Grace, Election, and Contingent Choice," pp. 269–277; *PRRD* 1: 123, 128–129; 3: 29. See also Van Asselt et al., eds., *Reformed Thought on Freedom.*

18 *Collatio,* in *Opera,* p. 486; *Works* 3: 57.

19. E.g., see Calvin, *Institutio* III.xxiii.7–9.

20. *Collatio,* in *Opera,* p. 498; *Works* 3: 74. Reflecting on his correspondence with Junius, Arminius reiterates the same point in a letter to Uytenbogaert. *Ep. ecc.* 19, pp. 33–35.

the necessary means for the preceding decrees of reprobation. In such a system of necessary sin, Arminius contends, God truly sins and is the only sinner.[21]

## B. The Effects of the First Sin

The immediate effects of the first sin are described in Genesis 3. These effects include the guilt of the two who actually committed the sin, indicated by their attempt to hide their naked shame. The apostle Paul gives the most extensive theological treatment in the New Testament of the lasting effects of this sin on humanity (especially in Romans 5). Yet the few answers that are given raise many more questions. Thus the topic has been the subject of heated debate throughout the history of the church. How exactly and to what extent does the first sin affect the rest of humanity? Since the time of Augustine, these enduring effects of the first sin on the human race have gone by the name *original sin*.

Two points are crucial for grasping Arminius's thoughts on original sin. First, he defines it primarily as a lack of original righteousness. Second, he further describes original sin as punishment, but not guilt.[22]

### B.1. *Absence of Original Righteousness*

What are the lasting effects of the first sin? Some consequences, such as pain and death, are strictly physical and are mentioned explicitly in Genesis 3. Spiritually, though, what is original sin? The medieval tradition

---

21. This is a recurring theme in Arminius's writings. E.g., see *Art. non.* X, in *Opera*, pp. 954–955; *Works* 2: 715–716; *Dec. sent.*, pp. 84–85, 101; *Works* 1: 629–630, 647–648; *Exam. Gom.*, pp. 154–158; *Works* 3: 654–658. Arminius himself was accused once of making God the author of sin, an irony which he described as a great wonder. See *Apologia*, art. 23, in *Opera*, pp. 168–170; *Works* 2: 37–40.

22. Arminius treats the topic of original sin primarily in *Disp. pub.* VII.15–16; XXXI.15; XXXII; *Disp. priv.* XXXI; *Apologia*, art. 13–14 and 31 (11), in *Opera*, pp. 153–155 and 180–182; *Works* 2: 10–14 and 57–61; *Quaestiones*, q. 3, in *Opera*, pp. 184–185; *Works* 2: 65; *Ep. ecc.* 81; *Works* 2: 69; *Art. non.* XII, in *Opera*, pp. 955–956; *Works* 2: 717.

On Arminius's thoughts regarding original sin, see Witt, "Creation, Redemption and Grace" pp. 478–488; Ellis, *Episcopius' Doctrine*, pp. 73–79, 178–179; Hicks, "Theology of Grace," pp. 32–41; Matthew J. Pinson, "Will the Real Arminius Please Stand Up? A Study of the Theology of Jacobus Arminius in Light of His Interpreters," *Integrity* 2 (2003): 129–133; Bangs, *Arminius*, pp. 339–340; Herbert McGonigle, "Arminius and Wesley on Original Sin," *European Explorations in Christian Holiness* 2 (2001): 96–100; Leon O. Hynson, "Original Sin as Privation: An Inquiry into a Theology of Sin and Sanctification," *Wesleyan Theological Journal* 22/2 (1987): 65–83.

wrestled with two main answers to this question.[23] On the one hand, Peter Lombard (ca. 1100–1160) articulated a view that also represents the opinions of Augustine and Hugh of Saint-Victor (ca. 1096–ca. 1142). Peter said that "original sin is a fault (*culpa*) which all contract who are conceived through concupiscence."[24] Indeed, according to Augustine and the Master of Sentences, original sin is concupiscence, that is, disordered desire or lust for the creation above the Creator.[25] The Lombard compares original sin to blindness. The defect of the eye is not apparent in the darkness of night, for one cannot tell the difference at night between a blind person and a person whose eyes function properly. Only when the light of day appears can the distinction be made and the defect becomes evident. In the same way, he says, the vice, or defect (*vitium*), of original sin is not apparent in children until they have reached a more advanced age, though it was there all along.[26]

On the other hand is the view espoused by Anselm of Canterbury (1033–1109) and taken up later by John Duns Scotus, William of Ockham (ca. 1285–ca. 1347), and Gregory of Rimini (ca. 1300–1358).[27] Speaking in the context of original sin, Anselm wrote that this "unrighteousness is nothing other than the absence of owed righteousness."[28] In a discussion of the various views, Thomas Aquinas summarized this latter perspective:

---

23. For a comprehensive historical survey of the doctrine of original sin, see Julius Gross, *Entwicklungsgeschichte des Erbsündendogmas*, 4 vols. (Basel: Ernst Reinhardt Verlag, 1960–1972). See also T. C. O'Brien, "Appendices," in *Summa Theologiae*, Volume 26, *Original Sin (1a2ae.81–85)* (New York: McGraw-Hill, 1965), pp. 105–161; Oberman, *Harvest*, pp. 121–123.

24. Peter Lombard, *Sententiarum libri quatuor* II.xxx.6, in *PL* 192: 722: "Peccatum itaque originale culpa est, quam omnes concupiscentialiter concepti trahunt."

25. Gross, *Entwicklungsgeschichte*, 3: 353; O'Brien, "Appendices," p. 129.

26. Peter Lombard, *Sententiae* II.xxx.8, in *PL* 192: 722: "Sicut enim in oculo caeci, in nocte vitium caecitatis est, sed non apparet, nec discernitur inter videntem et caecum, nisi luce veniente; sic in puero vitium esse non apparet, donec aetatis provectioris tempus occurrat." Cf. Augustine's comparison of blindness to sin in *De civitate Dei* XXII.i.2, in *PL* 41: 752.

27. Gross, *Entwicklungsgeschichte*, 3: 353.

28. Anselm of Canterbury, *De conceptu virginali et originali peccato* III, in *PL* 158: 436A: "Quod si ita est, et iniustitia non est aliud quam absentia debitae iustitiae." The longer variant reading puts the same idea more clearly: "Quod si ita est, originale peccatum non est aliud quam iniustitia, id est absentia debitae iustitiae." See also ibid. XXIV, in *PL* 158: 457C: "In hoc ergo sunt omnes pariter iniusti, quia nullam habent, quam omnis homo habere debet, iustitiam. Haec nuditas iustitiae descendit ad omnes ab Adam, in quo humana natura se spoliavit eadem iustitia." Cf. a similar articulation in idem, *De concordia praescientiae et praedestinationis nec non gratiae Dei cum libero arbitrio* III.13, in *PL* 158: 538–540.

"For original sin is the lack of original righteousness, as Anselm says. And so original sin is a certain privation."[29]

All scholastic theologians subsequent to Anselm wrestled with these alternatives. This tradition provides the context for Arminius's query:

> Is original sin only the lack (*carentia*) of original righteousness and of primeval holiness, with an inclination to sinning, which likewise formerly existed in humanity, although it was not so vehement nor so disordered as it now is, because of the lost favor of God, his curse, and the loss of that good by which [that inclination to sin] was driven back into the order? Or is it a certain habit contrary to righteousness and holiness that was infused (or a point of entry [*ingressus*] that was acquired) after that sin had been committed?[30]

Not content to make an exclusive choice, Alexander of Hales (ca. 1186–1245) proposed a third way that was taken up by Aquinas, Bonaventure (ca. 1217–1274), and Gabriel Biel (ca. 1425–1495).[31] This view seeks to mediate the previous alternatives. As Aquinas put it, "Original sin entails privation of original righteousness, and with this a disordered disposition in parts of the soul. Therefore it is not pure privation, but it is a certain corrupt habit."[32] This same view is also typical of Reformed orthodoxy. In fact, even the theologians who emphasized original sin as a positively corrupt habit generally acknowledged also the absence of original righteousness.[33]

Arminius, rejecting the first view, inclines toward the second view, declaring that it is "more probable that the absence alone [of original

---

29. *ST* Ia-IIae.lxxxii.1 obj. 1: "Originale enim peccatum est carentia originalis iustitiae, ut Anselmus dicit. Et sic originale peccatum est quaedam privatio."

30. *Art. non.* XII.2; in *Opera*, p. 956; *Works* 2: 717.

31. Gabriel Biel, *Collectorium circa quattuor libros sententiarum*, ed. Wilfridus Werbeck and Udo Hofmann, 4 vols. (Tübingen: Mohr, 1973–1984), II.xxx. q.2. art. 1; cf. Gross, *Entwicklungsgeschichte*, 3: 353–354.

32. *ST* Ia-IIae.lxxxii.1 ad 1: "ita etiam peccatum originale habet privationem originalis iustitiae, et cum hoc inordinatam dispositionem partium animae. Unde non est privatio pura, sed est quidam habitus corruptus."

33. E.g., see Du Moulin, *Anatome Arminianismi*, VIII.i–ii, pp. 46–47 (ET, pp. 51–52). See Aza Goudriaan, "The Synod of Dordt on Arminian Anthropology," in *Revisiting the Synod of Dordt (1618–1619)*, ed. Aza Goudriaan and Fred van Lieburg, Brill's Series in Church History, vol. 49 (Leiden: Brill, 2011), pp. 88, 101.

righteousness] is original sin itself."[34] Since, as T. C. O'Brien says, "The meaning of original sin depends on the meaning of original justice which is its positive contrast,"[35] it is important to understand what is meant by this "original righteousness" that Arminius and previous theologians claim is now lost. In the beginning, humanity was made in the image and likeness of God.[36] Some aspects of the *imago Dei* are essential to being human, including intellect, will, and affections. These essential properties, especially the faculties of the soul, are natural to humanity. Besides the natural, or essential, properties, other aspects of the *imago* are accidental; that is, one can still be human without them. These accidental, or supernatural, qualities are knowledge of God, righteousness, and holiness, which Arminius calls moral virtues and uses synonymously with the term *original righteousness*.[37] By virtue of being formed in the *imago Dei*, humanity before the fall was created in a state of original righteousness. On this general point of creation with original righteousness, Arminius was in agreement with his Reformed contemporaries, as well as with the great Christian tradition.[38] For Arminius, original righteousness meant the efficacious presence of the Holy Spirit to bring this knowledge of God and holiness, a gracious gift which then departed from the first sinners and their offspring.[39] It is this lack of original righteousness, and its absence now being passed on to human nature, that Arminius equates with original sin. In the end, Arminius seems to understand the

---

34. *Disp. priv.* XXXI.10. The statement from 1603 in *Disp. pub.* XXXII.5–6, emphasizing that original sin is not simply the absence of original righteousness (contra Anselm) but positive corruption that replaces righteousness, seems to be in tension with Arminius's later opinion reflected in other disputations and treatises. This apparent inconsistency may indicate a shift in Arminius's later perspective, or that he was not the primary author of *Disp. pub.* XXXII. On the authorship question in general and its relationship to this public disputation in particular, see Stanglin, *Missing Disputations*, pp. 43–100, especially 75–81.

35. O'Brien, "Appendices," p. 151.

36. Arminius treats the topic of the creation of humanity in God's image in *Disp. pub.* XXX; *Disp. priv.* XXVI; *Art. non.* VI, in *Opera*, pp. 952–953; *Works* 2: 711–713; *Collatio*, in *Opera*, pp. 524–525; *Works* 3: 112–114.

37. *Art. non.* VI.5, in *Opera*, p. 952; *Works* 2: 712; *Collatio*, in *Opera*, pp. 524–525; *Works* 3: 112–114; *Dec. sent.*, p. 79; *Works* 1: 625.

38. Cf. *Exam. Gom.*, p. 84; *Works* 3: 596; with *Canons and Dogmatic Decrees of the Council of Trent, Decretum de peccato originali*, 5th session, 1–2, in Schaff, *Creeds of Christendom*, 2: 84–85. Although Arminius uses *imago* and *similitudo* interchangeably, his distinction between the essential and accidental properties otherwise functions similarly to the common patristic distinction between *imago* and *similitudo*, respectively.

39. *Disp. priv.* XXXI.9.

difficulty of defining original sin, for even in his statement quoted above, he uses the language of probability (*verisimilius*) rather than full certainty. At any rate, we may say that Arminius, in his doctrine of original sin, stresses deprivation more than depravation.[40]

## B.2. Punishment, Not Guilt

To put the matter briefly, for Arminius, the claim that original sin is primarily a deprivation of original righteousness is accompanied by the claim that original sin itself does not make one liable to further punishment. But the modern reader who compares all the relevant passages in Arminius's writings must acknowledge a degree of ambiguity. Arminius's specialized vocabulary in this context can be confusing, and the inconsistency of the existing English translations tends to make matters worse. *Reus* is translated variously as "liable to," "guilty of," and "obnoxious to." *Reatus* is generally translated consistently as "guilt," but Bagnall's American edition at least once changes it to "penalty." And *culpa* is translated sometimes as "guilt," other times as "fault."[41]

Arminius believed that original sin is the *poena* (penalty, punishment) itself, which is preceded by the *reatus* (guilt) of Adam's actual sin, but original sin is not the guilt itself.[42] Subsequent to the guilt that the first couple merited, the punishment (*poena*) that they suffered is precisely the penalty that accrued to their posterity. Whatever punishment came to the first sinners has come down to all people.[43] All people are liable (*reus*) to eternal death, but it is not original sin per se that renders one liable to death. Original sin is the punishment for that liability, or guilt; it is the loss of original righteousness and holiness which then leads to actual sins.[44] All agreed that original sin is punishment; but to add guilt to its definition would

---

40. Hynson, "Original Sin," pp. 72–75, surveys Methodist theologians who, in contrast with Arminius but in line with Wesley, stressed depravation over deprivation.

41. See *Cap. VII Rom.*, III.i.2, in *Opera*, p. 905; *Works* 2: 631; *Disp. pub.* VII.16; *Disp. priv.* XXXI.1, 3, 5–6, 8–9; *Quaestiones*, q. 3, in *Opera*, pp. 184–185; *Works* 2: 65; *Apologia*, art. 31 (11), in *Opera*, p. 181; *Works* 2: 59; *Art. non.* XII, in *Opera*, pp. 955–956; *Works* 2: 717.

42. *Quaestiones*, q. 3, in *Opera*, pp. 184–185; *Works* 2: 65; *Apologia*, art. 31 (11), in *Opera*, p. 181; *Works* 2: 59.

43. *Disp. pub.* VII.16. Exactly how original sin is passed on to human souls is not especially important to Arminius's discussion of the topic. Cf. *Disp. pub.* VII.16 with *Disp. priv.* XXXI.11.

44. *Cap. VII Rom.*, III.i.2, in *Opera*, p. 905; *Works* 2: 631; *Disp. pub.* VII.16; XXXI.15; *Quaestiones*, q. 3, in *Opera*, pp. 184–185; *Works* 2: 65.

mean that God must again punish for the guilt. If this were the case, according to Arminius, original sin would then result in punishment, and would therefore entail an infinite cycle of guilt and punishment, without any actual sins ever intervening, which he considered to be an absurdity.[45]

## C. Total Inability and Actual Sins

What, then, is the condition of humanity after the fall? As a result of original sin, which for Arminius means the loss of original righteousness and the absence of the Holy Spirit's efficacious work, humanity after the fall and before regeneration possesses a strong inclination to commit sin.[46] Every part of the human soul has been negatively affected by the withdrawal of original holiness. Although Arminius never uses the phrase *total depravity*, nevertheless he teaches precisely what later Reformed writers mean when they use this phrase: the damage is "total" in the senses that no aspect of human nature—especially the intellect, will, and affections—remains unaffected and that no one is able to merit salvation. The mind (*mens*) has been struck blind (2 Cor. 4:4), unable to perceive the truth that otherwise should be plainly seen, and the affections of the soul (*affectus animi*) are slaves to Satan.[47] Not only is blindness given by God as penalty for sin (presumably through the loss of original righteousness), but also humanity's own actual sins merely add to the blindness.[48] Arminius's

---

45. *Apologia*, art. 31 (11), in *Opera*, pp. 180–182; *Works* 2: 57–61. Cf. *Ep. ecc.* 105, p. 197. Cf. also Du Moulin, *Anatome Arminianismi*, VIII.xii, p. 49 (ET, p. 55); with Peter Lombard, *Sententiae* II.xxx.5, in *PL* 192: 721.

46. *Art. non.* XII.2, in *Opera*, p. 956; *Works* 2: 717.

47. *Oratio de dissidio*, in *Opera*, p. 79; *Works* 1: 454–455.

48. *Ep. ecc.* 105, p. 197: "Quia poena habet rationem involuntarii, et peccatum voluntarium est; peccatum est actio peccantis, poena est passio eiusdem; per poenam redigitur peccatum in ordinem, at peccatum est ipsa summa inordinatio. . . . Sic excaecatio, quae est a Deo, poena est, non peccatum, quamquam inde existat aliud peccatum poenae maioris meritorium: at excaecatio quae est ab homine, qua homo sibi ipse excaecat oculos, peccatum est; et ab hac actione hominis et actione Dei existit unum apotelesma, quod dicitur excaecatio passiva, quae non est peccatum, sed poena et causa peccati, poena praecedentis, causa insequentis per remotionem prohibentis. Punit Deus adulterium Davidis per incestum Absolomi; at hoc istud dictum dicere non vult; notum enim est, Deum punire unum hominem per actum alterius, qui ab isto sine peccato non perpetratur." According to Goudriaan, "Synod of Dort," p. 89, the Synod of Dordt also stressed that, after the fall, the human intellect is "completely blind in spiritual matters."

emphasis on intellectual blindness is reminiscent of Peter Lombard's statement cited above. Original sin, accompanied as it is by the conditions of blindness and slavery, generates an "original propensity" to disobey God's law. This evil inclination, combined with human free choice, is a cause of further actual sins.[49]

Actual sins, in contrast to original sin, are personal sins committed by someone who has the right use of reason.[50] According to Arminius, although all sins merit death, not all sins are equal.[51] Among a variety of factors used to distinguish types of actual sins is the question of the motivating cause behind the sin. Sins may be committed out of ignorance, weakness, malice, or negligence.[52] Whatever the motivation for sin may be, in view of this postlapsarian enslavement to sin, Arminius emphasized the total inability of humans to turn to God on their own. The natural person does not will the good, indeed *cannot* will, think, or do the good.[53] Although natural faculties and hints of primeval wisdom remain in the intellect after the fall, "they cannot carry humanity to the knowledge and love of the true and saving good."[54] Whatever freedom remains to humanity after the fall, it is not sufficient by itself to turn to God. Divine grace must intervene.

## II. Divine Grace and Human Freedom
### A. Necessary, Resistible Grace

God's justice demands that sins receive a just penalty, but God the Son graciously substituted himself in the place of sinful humanity. How that grace acquired by Christ's atonement is communicated to humanity is a prominent topic for Arminius. Throughout his writings there appears a recurring refrain that fallen humanity without Christ has no ability, and thus no freedom, to choose spiritual regeneration. It is a pure gift from God. Human "free choice" (*liberum arbitrium*) is not the decisive factor;

---

49. *Disp. pub.* VIII.13; *Apologia*, art. 31 (11), in *Opera*, p. 181; *Works* 2: 59–60.

50. *Disp. pub.* VIII.1.

51. *Disp. pub.* VIII.9.

52. *Disp. pub.* VIII.5. Cf. *Ep. ecc.* 81, pp. 93–94; *Works* 2: 743–745.

53. *Cap. VII Rom.*, III.i.2, in *Opera*, p. 905; *Works* 2: 631; *Dec. sent.*, pp. 113–114; *Works* 1: 664.

54. *Disp. pub.* XXXIII.4.

rather, in the fallen condition, God's grace is "absolutely necessary" for a person to will the good.[55]

Arminius describes grace generally as God's disposition "to communicate his own good and to love the creatures, not out of merit or of debt, nor that it may add something to God himself; but that it may be well with the one on whom the good is bestowed (*tribuitur*), and who is loved."[56] Inasmuch as the intellect, will, and affections have been damaged by sin, grace must be infused into and positively affect every part of human nature to effect redemption.[57] In specifically soteriological contexts, Arminius uses a variety of modifiers to represent the distinctions and functions of grace. Although each modifying word reveals something significant and distinct about divine grace, Arminius classifies them into two main categories. In a passage in which he is attempting to clarify his opponents' use of the phrase *saving grace*, Arminius places in one category what he variously calls first (*prima*), prevenient or preceding (*praeveniens*), operating (*operans*), or knocking (*pulsans*) grace. To these he juxtaposes, in another category, second (*secunda*), subsequent or following (*subsequens*), cooperating (*cooperans*), or opening (*aperiens*) or entering (*ingrediens*) grace.[58] In other words, there is a grace that comes first, preceding any human decision, operating solely from God outside us (*extra nos*) in a monergistic way, and, to borrow imagery from Rev. 3:20, it stands at the door and knocks. In addition to this prevenient, operating, knocking grace, there is a second type of grace that follows the reception of the first grace and is therefore "cooperative" in a synergistic way, "opening" the door so that grace may "enter." Some scholars have denied that Arminius is a "synergist," yet his definition of subsequent grace is precisely "synergistic," which is simply the Greek equivalent of "cooperative" (derived from Latin).[59] Indeed, the order of

---

55. *Cap. VII Rom.*, III.i.2, in *Opera*, p. 905; *Works* 2: 631. For treatments of Arminius's teaching on grace, see Hicks, "Theology of Grace," pp. 52–68; Dekker, *Rijker dan Midas*, pp. 157–177; Ellis, *Episcopius' Doctrine*, pp. 79–84; Stanglin, *Arminius on Assurance*, pp. 77–83; Witt, "Creation, Redemption and Grace," pp. 515–677; Den Boer, *God's Twofold Love*, pp. 179–184.

56. *Disp. pub.* IV.69.

57 *Dec. sent.*, p. 113; *Works* 1: 664.

58. *Apologia*, art. 16, in *Opera*, p. 158; *Works* 2: 18.

59. On the one hand, Pinson, "Will the Real Arminius Please Stand?" pp. 134–135, denies that Arminius was a synergist, apparently defining it as a contribution of human *merit*. On the other hand, Hicks, "Theology of Grace," pp. 64–68, admits the synergism of Arminius, if it means including a human act of approval, not of merit. Cf. idem, "The Righteousness of Saving Faith: Arminian versus Remonstrant Grace," *Evangelical Journal* 9 (Spring 1991): 30.

grace to which Arminius alludes in Rev. 3:20 is based on Christ—"saving grace" personified—first knocking, and subsequently being received by the one opening the door, through which Christ enters. The initial contact of prevenient grace is wholly divine, but the subsequent grace entails a cooperative relationship.

The phrase *prevenient grace* is now almost exclusively associated with Wesleyan-Arminian theology. But Arminius's distinction between prevenient and subsequent grace was not his invention. The idea is anticipated in many passages of Scripture, and simply means that there is an unsolicited gift of divine grace "coming before" (*praeveniens*) any human willing, and there is grace "following after" (*subsequens*) the human acceptance of the first grace. Even if there was not complete consensus on its mode of operation, the doctrine of prevenient grace was common in the medieval church. Augustine discusses this concept in several passages.[60] In a famous anti-Pelagian treatise, the bishop of Hippo writes:

> Indeed we also work; but we cooperate with the one who works, because his mercy comes before (*praevenit*) us. But it comes before so that we may be healed, because it also follows after (*subsequetur*), so that having been healed, we may also be invigorated; it comes before so that we may be called, it follows after so that we may be glorified; it comes before so that we may walk piously, it follows after so that we may always live with him, because without him we can do nothing.[61]

The second Council of Orange (529), a defense of Augustinianism against semi-Pelagianism, states, "That grace is not preceded by merit. Recompense is due to good works if they are performed; but grace, to which we

---

Similarly, Witt, "Creation, Redemption and Grace," pp. 660–661, distinguishes between semi-Pelagian synergism and Erasmian synergism, classifying Arminius with the latter. Cf. also Bangs, *Arminius*, pp. 342–344; Muller, "Grace, Election, and Contingent Choice," p. 261; Olson, *Arminian Theology*, pp. 17–19.

60. E.g., see Augustine, *Sermones ad populum omnes* CLXXIV.iv.4, in *PL* 38: 942–943; idem, *Contra duas epistolas Pelagianorum* IV.vi.15, in *PL* 44: 620

61. Augustine, *De natura et gratia ad Timasium et Iacobum contra Pelagium* XXXI.35, in *PL* 44: 264: "Ubi quidem operamur et nos: sed illo operante cooperamur, quia misericordia eius praevenit nos. Praevenit autem ut sanemur, quia et subsequetur ut etiam sanati vegetemur: praevenit ut vocemur, subsequetur ut glorificemur: praevenit ut pie vivamus, subsequetur ut cum illo semper vivamus: quiae sine illo nihil possumus facere."

have no claim, precedes them, to enable them to be done."[62] The more immediate influence on Arminius comes from Thomas Aquinas, who explains, "Just as grace is divided into operating and cooperating according to the diverse effects, so also into prevenient and subsequent, in whatever manner grace is received."[63]

Like Thomas, Arminius also uses the terminology of *sufficient* and *efficient* grace to describe prevenient and subsequent grace, respectively. "This internal persuasion of the Holy Spirit is twofold. One is sufficient (*sufficiens*), the other is efficacious (*efficax*). When the former is exercised, one is *able* to will and to believe and to be converted. When the latter is applied, one *does* will, does believe, and is converted."[64] That is, prevenient grace is sufficient or adequate to make it possible for someone to receive Christ; efficient grace actually brings the possibility of salvation to realization.[65] This distinction is analogous to the acknowledgment that Christ's atonement is sufficient for all, but efficient only for the elect, that is, for those who appropriate its benefits. Arminius's theology implies that sufficient grace is available to all universally, perhaps counterfactually so, and through divine middle knowledge. The bestowal of the Holy Spirit for salvation, though, is not common to all, but to those who accept the gift of faith.[66]

Two points are worth reiterating. First of all, secondary, subsequent grace is dependent on primary, prevenient grace; God initiates conversion. Second, the operation of prevenient and subsequent grace is an ongoing process, never leaving humanity to make an autonomous decision.

---

62. *Canons of the Council of Orange*, canon 18, in *Creeds and Confessions of Faith in the Christian Tradition*, ed. Jaroslav J. Pelikan and Valerie R. Hotchkiss (New Haven, CT: Yale University Press, 2003), p. 695.

63. *ST* Ia-IIae.cxi.3 resp.: "Respondeo dicendum quod, sicut gratia dividitur in operantem et cooperantem secundum diversos effectus, ita etiam in praevenientem et subsequentem, qualitercumque gratia accipiatur." By the time of Thomas, the patristic use of the indicative verb (*gratia praevenit*) had shifted into a participial modifier (*gratia praeveniens*). Arminius is comfortable with both usages.

64. *Exam. Perk.*, in *Opera*, p. 665; *Works* 3: 315 (emphasis added). Cf. *Quaestiones*, q. 5, in *Opera*, p. 185; *Works* 2: 66.

65. Again alluding to Rev. 3:20 ("Behold, I stand at the door and knock"), and this time quoting Robert Bellarmine, Arminius writes, in *Exam. Perk.*, in *Opera*, p. 775; *Works* 3: 481: "The one who knocks at a door, certainly knowing that there is no one within who can open, knocks in vain, indeed, is foolish. But far be it from us to think this about God. Therefore, when God knocks, it is certain that a man can open, and by consequence he has sufficient grace."

66. *Ep. ecc.* 60, p. 113; *Works* 1: 747 n.

Prevenient, sufficient grace is both an external gift (for example, in the proclamation of the word) and an internal gift (operation on the heart).[67] It is not that the Holy Spirit bestows prevenient grace and then becomes a passive observer, as if "waiting to see whether a person will rightly use this power and believe the gospel." Rather, grace, not autonomous choice, has the greater role in persuading the human will and in continuing the process of helping a person receive the gospel.[68] To return to the illustration above, the point is that Christ does not simply knock and wait for a response, but he continues knocking, and even helps a person open the door, as the operation of prevenient grace indistinguishably evolves into a cooperation of subsequent grace.

Between Arminius and his Reformed contemporaries there is no real difference regarding the extent of sin and the need for grace. According to Arminius, divine grace accomplishes everything in the process of salvation and is absolutely necessary. "Without this special help of grace," Arminius writes, "it is most certain that nothing good can be done by any rational creature."[69] In agreement with his Reformed contemporaries, in his *Declaration of Sentiments* he said:

> I ascribe to God's grace the origin, the continuance, and the fulfillment (*het beghinsel, den voorgangh, ende de volbrenginghe*) of all good, even so far that the regenerate person himself, without this prevenient and stimulating, following and cooperating grace, can neither think, will or do good, nor also resist any evil temptation. From this it appears that I do not diminish God's grace by attributing too much to humanity's free will (*vryen wille*).[70]

Elsewhere he writes that without grace, free choice "cannot begin or complete any true and spiritual good."[71]

Arminius accepted that God's grace does everything attributed to it by his Reformed opponents. The question is not about the category of prevenient

67. *Apologia*, art. 8, in *Opera*, p. 145; *Works* 1: 764; *Ep. ecc.* 85, p. 158; *Works* 1: 764 n.

68. *Apologia*, art. 8, in *Opera*, p. 145; *Works* 1: 764–765.

69. *Exam. Perk.*, in *Opera*, p. 637; *Works* 3: 271.

70. *Dec. sent.*, pp. 113–114; *Works* 1: 664. This passage is quoted exactly in *Articuli Arminiani sive remonstrantia*, art. 4, in Schaff, *Creeds of Christendom*, 3: 545–549. Cf. the similarity of Erasmus, *Freedom of the Will*, p. 90.

71. *Epistola*, in *Opera*, p. 944; *Works* 2: 700.

grace or whether grace operates on the heart through the Holy Spirit. The question is about the mode of the operation, not about the essence of grace. The one difference that he stressed against his opponents was that this saving grace is not irresistible in its mode of operation. "But the only difference is located here, whether God's grace is an irresistible power (*onweder-standelijcke cracht*). That is the difference and it is not concerning deeds or operations which may be attributed to grace (which, after all, I acknowledge and teach as much as anyone ever did), but only concerning the mode of operation, whether or not it is irresistible."[72] Arminius, like so many theologians before him, is attempting to articulate an orthodox Christian perspective that reconciles the sovereignty of divine grace and the place of human freedom. In the task of restoring humanity, "God does these [good] things in us, but he does not perfect without us; he acts in us so that we may act."[73] Arminius put the same sentiment another way in an oral disputation: "Humanity determines itself, but not without grace; for free choice concurs with grace."[74] In the words of William G. Witt, since grace perfects nature and does not destroy it, grace therefore "neither competes with nor overwhelms creaturely realities."[75]

As Arminius observes, the mode of operation is the fundamental difference between the Arminian and Reformed orthodox doctrines of grace. For the Reformed, even if some do not prefer the phrase *irresistible grace*,[76] their belief is that God's grace cannot be resisted, and God will save whom God previously elects. God will grant grace and faith to the elect, and they will accept the irrevocable gift. Without any consent of human will, God

---

72. *Dec. sent.*, p. 114; *Works* 1: 664. Cf. *Dec. sent.*, p. 83; *Works* 1: 629.

73. *Disp. pub.* XXXIII.8: "Haec facit Deus in nobis, sed non perficit sine nobis, agit in nobis ut nos agamus."

74. As reported by Adrian van den Borre in *Ep. ecc.* 130, p. 226: "hominem se determinare, sed non sine gratia: concurrere enim liberum arbitrium cum gratia."

75. Witt, "Creation, Redemption and Grace," pp. 259, 316.

76. E.g., Festus Hommius reports that Gomarus resisted the word *irresistible* in the final conference with Arminius at The Hague. See Wijminga, *Hommius*, Bijlage G, pp. xiii–xiv: "An regeneremur potentia irresistibili. D. Gomarus reformavit statum propter ambiguitatem vocis irresistibilis." Cf. *Acta synodi Dordrechti*, fol. 006ʳ (ET, p. 31). But other Reformed theologians whose doctrine is consistent with that of Gomarus did not hesitate to use this word and concept. E.g., see William Prynne, *Anti-Arminianisme: Or the Church of Englands Old Antithesis to New Arminianisme*, 2nd ed. ([London,] 1630), pp. 74–75: "That the Elect doe always constantly obey, neither doe they, or can they finally or totally resist the inward, powerfull, and effectuall call or working of Gods Spirit in their hearts."

changes the will of the elect to desire God; as such, the sovereign divine will cannot be thwarted as it overrides the human will. For Arminius, though, salvation is by grace alone, but humans can resist the Holy Spirit—a fact that Arminius often pointed out from Scripture. That grace is a resistible gift does not make it a work of merit or any less a gift, contrary to the claim of his critics. Arminius wrote:

> We do not wish to do injury to divine grace, by taking from it anything that is of it; but let my brothers watch, lest they themselves do injury to divine justice by attributing to it what it refuses, or rather to divine grace by transforming (*transmutando*) it into something else which cannot be called grace. That I may in a word signify what must be proved by them, namely, that the grace that is necessary, sufficient, [and] efficient for salvation is [also] "irresistible," or acts with such power (*potentia*) that it cannot be resisted by a free creature.[77]

Arminius's claim is bold and clear: His opponents have done injury to saving grace by making it into a compelling, irresistible force. Instead, grace is a necessary, persuasive cause leading to salvation, not a coercive cause. God's sufficient grace may be offered to all people, irrespective of their choice, but irresistible saving grace, offered to a select few, is in conflict with God's love and with the freedom of human nature.[78] Therefore, Arminius writes, "Grace is not an irresistible force."[79] Again employing the analogy from Rev. 3:20, Arminius teaches that an unregenerate person may resist the Holy Spirit and grace, refusing to open the door of the heart on which Christ knocks.[80]

## B. Free Will and the Charge of Pelagianism

With respect to human (not divine) freedom, Arminius declares that human choice (*arbitrium*) can be free in three ways. First, there is freedom from internal and external necessity. Humanity is always free from necessity;

---

77. *Apologia*, art. 27 (7), in *Opera*, p. 177; *Works* 2: 52. Cf. *Dec. sent.*, p. 114; *Works* 1: 664; with idem, *Epistola*, in *Opera*, p. 944; *Works* 2: 700–701.

78. This is Arminius's claim, as reported from the eyewitness Festus Hommius in a letter to Sibrandus Lubbertus. The letter is printed in Wijminga, *Hommius*, Bijlage G, pp. xi–xv (here, xiv).

79. *Art. non.* XVII.13, in *Opera*, p. 959; *Works* 2: 722.

80. *Art. non.* XVII.5, in *Opera*, p. 958; *Works* 2: 721.

indeed, since choice is situated in the will, "there would not be will (*voluntas*) if it is not free (*libera*)."[81] Second, there is the possibility of freedom from misery, but this liberty applies only to humanity before the fall and in the eschaton. Third, there is freedom from sin.[82] How should the relationship between free choice and sin be understood?

Another traditional way for theologians to handle the question of human freedom, especially in relation to sin, was to consider free choice in three states or conditions: before the fall, after the fall, and after regeneration (sometimes adding a discussion of the fourth state of freedom from sin in the age to come). Arminius assumed these same human conditions when he dealt with the topic. After the fall and the deprivation of original righteousness in which humanity was able to avoid sin, humanity now exists in a state of corruption in which the will to good is useless without the assistance of divine grace.[83] Humanity's whole life "is utterly dead in sins,"[84] and fallen humanity needs God's grace to understand, will, and do the good.[85] Prevenient grace is, therefore, not prompted by preparatory works of any kind.[86] Prevenient grace comes first, enabling a fallen person's otherwise obstinate will to accept the grace. As many later Arminians have put it, Arminius stresses not free will as much as "freed will." The will is liberated by grace so that it might not resist the persuasive work of the Holy Spirit. As Arminius writes, "By the further help of grace [God] concurs with a person to will and do by action that good for which he receives sufficient powers, unless the person for his part sets up, or has set up, a barrier."[87] Salvation, in some ways, may be rightly described as a person not resisting God's grace.

It should be clear that, for Arminius, the human will plays no role at all in salvation without the liberating grace of God, which precedes and permeates the decision in such a way that the human turn toward God may never be called "autonomous." Nevertheless, this account of the human will's limited cooperation in salvation has been suspected of heresy. Arminius's teaching on grace, though it was consistent with the Christian tradition before him,

---

81. *Disp. pub.* XI.2.

82. *Disp. pub.* XI.2. On these different types of freedom, see Dekker, *Rijker dan Midas*, pp. 134–143.

83. *Disp. pub.* XI.7.

84. *Disp. pub.* XI.11.

85. *Dec. sent.*, pp. 112–113; *Works* 1: 659–660.

86. *Disp. pub.* XXXIII.4.

87. *Exam. Perk.*, in *Opera*, p. 637; *Works* 3: 272.

sparked controversy in his own day and continues to raise questions today. That Arminius was frequently misunderstood and maligned for his teaching on grace is apparent in the thirty-one articles falsely attributed to him, ten of which deal in some way with the theme of nature and grace.[88] The primary objection that Reformed theologians, then and now, have to Arminius's view of grace is that it ascribes too little to divine sovereignty and too much to human freedom, thus bordering on semi-Pelagianism, if not the heresy of full-blown Pelagianism. Since virtually every seventeenth-century opponent of Arminius and Arminianism labeled his doctrine of grace as "Pelagian," an exhaustive list should not be necessary. By way of example, though, consider this poignant, but typical, claim of Pierre du Moulin in 1619: "In Arminius we have Pelagius *redivivus.*"[89] Some scholarly literature today still perpetuates the charge of semi-Pelagianism.[90]

Are these epithets historically accurate? Arminius's relevant writings clearly demonstrate that he is no Pelagian.[91] He took great pains to distinguish his views from what he understood to be Pelagius's doctrines.[92] The issue may not be as clear-cut, at least at first glance, when it comes

---

88. See this classification in Dekker, *Rijker dan Midas*, p. 48.

89. Pierre du Moulin, *Anatome Arminianismi*, XXXV.vii, p. 298: "In Arminio habemus redivivum Pelagium" (ET, p. 335). On semi-Pelagianism and Arminius, cf. ibid., XLII, pp. 422–427 (ET, pp. 348–352). See also Gomarus, *Waerschouwinghe*, p. 36, who levels the charge of Pelagianism against his recently deceased colleague. It is also difficult to omit a reference to the droll title of that short book by Daniel Featley, *Parallelismus nov-antiqui erroris Pelagiarminiani* (London: Robert Mylbourne, 1626); ET: *Pelagius redivivus: Or Pelagius Raked out of the Ashes by Arminius and His Schollers* (London: Robert Mylbourne, 1626). Cf. a general discussion of the accusation in Bangs, *Arminius*, p. 338.

90. E.g., Carl Trueman, *John Owen: Reformed Catholic, Renaissance Man*, Great Theologians (Burlington, VT: Ashgate, 2007), p. 27, takes it for granted that Arminianism was "a movement of semi-Pelagian soteriology." The extent to which this might be true of later Remonstrant theology and various movements of "Arminianism" (e.g., English Arminianism) is beyond the scope of this discussion, but at any rate should not be confused with the theology of Arminius.

91. E.g., note the conclusions of Dekker, *Rijker dan Midas*, p. 156: "Vanuit zijn eigen definitie van 'pelagianisme' is zijn theorie [of human freedom] niet pelagiaans." Ibid., p. 176: "Mijn conclusie is derhalve, dat Arminius op dit punt [of grace] geen 'pelagianisme' kan worden verweten." See also Ellis, *Episcopius' Doctrine*, p. 179: "Strong affirmations of the necessity of the Spirit in all aspects of salvation disallow accusations of either Pelagian or Semi-Pelagian theology."

92. See especially *Cap. VII Rom.*, III, in *Opera*, pp. 904–912; *Works* 2: 629–642; *Epistola*, in *Opera*, p. 944; *Works* 2: 700; *Apologia*, art. 29–30 (9–10), in *Opera*, pp. 178–180; *Works* 2: 55–57; *Dec. sent.*, pp. 116–118; *Works* 1: 672–691. See also C. Brandt, *Life*, pp. 68–69. The early Remonstrants (Arminius's theological heirs in Holland) felt the same burden. Because of such accusations aimed at the Remonstrants, Hugo Grotius and Gerardus Vossius engaged in detailed study of Pelagianism and published works vindicating the Remonstrants from this charge. See Israel, *Dutch Republic*, p. 440: "The aim of [Gerardus] Vossius' 800-page *Historia Pelagianismi* (Leiden, 1618) was to prove that Remonstrants were not Pelagians."

to the charge of semi-Pelagianism.[93] "Semi-Pelagianism," which in Arminius's day was a recent neologism, properly denotes the attempt of some fifth-century Gallic monks to reconcile the roles of divine grace and human freedom in salvation, typically carried out in a markedly anti-Pelagian way.[94] Unlike Pelagianism, which is understood to entail a denial of both original sin and the distinction between nature and grace, semi-Pelagianism acknowledges the lingering ill effects of the fall on human nature as well as the need for an internal operation of special grace; but unlike Augustinianism, this saving grace comes in response to the human will. Therefore to the Reformed, who allowed little room for the human will in salvation, Arminius, who granted the possibility of human cooperation in salvation, seemed to be simply a semi-Pelagian *redivivus* whose lip service to Augustinian orthodoxy could not mask his affinities for Pelagianism.

Is this common claim—that Arminius was a semi-Pelagian who granted too much to human free will—warranted? It all depends on how semi-Pelagianism is defined. Arminius noted this ambiguity in his own day. One can easily condemn a doctrine under the pretext of Pelagianism, "if one may invent semi- [that is, half-] Pelagianism, one-fourth Pelagianism, three-fourths, five-twelfths, and thus and so on." He goes on to admit a continuum between a heretical opinion and its absolute opposite, and that whatever contains a lesser degree of heresy is, by definition, closer to the truth, which is often the mean between two extreme opinions.[95] In this passage, Arminius characterizes his opponents' method as nothing more

---

93. F. Stuart Clarke, "The Theology of Arminius," *London Quarterly and Holborn Review* 185 (Oct. 1960): 249–250, refers to semi-Pelagianism as "the most plausible misunderstanding of the theology of Arminius."

94. For more on semi-Pelagianism, see Rebecca Harden Weaver, *Divine Grace and Human Agency: A Study of the Semi-Pelagian Controversy*, Patristic Monograph Series, vol. 15 (Macon, GA: Mercer University Press, 1996); William S. Babcock, "Grace, Freedom and Justice: Augustine and the Christian Tradition," *Perkins Journal* 26/4 (1973): 1–15; S. J. McKenna, "Semi-Pelagianism," in *New Catholic Encyclopedia*, 2nd ed., 15 vols. (Detroit: Thomson/Gale, 2003), 12: 899–901; Augustine M. C. Casiday, "Grace and the Humanity of Christ according to St Vincent of Lérins," *Vigiliae Christianae* 59/3 (2005): 298–314. See also Mathijs Lamberigts, "Le mal et le péché. Pélage: La rehabilitation d'un hérétique," *Revue d'histoire ecclésiastique* 95 (2000): 97–111; idem, "Pelagianism: From an Ethical Religious Movement to a Heresy and Back Again," trans. John Bowden, in *"Movements" in the Church*, ed. Alberto Melloni (London: SCM Press, 2003), pp. 39–48; Susan E. Schreiner, "Pelagianism," in *The Oxford Encyclopedia of the Reformation*, 4 vols., ed. Hans J. Hillerbrand (New York: Oxford University Press, 1996), 3: 238–241.

95. *Apologia*, art. 30 (10), in *Opera*, p. 179; *Works* 2: 56–57.

than a common rhetorical device—attaching Arminius's name to that of a famous heretic (in this case, Pelagius) in order to discredit his teaching.

Besides its negative use as an *ad hominem* argument, semi-Pelagianism can mean something more than a mere insult, and it is legitimate to inquire into Arminius's relationship to this teaching. Although Arminius never offers a direct evaluation of semi-Pelagianism, it is certainly possible to compare and contrast it with his own teaching. Similarities are present, particularly in the attempt to reconcile the necessity of God's grace and humanity's participation in salvation. Indeed, these similarities are common to the vast majority of the Christian tradition.[96] But if semi-Pelagianism means that the will, by nature and external grace alone, can sometimes move positively toward God, and if it thus implies "the priority of the human will over the grace of God in beginning the work of salvation,"[97] then Arminius is no semi-Pelagian.

To be sure, it is possible to find an isolated passage in Arminius and to construe it as a semi-Pelagian sentiment. For example, in an early writing, Arminius considers Matt. 13:12 ("Whoever has, it will be given to him and made to abound") and suggests that God gives "supernatural grace to the one who rightly uses the natural light."[98] Elsewhere, though, Arminius clarifies that "nature, utterly destitute of grace and God's Spirit," cannot move humanity to glorify God, but instead inclines to worldly things.[99] Arminius affirms that fallen humanity requires a prevenient, internal operation of God's grace so that it may be liberated to accept salvation freely.

The very first controversy of Arminius's ministry also concerned this accusation of (semi-)Pelagianism. The typical Reformed view of Romans 7 interpreted the "ego" ("I") as a regenerate Christian who continues to struggle with sin. Instead, Arminius interpreted the "ego" of Romans 7 as a not yet regenerate person, for a Spirit-filled Christian cannot rightly be

---

96. Weaver, *Divine Grace*, p. 69, speaks of "the novelty of the Augustinian position" on grace, which emphasizes the sovereignty of grace to the near exclusion of human participation.

97. This is the "pivotal problem of Semi-Pelagianism," according to McKenna, "Semi-Pelagianism," pp. 900–901. It is debatable whether classic semi-Pelagians, such as John Cassian and Vincent of Lérins, would truly fit this description.

98. *Exam. Perk.*, in *Opera*, p. 754; *Works* 3: 449. Goudriaan, "Arminian Anthropology," pp. 90–91, points to this passage in order to demonstrate Arminius's discontinuity with Reformed theology (at Dordt).

99. *Apologia*, art. 15, in *Opera*, p. 156; *Works* 2: 15.

described as enslaved to indwelling sin (Rom. 7:14, 20).[100] Arminius was not implying that a person can know the good and struggle to do it apart from grace, as his opponents charged. Rather, the "ego" of Romans 7 has received first grace and, through holy despair of keeping the law, is on the way to trusting in Christ for salvation and receiving the grace of regeneration. Not only is his interpretation anti-Pelagian, a point which he explains at length,[101] but throughout his treatise on Romans 7 he appeals to the Christian tradition with numerous quotations to show that his teaching is the historic norm, in line with all the early church fathers, including the early Augustine, as well as many medieval theologians.

Nowhere is his rejection of semi-Pelagianism clearer than when he responds to the charge that he favorably taught the late medieval maxim, "God will deny his grace to no one who does what is in him."[102] This slogan was made famous by followers of William of Ockham, such as Gabriel Biel, who said that God, out of his own liberality, grants "first grace" to the one who does what is in him.[103] Appealing to various biblical passages, Biel explains what it means for one to do what is in him and how God necessarily responds to the human initiative.[104] For Biel, God's positive response is not absolutely necessary but is contingently necessary based on the gracious condition: "If a man does what is in him, God gives grace."[105] As the accusation stands, and as it was explained by Biel, since it omits prevenient grace from the beginning of conversion, this phrase is properly semi-Pelagian.[106] For Biel, grace is not the root, but the fruit, of

---

100. See *Cap. VII Rom.*, I.ii (verse 14).4, in *Opera*, pp. 840–841; *Works* 2: 516–517, passim. Cf. Clarke, *Ground of Election*, pp. 16–19.

101. *Cap. VII Rom.*, III, in *Opera*, pp. 904–912; *Works* 2: 629–642.

102. *Apologia*, art. 17, in *Opera*, p. 158; *Works* 2: 19: "Deus gratiam suam nemini negabit facienti quod in se est."

103. Biel, *Sententiae* II.xxvii q. 1 art. 2 conc. 4: "Quia actum facientis quod in se est Deus acceptat ad tribuendum gratiam primam, non ex debito iustitiae, sed ex sua liberalitate."

104. Biel, *Sententiae* II.xxvii q. 1 art. 2 conc. 4: "Converti ad Deum, appropinquare Deo, aperire illi est facere quod in se est. Convertitur autem Deus ad hominem, appropinquat ei et intrat habitando in eo et cenando cum illo per gratiam, quam infundit." Biel's descriptions allude to Zechariah 1, James 4, and Revelation 3, the last of which (Rev. 3:20) Arminius also used in his description of grace (see above pp. 152–153, 157). Unlike Arminius, Biel, it seems, neglected the part about Christ knocking first.

105. Biel, *Sententiae* II.xxvii q. 1 art. 3 dub. 4: "Si homo facit quod in se est, Deus dat gratiam."

106. On the history and development of this axiom through the early scholastic period, see Artur Michael Landgraf, *Dogmengeschichte der Frühscholastik*, 4 vols. (Regensburg: Verlag

preparatory good works.[107] For this reason, Arminius rejected the statement in question, reiterating that grace must *precede*, as well as accompany and follow, the process of conversion. Instead, on the basis of passages such as Matt. 13:12, Arminius cannot accept the statement as it stands, but, if he is to be charged with it, wishes to drastically modify the original statement to say, "To the one who does what he can through the first grace already conferred on him," God will grant further grace.[108] In other words, what the late medieval maxim lacks is the primary grace that must precede any human impulse toward God. Arminius's insistence on the necessity of first grace is the wedge between his view and Biel's, and Arminius clearly stands on the Reformed-Protestant side of that chasm. Arminius's "modification" of Biel's sentiment comes closer to rejection than retention.[109]

Despite Arminius's clear teachings on the matter, some scholars continue to claim that "human will was central to Arminianism," and that "Arminian theology gravitates toward anthropocentrism."[110] On the contrary, whatever prominence Arminius may seem to grant to free will is motivated by three things, none of which is anthropocentric. First of all, if humanity is not free but determined, then the responsibility for sin

---

Friedrich Pustet, 1952–1956), I/1: 249–264. For its use in the late medieval nominalist Gabriel Biel, see Oberman, *Harvest*, pp. 129–145, who also concludes that Biel is semi-Pelagian (ibid., pp. 177, 426); and Harry J. McSorley, "Was Gabriel Biel a Semipelagian?" in *Wahrheit und Verkündigung*, ed. Leo Scheffczyk, et al. (Munich: Verlag Ferdinand Schöningh, 1967), pp. 1109–1120.

107. Oberman, *Harvest*, p. 141. Cf. ibid., p. 161: "Biel has a high regard for man's natural capacities even outside the state of grace."

108. *Apologia*, art. 15, 17, in *Opera*, pp. 157–159; *Works* 2: 16, 19–20. According to Steinmetz, *Luther in Context*, p. 63, the early Luther attempted to retain some of Biel's formulations and to invest them with new meaning, but he later rejected such formulations as irredeemable.

109. This interpretation appears to differ from that of Blacketer, "Arminius' Concept of Covenant," 205–207, who portrays Arminius's position as "in fact very close to that of Biel." But Arminius's drastic modification of Biel's statement is not an endorsement of it; rather, he has taken the charge as stated against him and demonstrated how the slogan must be completely reworked beyond its original intention in order to represent his own belief. Admittedly, as Blacketer draws the lines, Arminius is closer to Biel when it comes to a resistible operation of grace that is universally (even if counterfactually) available. But this catholic similarity between Arminius and Biel against the Reformed says less about any Pelagian tendencies of Arminius than it says about the peculiar view of grace among the Reformed.

110. Goudriaan, "Arminian Anthropology," p. 105; idem, "Justification by Faith and the Early Arminian Controversy," in *Scholasticism Reformed: Essays in Honour of Willem J. van Asselt*, ed. Maarten Wisse, et al., Studies in Theology and Religion, vol. 14 (Leiden: Brill, 2010), pp. 177–178.

and evil lies elsewhere. Since it is regarded as blasphemous to charge God as the author of evil, then human freedom must be maintained as the primary culprit in sin. Second, freedom is maintained throughout the process of salvation, for grace is intended to perfect and fulfill human nature. The nature of grace as an extravagant, undeserved—yet resistible—gift requires the freedom to reject it. Grace, freely given and freely received (that is, not resisted), is not a coercive power that supplants human nature. Here, though grace and freedom go hand in hand, Arminius is more interested in preserving the nature of grace than in merely promoting the notion of human freedom. Finally, affirming human freedom upholds the mutuality of relationship between God and humanity that is everywhere evident in Scripture. It is a reciprocal and joyous love that characterizes both God's actions toward humanity and the human response enabled by grace. The ground of human freedom is the chief good toward which the human will is created to incline. Thus, God's righteousness, grace, and relational love—all three of which circumscribe human freedom as emphases in Arminius's theology—are central and reveal the decidedly *theological* (not anthropocentric) interest of Arminianism.[111] If Arminius is to be known as a "theologian of freedom," as he is often called,[112] then the deeper motivations beneath the surface must likewise be acknowledged, and he could just as well be called a "theologian of grace."

In sum, there is no question about Arminius's opposition to Pelagianism, and no serious historian or theologian today believes Arminius to be a Pelagian. With regard to semi-Pelagianism, although there are some similarities, the question is answered on historical grounds. Semi-Pelagianism locates the beginning of faith (*initium fidei*) within humanity; Arminianism locates it in God's gift of first grace. What is clear is that Arminius himself rejected semi-Pelagianism, and the burden of proof remains on those who would continue to assert otherwise.

---

111. Cf. C. Graafland, *Van Calvijn tot Barth: Oorsprong en ontwikkeling van de leer der verkiezing in het Gereformeerd Protestantisme* (The Hague: Boekencentrum, 1987), p. 92, who states that, for Arminius, the doctrine of God is revealed in divine grace and righteousness.

112. Thus, Dekker, *Rijker dan Midas*, p. 237. It is not just the opponents of Arminianism who seem to exaggerate Arminius's emphasis on human freedom. E.g., recall the title of the collection of essays marking the four-hundredth anniversary of Arminius's birth: *Man's Faith and Freedom*. In his review of this book, Bangs noted that "the many qualifications with which he [Arminius] surrounded human freedom are ignored." Bangs, "Recent Studies," 428.

## III. Faith and Justification

Though Arminius treats the topics of faith and justification in discrete disputations,[113] it is difficult to treat them separately here, especially in light of the accusations that Arminius's opponents made about the role of faith in his teaching on justification. Before engaging that debate, observe what Arminius says about the nature of faith. It is through faith that sinful humanity becomes united to Christ and enjoys communion with all his benefits.[114] Faith is the "assent of the soul produced in sinners by the Holy Spirit through the gospel . . ., by which they acknowledge Jesus Christ as Savior destined and given to them by God."[115] Justifying faith is a matter of trusting that Jesus Christ is the Savior of those who believe, including oneself.[116] This saving faith comes to sinful humanity as a result of God's call.[117] God calls humanity to salvation by his word, which is communicated either through ordinary human means, such as preaching, or through the extraordinary (and thus atypical) means of direct illumination by the Holy Spirit.[118] However God's word may come to someone and produce saving faith, that faith is produced by the Holy Spirit, whom Arminius calls the "author of faith."[119] As Hicks puts it, faith is not a righteous act of merit, but an active reception of merit.[120]

---

113. Arminius treats the topics of faith, justification, and various issues related to them in *Disp. pub.* XIX, XXXVIII–XL; *Disp. priv.* XLIV–XLVIII; *Dec. sent.*, pp. 123–125; *Works* 1: 695–700; *Apologia*, art. 1–2, 4, 24–27 (4–7) in *Opera*, pp. 135–140, 171–177; *Works* 1: 738–742, 745–750; 2: 42–52; *Quaestiones*, q. 6, in *Opera*, pp. 185–186; *Works* 2: 67 and 70; *Art. non.* XIX, XXII–XXIII, in *Opera*, pp. 960–964; *Works* 2: 723–724, 726–729; *Ep. ecc.* 46, 56, 60, 70–71, and 81; and *Epistola*, in *Opera*, pp. 944–945; *Works* 2: 701–702. See also the discussion in Hicks, "Theology of Grace," pp. 79–106; Stanglin, *Arminius on Assurance*, pp. 95–102, 105–110.

114. *Disp. pub.* XXXIX.14.

115. *Disp. pub.* XXXVIII.1.

116. *Art. non.* XIX.6, in *Opera*, p. 960; *Works* 2: 723.

117. On vocation to salvation, see *Disp. pub.* XVI; *Disp. priv.* XLII. See also Hicks, "Theology of Grace," pp. 42–52; Stanglin, *Arminius on Assurance*, pp. 93–94.

118. *Disp. priv.* XLII.4. Arminius frequently expresses this sentiment, noting that it is common among the Reformed. Cf. *Disp. pub.* XVI.5, 13; XXXVIII.7; *Apologia*, art. 18, in *Opera*, pp. 159–160; *Works* 2: 20–22; with Franciscus Gomarus, *Disputationum theologicarum vigesima-tertia, de fide iustificante*, Henricus H. Geisteranus, Jr., respondens, ad diem 15 October 1603 (Leiden: Joannes Patius, 1603), theses 5–6.

119. *Disp. priv.* XLIV.6.

120. Hicks, "Theology of Grace," pp. 92–93.

Arminius is unwavering in his insistence that faith is a result of God's grace; that is, "Faith is a gracious and gratuitous gift of God."[121] The certainty that accompanies the assent of faith is not produced by rational argumentation but by a supernatural gift from God.[122] Arminius expresses his view of faith as a divine gift in the following analogy (*similis*):

> A rich man gives a poor and famishing beggar alms by which he may be able to sustain himself and his family. Does it cease to be a pure, undiluted gift (*donum purum putum*) because this beggar extends his hand for receiving? Can it be said with propriety (*commode*) that the alms depended partly on the liberality of the one giving and partly on the liberty of the one receiving, though the latter would not have had the alms unless he had received it by extending the hand? Can it be rightly said, because the beggar is always prepared for receiving, that he can by [any] mode will to have the alms or not have it? If these things cannot be truly said, how much less about the gift of faith, for whose receiving many more acts of divine grace are required.[123]

His chief point is that a donation of money, like faith, is still a pure gift, even if the beggar is ready to receive it. Simply to receive alms is not equivalent to deserving or earning it; neither is it a coerced, irresistible deposit into a bank account. Faith is a gift for those who do not refuse it, which becomes a condition of election. As Evert Dekker puts it, for Arminius, "free judgment of the will functions as condition, never as contribution."[124] Arminius acknowledges that the comparison breaks down, and particularly because *more* grace is required than the brief parable indicates. According

121. *Art. non.* XIX.9, in *Opera*, p. 960; *Works* 2: 723. Cf. *Quaestiones*, q. 6, in *Opera*, pp. 185–186; *Works* 2: 67; *Apologia*, art. 4, in *Opera*, p. 140; *Works* 1: 750; *Ep. ecc.* 60, p. 112; *Works* 1: 746 n.

122. *Disp. pub.* XXXIX.4–5.

123. *Apologia*, art. 27 (7), in *Opera*, p. 176; *Works* 2: 52. Luther also describes the recipient of grace as a beggar. See Luther, *De captivitate Babylonica Ecclesiae praeludium*, in *D. Martin Luthers Werke: Kritische Gesamtausgabe*, 66 vols. (Weimar: Hermann Böhlau, 1883–1987), 6: 519. This reference indicates Protestant precedent for Arminius's analogy; it is not to claim that Arminius agreed with Luther on the beggar's "role" in salvation. More proximate to Arminius's intention is Erasmus's analogy of a father helping his son. See Erasmus, *Freedom of the Will*, p. 91. Erasmus offers other analogies in *Freedom of the Will*, p. 79. Dirck Coornhert also employed a beggar analogy. See Dekker, *Rijker dan Midas*, p. 173 n. 51.

124. Dekker, *Rijker dan Midas*, p. 177: "Het vrije wilsoordeel functioneert als voorwaarde, nooit als bijdrage."

to his doctrine of grace, there are other gifts and persuasions that precede this gift of faith and prepare the liberated will to receive it, thus ruling out a semi-Pelagian interpretation of the analogy. That is, when the donor gives and the beggar receives alms (that is, faith), it is neither the first nor the final contact between the two.

Along with communion with Christ and sanctification, justification is an effect of faith. These benefits are the promise of the new covenant in Christ.[125] The doctrine of justification is meant to explain how sinners can stand before God and be considered righteous. For Arminius, justification is God's gracious action of imputing Christ's righteousness to the elect.[126] This imputation, therefore, originates *extra nos* (outside us), not *in nobis* (within us).[127]

Arminius agreed with his Reformed contemporaries regarding the chief points of the doctrine of justification. Arminius could not have stated more plainly that justification does not hinge on good works, whether before or after faith. Good works are not a causal factor in justification.[128] The meritorious and material cause of justification is Christ's righteous obedience.[129] Whether it is Christ's passive obedience only that is imputed, or also his active obedience, Arminius does not dispute.[130] The end, or goal, of justification is the salvation of those justified and the demonstration of divine justice and grace.[131] Arminius, like his colleagues, considered faith to be the instrumental cause of salvation on our part.[132] How that faith functions as a means of justification, though, became a topic of controversy. What does the apostle Paul mean when he writes, "Faith is reckoned [or imputed] for righteousness" (Rom. 4:5)? Franciscus Gomarus and other opponents of Arminius took the phrase as a metonymy to mean that the righteousness of Christ is imputed to us, but Arminius took

---

125. *Disp. priv.* XLVIII.1.

126. *Disp. pub.* XL.7; *Disp. priv.* XLVIII.2.

127. *Disp. pub.* XL.23.

128. *Disp. pub.* XL.11, 13–14; XLIII.11–13.

129. *Disp. priv.* XLVIII.5. Cf. Gomarus, *Theses theologicae de iustificatione hominis coram Deo*, Isaacus Diamantius respondens, 20 March 1604 (Leiden: Joannes Patius, 1604), thesis 11, who has Christ's righteousness and satisfaction as the material cause of justification.

130. *Epistola*, in *Opera*, p. 945; *Works* 2: 701; *Dec. sent.*, p. 123; *Works* 1: 696; *Art. non.* XXIII.4, in *Opera*, pp. 962–963; *Works* 2: 726–27.

131. *Disp. priv.* XLVIII.9. Cf. Gomarus, *De iustificatione*, thesis 15.

132. *Disp. pub.* XL.31; *Disp. priv.* XLVIII.7.

the words of the apostle at face value and said that faith is imputed for righteousness.[133] On the basis of Rom. 4:3, Arminius asserts that, although faith is in one sense the instrument of justification, it is "believing," or faith as an action, that is imputed for righteousness.[134] According to Arminius, though Christ's righteousness is reckoned to us, it does not make sense to say that it is reckoned or imputed *for righteousness*, since what is being reckoned is righteousness itself. Arminius acknowledges that Christ's righteous obedience is reckoned for us and is the foundation of our righteousness; only it is not imputed for righteousness.[135] Arminius agrees with and offers his subscription to Calvin's discussion of this point in *Institutes*, and he is disappointed that his opponents have found his own articulation of this doctrine, given in the very words of the apostle, to be unorthodox.[136] In Arminius's estimation, it is a minor point of disagreement that does not warrant such controversy.

Nevertheless, Arminius's detractors persisted in making it a point of contention. The alleged consequence that his opponents drew from his statement was that Arminius excluded Christ and his righteousness from justification and that justification is attributed to the worthiness of faith.[137] In a similar vein, Aza Goudriaan interprets this debate as evidence that "Arminianism tended to focus on human ability and human free will," and that "the insistence on human activity" means that "the sovereign predestination of God and the work of Christ are both re-defined or put into the background." He goes on to write:

> In this way, Arminian theology gravitates toward anthropocentrism (in the human act of faith) rather than to Theo-centrism (as articulated, for instance, in a sovereign divine predestination of individuals) or Christo-centrism (as expressed, for example, in a justification of believers by imputation of the work of Christ).[138]

---

133. For a survey of this debate, especially reported from the perspective of Gomarus, see Goudriaan, "Justification by Faith," pp. 155–178.

134. Arminius articulates his perspective on this debate in *Epistola*, in *Opera*, pp. 944–945; *Works* 2: 701–702; *Apologia*, art. 24 (4), 26 (6), in *Opera*, pp. 171–173, 175–176; *Works* 2: 42–45, 49–51; and *Dec. sent.*, pp. 124–125; *Works* 1: 697–700.

135. *Epistola*, in *Opera*, p. 945; *Works* 2: 702.

136. *Dec. sent.*, pp. 124–125; *Works* 1: 700.

137. *Epistola*, in *Opera*, p. 945; *Works* 2: 701.

138. Goudriaan, "Justification by Faith," pp. 177–178.

However, quite the opposite is true. As we have already demonstrated, Arminius denies any role for autonomous free choice in salvation, and he insists that the act of believing is a pure, unmerited gift of God's grace. Faith is no work of merit. Indeed, for Arminius, this is the very reason that faith is graciously "imputed" for righteousness, because there is absolutely nothing worthy or righteous originating on the human side. Faith as an action is not the ground of justification.[139] And to the charge that he has removed Christ from justification, Arminius repeats that Christ is the meritorious cause of justification and that God's gracious esteem toward us "is not outside of Christ, but with respect to Christ, in Christ, and because of Christ."[140] Attempts to implicate Arminius as heterodox on the basis of his statements on faith and justification appear to be unsuccessful.[141]

## IV. Union with Christ

The immediate effect of saving faith is union with Christ. For Arminius, the theme of union between God and humanity is of vital importance; he calls it the end, or purpose, of theology. The salvation of humanity and the glory of God are both contained in this ultimate end, humanity's "union with God and Christ."[142] Union with Christ is requisite for salvation, for Christ can communicate his blessings only to those who are united with him.[143] Arminius defines this union as a

---

139. Hicks, "Theology of Grace," p. 100.

140. *Epistola*, in *Opera*, p. 945; *Works* 2: 702.

141. E.g., see the unsuccessful attempt to demonstrate Arminius's doctrine of justification as outside Reformed orthodox bounds in Robert A. Peterson and Michael D. Williams, *Why I Am Not an Arminian* (Downers Grove, IL: InterVarsity Press, 2004), p. 109 (emphasis added): "[Arminius] consistently affirmed that the initiative in salvation is God's, that salvation is a response to God's preceding grace, and that salvation is by grace alone through faith alone. Yet the *faith* that saves (the "*instrumental cause*" of justification) *properly belongs to human beings*. Between the universal love of God for the world and the application of salvation to particular persons stands the active *faith* of the sinner as the *essential determining cause of salvation*." As the documents prove, all the Leiden theologians agreed that faith is the instrumental cause that properly belongs to human beings, even if it is given by God, but no one called faith the "essential determining cause." See Stanglin, *Arminius on Assurance*, pp. 105–110. A particularly stirring example of similar inaccuracies from another author is cited in ibid., p. 240 n. 1.

142. E.g., see *Oratio secunda*, in *Opera*, pp. 49–50; *Works* 1: 362–364; *Disp. priv.* XLII.9. For a fuller discussion of union and communion with Christ, see Stanglin, *Arminius on Assurance*, pp. 103–105.

143. *Disp. priv.* XLV.1.

mystically essential conjunction by which believers—being connected, by God the Father himself and Jesus Christ through the Spirit of Christ and of God, immediately to Christ himself, and through Christ to God—become one (*unum*) with him and with the Father and [become] participants of all his good things, to their own salvation and the glory of Christ and of God.[144]

The connection of redeemed humanity with God is thoroughly Trinitarian, but it is primarily with Christ. Arminius specifies the kind of union he has in mind. Union and communion with God are made possible only because of the incarnation, in which God became human.[145] It involves essence, therefore, inasmuch as believers share the human nature of Christ and appropriate his benefits. At the same time, it is not a combining of God and humanity into one essence or nature, nor is it the absorption of humanity into God. Like a marriage, the union does not destroy the individual essences, but mystically joins Christ and his people (Eph. 5:32).[146] In other words, it is a conjunction, but not a combining, of essences. The benefits of union with Christ begin in this life with the communion or sharing of his benefits. Those in union with Christ participate in the benefits of his death—particularly the abolition of death, sin, and the law—and in the benefits that flow from his new life.[147] This union and its fruits, which are presently experienced by the regenerate, anticipate eschatological fulfillment. The final, ultimate result of this union will be the beatific vision of God in Christ, when God's presence and goodness will be directly accessible to the human understanding and will. "By this union the understanding gazes upon God himself and all his goodness and inestimable beauty, as though face to face with the clearest vision."[148]

## V. Sanctification
### A. Renewed Righteousness

The results of faith and union with Christ are justification and sanctification (the former of which was discussed above in conjunction with faith).

---

144. *Disp. priv.* XLV.3. Cf. *Oratio prima*, in *Opera*, p. 37; *Works* 1: 340.

145. *Oratio prima*, in *Opera*, p. 37; *Works* 1: 340.

146. *Oratio secunda*, in *Opera*, pp. 49, 52; *Works* 1: 362, 367.

147. *Disp. priv.* XLVI–XLVII.

148. *Oratio secunda*, in *Opera*, p. 50; *Works* 1: 362–363.

Sanctification and assurance are topics that are proper to the Christian life. Arminius defines *sanctification* as separation from common use for the sake of divine use, consisting in the mortification of the old person and the vivification of the new. This process involves purification from sin in order that the believer might serve God in newness of life.[149] Arminius endorses the "third use of the moral law," directed toward the regenerate as a rule for godly living.[150] He describes good works as deeds done by the regenerate—or those whom God is moving toward regeneration—through the operation of the Holy Spirit.[151] God remains the primary cause of good works, with regenerate humans cooperating as the secondary efficient cause.[152] God's people do not perform good deeds in order to be justified or to accrue merit before God.[153] Nevertheless, though good works play no causal role in justification, there are many reasons for doing good: these works are done (1) for the glory of God; (2) for our own good, to make ourselves more certain of our faith and election, rendering our calling firm; and (3) for the good of our neighbors, both believers and unbelievers.[154] On these causes and reasons for good works, Arminius's colleagues in Leiden were in agreement with him.[155]

Recall that Arminius, like the Western tradition before him, distinguished three conditions of humanity and freedom: prelapsarian innocence, subsequent corruption, and renewed righteousness. In the state of corruption, humanity is completely dead in sin. In the third state of regeneration, however, Arminius was more optimistic than his opponents about the efficacy of sanctification. All Reformed theologians agreed that a change occurs in regeneration, but Arminius described free choice in the regenerate state as "far different" from the state of corruption. No longer can a regenerate person be described as "enslaved to sin" (Rom. 7:14). It is called a state of "renewed righteousness" because the original righteousness

---

149. *Disp. priv.* XLIX.1, 5, 9–10.

150. *Disp. pub.* XII.5. Arminius deals with the topic of good works in *Disp. pub.* XLII–XLV; *Disp. priv.* LXX–LXXIX; *Apologia,* art. 15–17, and 29 (9), in *Opera,* pp. 156–159 and 178–179; *Works* 2: 14–20 and 55–56; *Quaestiones,* q. 9, in *Opera,* p. 186; *Works* 2: 68; *Ep. ecc.* 81; *Works* 2: 70–71; and *Art. non.* XXIV, in *Opera,* p. 964; *Works* 2: 729.

151. *Disp. pub.* XLIII.1; *Apologia,* art. 16, in *Opera,* p. 157; *Works* 2: 17.

152. *Disp. pub.* XLII.3–4.

153. *Disp. pub.* XLII.13; XLIII.11–13.

154. *Disp. pub.* XLII.10. In *Disp. pub.* XII.5, Arminius enumerates nine reasons for doing good.

155. E.g., see Lucas Trelcatius, Jr., *Disputationum theologicarum quarto repetitarum vigesima-septima de bonis operibus et meritis eorum,* Ricardus Janus Neraeus respondens, 4 March 1606 (Leiden: Joannes Patius, 1606).

that had been lost has now returned, and the consequent sanctification is produced by the Holy Spirit. Having now received "new light and knowledge of God and of Christ and of the divine will," having been stirred by "new affections, inclinations, and motives," implanted with "new powers," "freed (*liberatus*) from the kingdom of darkness," this regenerate person now "loves and embraces what is good, righteous, and holy."[156] Arminius reminds his readers that the work of regeneration and illumination is gradual, not completed in one moment, and that, just as the beginning of all good is from God through his Spirit, so is the continuance and perseverance in good the gift of the Spirit.[157] Although he admits that it is strictly possible for the regenerate to fulfill the moral law perfectly in this life,[158] Arminius does not leave the impression that such perfection actually happens often, if at all. Rather than spending time debating the possibility of perfection, however, Arminius would prefer Christians to spend their energy encouraging one another to strive toward the mark of perfection.[159]

## B. Possibility of Apostasy

Arminius acknowledged perseverance in the sense that the truly elect will persevere in their saving faith to the end. The question is whether he thought a person with true, saving faith could lose that faith, or could sin in such a way as to fail to persevere and thus forfeit his or her salvation. Because of its relationship to the topic of sanctification (and assurance, below), this question of the possibility of apostasy is worth pursuing briefly.

A few readers of Arminius remain agnostic regarding his view of apostasy, for Arminius himself was ambiguous at times, indicating his own need for more study of the issue. But most scholars agree that Arminius taught that true believers can fall away. There remains some debate, though, about Arminius's view of how this happens and whether the

---

156. *Disp. pub.* XI.12.

157. *Disp. pub.* XI.13–14.

158. *Art. non.* XX.4, in *Opera*, p. 961; *Works* 2: 724–725. See also the discussion in *Quaestiones*, q. 9, in *Opera*, p. 186; *Works* 2: 68; *Dec. sent.*, pp. 116–118; *Works* 1: 672–691, where Arminius shows his concurrence with Augustine on this matter.

159. *Apologia*, art. 29 (9), in *Opera*, p. 179; *Works* 2: 56. For a fuller discussion of the state of the regenerate and Christian perfection, see Stanglin, *Arminius on Assurance*, pp. 120–130.

fallen can ever be brought back to salvation.[160] Taking the entire body of his writings into account, it is clear that Arminius assumed that true believers can fall away, and that, in most cases, they can be brought back.

One should observe two important sets of distinctions when it comes to apostasy. The first distinction is that between the possibility and the actuality of apostasy. Arminius explicitly acknowledges that it is strictly possible for a true believer to fall away, and he never publicly denies that apostasy actually happens. In the most famous passage on this topic, found in the *Declaration of Sentiments*, Arminius denies that he ever publicly *taught* that final apostasy *actually* happens. When pressed to *speculate* whether it does actually happen, Arminius equivocates. But he never denies the *possibility* of apostasy. It is true that the common English translation of Arminius's *Declaration of Sentiments* has him denying even the possibility, but this is an unfortunate addition into the text that is represented neither in the Latin (the basis of James Nichols's English translation) nor in the Dutch original. The second distinction to be observed is between the elect and the believer. Arminius defines the *elect* as a believer who perseveres; therefore, every elect person is a believer, but not every believer is elect. A true believer (*simpliciter*) might not persevere, and thus would not be elect. In the end, there is really little question that Arminius believed in the possibility of apostasy for a true believer, and he even gave biblical examples to show that it has actually happened.[161]

How, then, does a once sincere believer forfeit salvation? What conditions must obtain for apostasy to become actual? The most obvious way for a believer to apostatize is by rejecting the faith and renouncing Christ explicitly, thus becoming an unbeliever.[162] If, as Arminius taught, a person has a say in her faith, and salvation may rightly be described as not resisting the grace which is by definition resistible, then a person may at any time resist that grace. One need only recall the energy with which Arminius insisted that for grace to be grace, it must be resistible. Arminius's famous beggar analogy may be illustrative. To make the point that faith is a pure gift

---

160. E.g., Stephen M. Ashby, "A Reformed Arminian View," in *Four Views on Eternal Security*, ed. J. Matthew Pinson (Grand Rapids, MI: Zondervan, 2002), pp. 137, 180–187, who claims to hold the views of Arminius himself, claims that true believers can lose salvation only by renouncing faith, after which they cannot be restored.

161. On these distinctions, see *Dec. sent.*, p. 115; *Works* 1: 667; *Apologia*, art. 1–2, in *Opera*, p. 136; *Works* 1: 741–742; *Quaestiones*, q. 8, in *Opera*, p. 186; *Works* 2: 68. Cf. Stanglin, *Arminius on Assurance*, pp. 132–134.

162. E.g., see *Exam. Perk.*, in *Opera*, pp. 758–762; *Works* 3: 455–460.

from God, Arminius said that a beggar reaching out his hand to receive freely has not thereby earned the alms received. To extend this analogy, a beggar could refuse the alms initially or at any time after receiving the gift. The gift is resistible at the beginning of the conversion process, and at every step along the way after conversion. But it is still a gift, even if it is retained.

Granting that Arminius unequivocally taught that faith, the acceptance of which is the primary condition of election on the human side, can be renounced, resulting in the loss of salvation, it is important to examine whether a person can sin in such a way as to lose salvation. Some interpreters grant the notion of apostasy through renunciation of faith but deny that Arminius would allow for other sins to affect one's status before God. Contrary to this opinion, however, there are three pieces of evidence that indicate that Arminius did believe that certain sins of commission could result in apostasy.

First, there are clear passages in which Arminius connects certain sins of commission with apostasy, particularly using the example of David as an illustration. David clearly committed grievous sins without explicitly renouncing his faith; yet, according to Arminius, he fell and needed restoration.[163] Second, as noted above, Arminius distinguishes four different motivations for sin, the worst of which causes a fall from grace. This sin he designates as arising "out of malice" (*ex malitia*). Whether such a sin of apostasy can be forgiven depends on the object of malice. If the sin arises out of malice for the law and causes one to fall away, it is forgivable. If the sin, however, arises out of malice for Christ, the consequent apostasy is unforgivable.[164]

Third, Arminius observes that sinful deeds arising from malice indicate a lack of actual saving faith, even if the habit (*habitus*) of faith is present. This point reveals that the root problem is the lack of faith, but this lack of faith is manifest in malicious sins of commission.[165] In a sense, then, it is true, as Arminius says, that believers, as long as they remain believers, cannot lose salvation. But these passages from Arminius indicate that certain sins are inconsistent with saving faith. These sins either lead to or, perhaps more precisely, reflect the absence of active faith (even if the *habitus* remains present). Arminius is clear that some who fall away,

---

163. *Exam. Perk.*, in *Opera*, pp. 763–764; *Works* 3: 463–464; *Disp. pub.* XI.14; *Art. non.* XXI.3; *Works* 2: 725.

164. *Disp. pub.* VIII.5; *Ep. ecc.* 45, pp. 93–95; *Works* 2: 743–750.

165. *Ep. ecc.* 81, p. 151; *Works* 2: 70; *Exam. Perk.*, in *Opera*, pp. 763–764; *Works* 3: 463–464.

like David and Peter, can be brought back from apostasy to repentance and a state of forgiveness.[166] Others, like Judas, who was malicious against Christ himself, cannot be restored.[167]

## C. Justification and Sanctification

In light of Arminius's affirmation of the possibility of apostasy, what is the relationship between justification and sanctification? One option bases sanctification entirely on the past event of justification. This option puts all the focus on justification, which could result in a reductionistic view of sanctification. Such a view ends up collapsing sanctification into justification. A person is thought to be sanctified enough, simply by virtue of justification. Perhaps another way of considering this view is that sanctification is completely severed from justification, and there is no relationship between the two. In any case, this reductionistic view of sanctification expects little or no progress in Christian holiness. If unchecked, this perspective could produce the kind of presumptuous security against which Arminius warned. This is expressed popularly as "once saved, always saved."

A second way of thinking about the relationship between justification and sanctification is to base justification on sanctification. This option makes sanctification a pre-condition for justification; one is justified by virtue of sanctification. Some interpreters have mistakenly attributed this view to Arminius. But Arminius rejected this option for at least two reasons. First of all, the apostle Paul states that we are saved by grace through faith, created in Christ Jesus to do good works (Eph. 2:8–10). In other words, good works are not a causal factor in obtaining or maintaining salvation. We are already saved; therefore, we want to do good works, and we do them. Arminius agreed that justification cannot be conditioned on good works.[168] Second, if assurance is based on the quality and quantity of good works, then one will never be assured. This perspective could produce a feeling of despair that can be summarized as "once saved, barely saved." For this and other reasons, Arminius did not base justification on sanctification.[169]

---

166. Arminius makes it clear that one can fall away and be restored through repentance and forgiveness. See *Disp. pub.* XI.14; *Ep. ecc.* 45, pp. 92–93; *Works* 2: 740 and 742–743; *Exam. Perk.*, in *Opera*, p. 759; *Works* 3: 456.

167. For a fuller discussion of apostasy, see Stanglin, *Arminius on Assurance*, pp. 130–139.

168. E.g., see *Disp. pub.* XII.5.

169. Contra J. V. Fesko, "Arminius on Union with Christ and Justification," *Trinity Journal* n. s. 31 (2010): 219, who claims that, for Arminius, "Justification hinged upon the believer's

Instead, a balance must be sought. Just as justification is predicated on faith, sanctification must also be based on faith. Arminius declared that they are both effects of faith. The relationship is this: faith is the link between justification and sanctification. As a resistible gift of God's grace, faith is the condition of election and justification, and it is a necessary part of sanctification. Final justification is realized in time for the one who perseveres in faith.[170] As Arminius noted, it is when active faith ceases in the life of sanctification that a person's salvation is in jeopardy. Sin out of weakness can be consistent with active faith; sin out of malice is not. The motivation of the heart is the key. The criterion for sanctification is not the *quantity* of good works, but their *motivation*—holiness being pursued out of true faith and fervent love. This faith is one that works, as the Epistle of James reminds us.

## VI. Assurance

Broadly speaking, there are two kinds of questions one can ask about salvation. On the one hand, when one asks about objective, factual matters of salvation—what salvation is, how it is accomplished, how I can be saved—these are questions about the ontology of salvation that divine revelation addresses. On the other hand, when one asks the more subjective question about assurance of one's own salvation—how I can know that I am saved—this is an epistemological question. The objective matter of fact has become the existential question of the individual before God. Here Scripture also provides some answers, but given the uniqueness of each individual, the epistemological, existential question is between that individual and God, and it can become a significant pastoral problem.

Protestant churches in general, and Reformed Churches in particular, considered themselves to be restoring true assurance of salvation to God's people. The opening question of the Heidelberg Catechism is but one striking illustration of the importance of personal assurance in Reformed theology: "What is your only *comfort* in life and death?"[171] In general, for

---

sanctification." He goes on to imply that, for Arminius (as for N. T. Wright), "the ground of final justification" is "the Spirit-wrought works of the believer" (ibid., 222). Rather, Arminius observed that final justification is manifest for the one who perseveres in "faith," not works. *Disp. priv.* XLVIII.12.

170. *Disp. priv.* XLVIII.12.

171. Zacharias Ursinus and Caspar Olevianus, *The Heidelberg Catechism*, Q & A 1, in Schaff, *Creeds of Christendom*, 3: 307–355 (emphasis added).

the Reformed, assurance is based on the doctrine of God's unconditional election and his gift of perseverance. "Getting in" is not based on good works, and neither is "staying in." God's sovereign election is irrevocable, and he will save whom he chooses. Salvation is in no way dependent on the fallible believer, and that should be reassuring. As we will see, however, such assurance was often elusive.

## A. Pastoral Problems with Reformed Soteriology

*Certitudo*, or certainty, was the standard Latin term that denoted assurance. Certainty (*certitudo*) of salvation may be defined as assurance of one's personal salvation made in one's heart by the Holy Spirit. When it came to this certainty, or assurance, in the context of Reformed soteriology, Arminius observed two pastoral problems during his ministry in Amsterdam, which he referred to as the two "pests of religion and of souls," and the "two fiery darts of Satan."[172]

The first problem was that many people in Arminius's Amsterdam congregation had no confidence in their election. They feared for their salvation, lacking that divine comfort they desired in life and in death. Arminius recounts the story of parishioners to whom he ministered during the outbreak of the plague in Amsterdam in 1602. He visited the homes of two separate people, each of whom, deathly ill, was suffering spiritual torment from lack of assurance of salvation. Arminius described both sufferers as true believers who, of all people, should have rested assured in their salvation. Yet, at this crucial time when they needed assurance most, they could not find it.[173]

Arminius called this the state of *wanhope* (Dutch) or *desperatio* (Latin), that is, as both words literally mean, "despair" or "lack of hope."[174] Despair is the very state of mind to which the Roman Church's penitential system supposedly led, the hopelessness that Martin Luther was trying to escape and that Protestant churches were seeking to assuage. How could Christians, who were saved not by their own goodness but by Christ's imputed righteousness, ever fall victim to despair?

---

172. *Disp. priv.* XLIII.8; *Dec. sent.*, p. 93; *Works* 1: 637. Cf. *Disp. priv.* XXXIX.9, where Arminius calls these "the two greatest evils to be avoided in all religion."

173. *Ep. ecc.* 56, pp. 106–107; *Works* 1: 176.

174. See Arminius's description in *Dec. sent.*, p. 93; *Works* 1: 638.

For Arminius, the problem lies first with the Reformed conviction that saving faith includes not only knowledge and assent, but also *fiducia*, or confident assurance. In other words, assurance is, by definition, thought to be a necessary component of saving faith.[175] Under this assumption, if a person has belief in Christ as Savior, and believes that Christ's righteousness may be imputed to him by faith, and the person desires this salvation, but only lacks certainty of that salvation, then the person may begin to question his faith altogether, and wonder whether he is one of the elect. After all, if a person seems to be missing a key component of saving faith—assurance—then she would doubt the strength of her conviction and would tend to despair. Arminius contested this assertion that led Christians to despair. Instead, he distinguished assurance (*fiducia*) from faith (*fides*), declaring that assurance follows as the ordinary result of saving faith, but is not necessarily simultaneous with faith.[176]

But what about when doubts creep in and assurance is weak? The typical Reformed response is that faith can be weak in this life, and since assurance (*fiducia*) is part of faith, then it is no surprise that assurance can be weak as well. This response provides little consolation, however, because of a second doctrine—the doctrine of temporary faith, as taught by Calvin and other Reformed theologians. Even the reprobate can have a temporary faith that can appear genuine to themselves (that is, not hypocritical) and can resemble the true faith of the elect. It is the great correspondence between temporary and true faith that undermines assurance so thoroughly. Calvin asserted that a person could seem to others to have faith, indeed could think himself to possess saving faith, when it was really only a faith temporarily granted by God that was not meant to persevere but instead would be withdrawn by God. The person who appeared to fall away was never elect in the first place, but only possessed temporary faith. The common biblical example is Simon Magus (Acts 8), whose belief was soon shown to be fraudulent. Such a person is self-deceived, and, despite all present appearances to the contrary,

---

175. E.g., Gomarus, *De fide*, theses 7–10, who makes *fiducia* a necessary part of faith.

176. *Ep. ecc.* 70, p. 134; *Works* 1: 176–177 n.; *Disp. pub.* XXXVIII.1; XXXIX.3; *Disp. priv.* XLIV.5. For a fuller discussion of *fides* and *fiducia* in Arminius, see Stanglin, *Arminius on Assurance*, pp. 98–100. Muller, "Priority of the Intellect," 55–72, examines the intellectualist inclination of Arminius's soteriology and sees Arminius's separation of *fiducia* from the definition of faith as an indication of his intellectualism. The Thomistic influence of soteriological intellectualism would, of course, fit well with his intellectualist view of the divine life (see chapter 2).

lacks genuine faith. Thus, one can never be assured that the present sense of faith is genuine.[177]

When combined with a third doctrine—the doctrine of unconditional reprobation—this undermining of assurance can be devastating. The Reformed doctrine of unconditional election claims that God chooses whom God wills to save, based not on their good works, their foreseen faith, or even their willing assent. The necessary corollary to this election is that God unconditionally reprobates, or perhaps "passes over," the remainder of humanity, the result of which is condemnation. The only way to escape condemnation is to be chosen by God. But, as Arminius observes, since that election is (apart from God's absolute and sovereign will) unconditional, there is nothing that reprobates can do to be in a saved relationship with a God who has not chosen them.[178]

Therefore, at best, on the Reformed account, one can have only probable assurance of final election. The doctrine of unconditional reprobation, combined with the acknowledgment of the category of temporary faith, undermines assurance and leads to despair. Since humans cannot peer into the secret will and decrees of God, it is impossible to know for sure that we are elect and not simply self-deceived by temporary faith. At certain moments in life, most Christians can easily wonder whether they are saved, and perhaps be persuaded that they are not. From a Reformed perspective, if one ever doubts one's election or suspects temporary faith, there is little recourse. With the type of despair produced by the late medieval Roman Church, the people could conceivably be satisfied with more good works. In a Reformed context, however, such people might conclude that they are unconditionally reprobate, leading to an inescapable despair that provides no hope of salvation, and giving little reason for them to attempt to be saved. As the saying goes, "Damned if you do; damned if you don't."

In addition to the problem of despair, the second problem that Arminius witnessed was the exact opposite of the first. In his opinion, many believers were over confident of their own salvation. Once again, Arminius appealed to his pastoral experience. He recalled times when he admonished Christians

---

177. On the Reformed doctrine of temporary faith, see Stanglin, *Arminius on Assurance*, pp. 182–187; David Foxgrover, "'Temporary Faith' and the Certainty of Salvation," *Calvin Theological Journal* 15/2 (1980): 220–232.

178. *Dec. sent.*, p. 87; *Works* 1: 632.

to abandon their sinful ways and repent, only to be reminded by his parishioners that sin is always a part of the Christian life, even for Paul (as the
typical Reformed interpretation of Romans 7 would have it), and that one
should not care much, since God would be gracious.[179]

Arminius called this state *sorgloosheyt* (Dutch) or *securitas* (Latin), that
is, as both words mean, "security" or "lack of care."[180] The word literally
means "carelessness," including the idea of neglecting something that
really does deserve attention. *Security*, a term that in the Christian tradition
normally had negative connotations of negligence, presumption, and ar-
rogance, was increasingly used by Reformed theologians in a novel way to
indicate a positive virtue.[181] Like so many other Christians before and after
him, such a careless attitude frustrated Arminius during his time as a
pastor and preoccupied him for years to come. He considered arrogant
security to be even more dangerous in the Reformed Churches than the
problem of despair. What prompted this common mind-set of security in
Reformed Churches? How did it get to this point?

It is to be expected that a movement that was reacting against a lack of
assurance of salvation, in its attempt to restore true assurance, could fall into
the opposite danger of overemphasizing confident certainty. Like the first
problem of despair, this tendency toward security is the result of the distinctive combination of three Reformed teachings. The first point concerns the
efficacy of sanctification. For the Reformed, although the regenerate person
can make steps toward sanctification with the help of the Holy Spirit, they
are baby steps; progress is minimal. The standard Reformed interpretation
of Romans 7, read as the autobiographical account of the regenerate apostle
Paul, supports the notion that sin is an ongoing and prominent struggle in
the Christian life. Having comparatively little expectation of personal sanctification could imply that sin is in some sense normal and, therefore, not of
grave concern to the individual Christian. For his part, Arminius contested
this reading of Romans 7, interpreting the person weighed down with sin
as someone not yet regenerate, because sin cannot dominate the life of a
regenerate person, as is described in this passage.[182]

---

179. *Cap. VII Rom.*, V.i.2, in *Opera*, p. 921; *Works* 2: 659–660.

180. See Arminius's description in *Dec. sent.*, p. 93; *Works* 1: 637.

181. This historical sketch is provided in Stanglin, *Arminius on Assurance*, pp. 152–173.

182. *Cap. VII Rom.*, V.i.2, in *Opera*, p. 921; *Works* 2: 659.

The second Reformed doctrine that led to security is unconditional election, along with its corollary of irresistible grace. After all, if one is elect from eternity, and if that election has no condition on the human side, there is nothing that can be done in time to separate the elect from the love of Christ. If one is confident in one's election, then salvation is secure. What's more, if it is wrong to doubt one's election and virtuous to be confident, and if assurance is a component of faith, then it may yet be more virtuous to be more confident.

Unconditional election and irresistible grace can promote security, especially when combined with a third doctrine, the perseverance of the saints, which is a predictable corollary of unconditional election. If a person becomes part of God's chosen covenant people by *irresistible* grace alone, apart from good works, then no amount of evil works or lack of good works can nullify that election and covenant. According to Arminius, if one affirms the impossibility of apostasy, this doctrine does not console as much as it engenders carelessness with regard to sin, which, for Arminius, is a dangerous indication of "carnal security" (*securitas carnalis*).[183] Therefore, the normalcy of sin in the Christian life, along with the doctrines of unconditional election and eternal security, could foster an attitude of "saved if you do; saved if you don't." This lack of concern over the presence of sin is the very thing that could precipitate a fall.[184]

The attitude of thinking of oneself as hopelessly reprobate or, conversely, sitting securely in sin while grace abounds, is not the pastoral aim of Reformed theology. But Arminius was serious about these attitudes being the fair implications of Reformed soteriology. Though they may not be the intended outcomes, they are the logical outcomes. And if these consequences are validly inferred, then there is something wrong with the theology. As Arminius himself said, "Nothing can be true from which a falsehood may by good consequence be concluded."[185] For example, Arminius thought supralapsarianism to be erroneous, among other reasons, because it implies that God is the author of sin, though the Reformed denied this

183. *Art. non.* XXII.4–5, in *Opera*, p. 962; *Works* 2: 726.

184. For a full discussion of *desperatio* and *securitas*, see Stanglin, *Arminius on Assurance*, pp. 149–193.

185. *Cap. VII Rom.*, in *Opera*, p. 825; *Works* 2: 490. Cf. *Dec. sent.*, p. 61; *Works* 1: 609.

implication.[186] Likewise, Reformed soteriology, with its combination of distinctive doctrines, is flawed because it leads people to believe that there is
nothing they can do to affect their salvation, either positively or negatively.
Such a belief justifiably places one in either despair or security, and it is not
enough simply to point out the dangers.[187] For Arminius, something must
change.

## B. Assurance as a Point of Departure

It should be clear, then, how important the doctrine of assurance was to
Arminius, and how it became a point of departure for some of his more
well-known teachings. Not that assurance was his sole concern or that it
was anything like the center of his theology, but it was a pressing, pastoral
problem that motivated him to reexamine the theological assumptions
connected to it and to articulate a doctrine of God, creation, and predestination that promotes a healthy, more balanced assurance of salvation. For
example, Arminius claimed that a correct doctrine of predestination
should lead to a balanced perspective on assurance. He wrote, "There is
great use for this doctrine [of predestination] handed down from the Scriptures. For it serves to establish the glory of God's grace, to comfort afflicted
consciences, to upset the impious and drive away their security."[188] In
other words, the solution will require more than simply a word of encour-
agement to the desperate or a word of admonition to the secure, more
than a superficial bandage. The problem is with the doctrines that lead to
these wrong attitudes. Hence, Arminius's theological concerns cannot be
understood fully without giving attention to the practical concerns that
sometimes motivated and always informed them.

The pivotal, practical question at stake with assurance concerns one's
relation of dependence: On what is a person dependent? Despair is

---

186. See Gomarus's denial of this charge in *Disputationum theologicarum decima-quarta, de
libero arbitrio*, Samuel Gruterus respondens, 19 March 1603 (Leiden: Joannes Patius, 1603),
thesis 10: "Unde sequitur eum [Adamum] nulla coactione aut necessitate ad peccandum
adductum fuisse, cum aliter agere potuerit si voluisset; sed causam propriam et per se in
voluntate ipsius positam fuisse." See also *Exam. Gom.*, pp. 153–154; *Works* 3: 654.

187. Such typical warnings gained confessional status in the Church of England's Thirty-
Nine Articles. See *Articuli XXXIX. Ecclesiae Anglicanae. A.D. 1562*, art. XVII, in Schaff, *Creeds
of Christendom*, 3: 497–498.

188. *Disp. pub.* XV.14.

grounded in nothing, based on no foundation, and is therefore the absence of hope (*wanhope/desperatio*). Security is grounded on something, but it is a *false* thing, an inadequate foundation. Unlike despair, which signifies a lack of hope, the secure person relies on a false hope, a hope that is misplaced (*sorgloosheyt/securitas*). To place hope on a false foundation is no better than to have no foundation at all. Both tendencies undermine true assurance. Security, though, is worse than despair, for a secure person does not know that the foundation is misplaced and false, remaining blissfully unaware of the dangerous condition. For Arminius, the goal is to avoid both of these extremes and to ground one's hope on something solid. What does true assurance look like? On what is it grounded?

## C. A Posteriori Grounds of Assurance

Arminius delineated four testimonies of salvation that could bolster a person's assurance. They function as grounds of assurance for the Christian who is sick with despair or negligent in security. They are not the ultimate foundation of *salvation*, but we may name them legitimate grounds of *assurance* inasmuch as they bear witness to and confirm one's salvation. They are a posteriori in the sense that they are pieces of evidence that point back to the ontological reality of salvation, just as good fruit bears witness to the quality of a good tree.[189]

The first such mark is the sense of faith (*sensus fidei*). Faith is a simple sign of a person's election. People should ask themselves if they have faith. If the answer is affirmative, and if such faith is a gift of God to the elect, then they can rest assured of their election, for God saves believers. To express it logically, "God will save believers. I believe. Therefore, God will save me." This simple introspective exercise is the so-called "reflex act of faith," and is a form of a classic practical syllogism (*syllogismus practicus*) that became prominent among the Puritans.[190]

The second a posteriori ground of assurance is the internal testimony of the Holy Spirit (*internum testimonium Spiritus sancti*). The Spirit of God bears witness in our hearts that we are his children, enabling us to cry out "Abba, Father" (Rom. 8:15–16). This adoption as God's children is one of

---

189. On these a posteriori testimonies, see Stanglin, *Arminius on Assurance*, pp. 198–213.

190. For an instance of Arminius using this in a pastoral situation, see *Ep. ecc.* 56, p. 107; *Works* 1: 178.

the benefits that flows from the union and communion of believers with Christ.

The third testimony of salvation is the struggle (*lucta*) of the Spirit against the flesh, a prominent theme in Arminius's writings. The fact that one wrestles with worldly temptations, and is not completely overcome without a fight, is a sign of the sanctifying grace of God. This struggle with sin, which could conceivably lead a person to discouragement, is interpreted instead as an indication of a healthy spiritual life that is seeking righteousness.

The final indication of salvation is the desire to engage in good works (*bona opera*). This testimony is the external counterpart to the internal struggle against the flesh. The true child of God wants to show love to neighbors; this is the proper effect of faith.

These four testimonies of salvation are not distinct to Arminianism. Reformed contemporaries of Arminius appealed to the same four marks of salvation to confirm and assure one's election.[191] The difference between the two camps lies especially in the a priori assumptions about the God who grounds salvation and its assurance.

## D. A Priori Ground of Assurance

These four a posteriori testimonies are never described as the foundation of salvation; they are simply grounds for assurance, answering the epistemological question. Because they are subjective to the inquirer, the extent of certainty provided by these testimonies may fluctuate. In his search for

---

191. Cf. the substantially identical lists of Arminius and Gomarus. Cf. *Disp. pub.* XXXVIII.15: "Hanc autem Fidem vere fideles habere se sciunt. 1. Ex ipso sensu Fidei, quod docent insignia attributa et nomina, quibus insignitur Fides in Scripturis. Tribuitur enim illi πληροφορία, παρρησία, πεποίθησις, dicitur ὑπόστασις, ἔλεγχος, quae fidei non competunt, si credens ignoret se credere. 2. Ex Spiritus Sancti in illis habitantis testimonio, testatur enim una cum spiritu nostro quod sumus Filii Dei. At Filii Dei non nisi per Fidem in nomen Christi sumus. 3. Ex lucta Fidei cum dubitationibus et spiritus cum carne. [4.] Denique ex effectis spei et charitatis erga Deum et proximum, operumque ex illa charitate promanantium." And *Disp. pub.* XXXIX.16: "tum minorem pro certa habemus, non modo ex fidei ipsius sensu, et testimonio tum Spiritus S[ancti] testificantis et conscientiae nostrae, sed etiam ex lucta fidei in dubitationibus, illiusque victoria, et tota vita nostra." With Gomarus, *De fide*, thesis 20: "Hac fide iustificante qui sunt praediti, etiam se ea praeditos esse certo cognoscere possunt, et ex certis hisce τεκμηρίοις cognoscunt: Primum est *Internum* Spiritus Sancti *Testimonium*; Secundum *Verus* ipsius fidei *Sensus*, credens enim scit se credere; Tertium *Mutua* Carnis et Spiritus *lucta*, Quartum *Omnia* Posteriora et pleraque etiam Priora fidei *Effecta*; posito enim Effectu ponitur causa." In *Disp. pub.* XXXVIII.16, Arminius also lists many signs that are contrary to saving faith.

assurance between the two extremes of despair and careless security, Arminius turned his attention to a matter that is fundamental, a priori, and not subject to fluctuation, namely, the doctrine of God. The significant distinction between Arminius and his Reformed contemporaries begins here, with their contrary views of God and his intentions for creation. As it turns out, theology proper has an enormous impact on the doctrine of salvation.[192]

In several places throughout his writings, Arminius assumes two objects of the divine will, and therefore, the divine love: (1) God primarily loves himself and the good of righteousness (or justice); and (2) he secondarily loves the creature and its blessedness.[193] God's love for himself is not a kind of egoism; the affirmation simply recognizes that God always inclines toward the good, and primarily toward the chief good.[194] The origin of this notion goes back to Thomistic intellectualism, wherein the will is directed toward the intellectually known good. By implication, not only does God incline toward his own goodness, but creation, the communication of God's goodness, is also an object of God's willing. Therefore, God's will inclines toward himself first, and toward other things second. Creation is not a primary end in itself or on an equal plane with God, but it does enjoy status as a secondary end within the will of God, who wills and enjoys the blessedness of the creature. In other words, God's will tends toward himself and his creation, and since God's will is loving, his love inclines toward himself and his creation. Arminius calls this the twofold love of God (*tweederley liefde Godes*).[195]

The Reformed are more reluctant than Arminius to describe God's affection toward the whole human race as "love." For Arminius's opponents, God's loving will does not extend to all humanity for the purpose of salvation. His will concerning election and the basis of this will are inscrutable. This assumption is especially prominent in the supralapsarian form, in

---

192. On the a priori grounding of assurance, see Stanglin, *Arminius on Assurance*, pp. 213–231.

193. *Disp. pub.* IV.67; XII.4; XVII.4; *Disp. priv.* XX.4–5; *Art. non.* II.3–5, in *Opera*, p. 949; *Works* 2: 707; *Dec. sent.*, pp. 90–94, 110; *Works* 1: 634–638, 656; and from his final conference in The Hague (August 1609), reported by Hommius, in Wijminga, *Hommius*, Bijlage G, pp. xii, xiv.

194. E.g., *Disp. pub.* IV.50: "The supreme good (*summum bonum*) is the first, foremost, and direct object of the divine will."

195. On God's twofold love, see Stanglin, *Arminius on Assurance*, pp. 89–91, 219–231. Cf. Den Boer, *God's Twofold Love*, pp. 154–166.

which God creates the reprobate only as a means for their destruction. Arminius disagrees when he writes, "God's first action toward some object, whatever it may be, cannot be its casting away or reprobation to eternal misery."[196] Rather, God loves good before hating evil, and hates evil only because he first loves good.[197] God has freely—not of necessity—obliged himself to creation as an object of his loving will. Although God has the ability per se to create in order to reprobate, he relinquishes the right or authority to ordain harm for the creature unless justified by the creature's sin.

According to Arminius, God's love of righteousness and his love of the creature have priority in his will and decree, but the love of righteousness comes first. As such, God hates no creature, except because of sin.[198] Just as God antecedently wills all humanity to be saved, but consequently wills to punish unbelievers, so his antecedent love is for the salvation of all, but, after sin, his saving love is consequently directed toward those who are in Christ through faith. Although all are not consequently saved, all are equally loved antecedently by God for the purpose of eternal fellowship.

Arminius appeals to Heb. 11:6 as a reflection of God's twofold love of righteousness and the creature, and as a guard against the two fiery darts of Satan—security and despair. The passage declares that God rewards those who seek him out. On the one hand, if one truly believes that God will reward only those who seek him, a belief based on God's love of righteousness, which is greater than his love of the impenitent creature, then seeking God is encouraged and careless security is prevented. On the other hand, if one truly seeks God, one should not despair, because God has promised the reward to seekers. The believer who seeks God has no need to worry about a secret will (*voluntas arcana*) of God to reprobate, for God is eager to reward the faithful. The divine *beneplacitum* is God's "good pleasure," which Arminius defines as God's "benevolent affection."[199] Whereas the Reformed place the cause of both election and reprobation in the divine *beneplacitum* (good pleasure) and appeal to mystery concerning God's will to elect and reprobate,[200] Arminius declares that God's desire to save all

196. *Exam. Gom.*, p. 76; *Works* 3: 590.

197. See *Exam. Gom.*, p. 59; *Works* 3: 574–575.

198. *Art. non.* II.4, in *Opera*, p. 949; *Works* 2: 707.

199. *Disp. pub.* XV.4.

200. E.g., see Kuchlinus, *De divina praedestinatione*, theses 15, 21.

people is well-known because it has been revealed in Christ. For assurance, one need only look to Christ and the God of love and grace that he reveals.

Once again, it is the doctrine of God's nature that shapes Arminius's soteriology. The Dutch scholar C. Graafland admits that, vis-à-vis Reformed theology, Arminius introduced a "deeply radical variation" of the doctrine of God.[201] In sum, Arminius's claim is that God's act of creation is a free act of love and grace for the purpose of eternal communion, an act in which God obliges himself to creation for its benefit. His love of the creature, however, is second only to his love of justice, with the result that he will never condemn a believer or ignore the sins of the impenitent unbeliever. With this affirmation about God, believers may rest assured that God loves them, genuinely desires their redemption, and has promised to save them.

Finally, it is worth summarizing the contrast between the Arminian and the Reformed accounts of assurance. The Reformed, once assured, should have a kind of permanent assurance, a final assurance that election renders a fall impossible. The problem, as Arminius has shown, is that such assurance is difficult if not impossible to attain, particularly since God's desire for the salvation of any given individual cannot be assumed, and the matter is inscrutable. The a posteriori testimonies mean little if God does not desire one's salvation. The divergence between the competing visions is rooted in the doctrine of God.

As with the Calvinist, the Arminian also may not have final assurance of what the future holds, but, according to Arminius, the decisive advantage is with regard to present assurance. For the Arminian, one point is indubitable and unassailable: God loves each person for the purpose of eternal fellowship and desires the salvation of all. The divine "yes" that initiates and completes the process of salvation is, by God's grace, answered by the human "yes." Agnosticism about the future state of one's faith should not undermine present assurance. On an Arminian account, this fact should not be troubling, for this is how every other relationship in life is handled. For example, despite one's intentions and vows, one cannot absolutely guarantee permanent commitment to a spouse in the future or know with certainty one's own level of commitment to that spouse fifteen years from this moment, any more than one can know such things about one's commitment to God. Yet this does not undermine present assurance. It is enough to know oneself to be committed right now and that one

---

201. Graafland, *Van Calvijn tot Barth*, pp. 92-93.

has a say in the relationship, that there is no intention of shirking the commitment, and that God will help a person remain faithful.

In summary, Arminius discerned and described two common dangers with respect to assurance, both of which were more than theoretical, for he witnessed them as prevalent in Reformed Churches. His attempt to chart a middle way between despair and careless security, to reinstate a healthy doctrine of assurance in the church, is worthy of consideration. Arminius reminds us that not only can we look to the fruit of the Spirit in our lives, but we can look primarily to the God who has created us for eternal communion, accomplished redemption in Christ to reconcile us, and provided grace through the Holy Spirit to draw us into his presence. According to Arminius, proclaiming the truth about God and his works of love through Christ in creation and predestination will lead to this salutary assurance.

## VII. Conclusion

For Arminius, human nature has lost the original righteousness in which it was created, and each of its parts has been tainted by sin. As a result, fallen humans are utterly unable to save themselves and are completely helpless without God's prevenient and subsequent grace. Humanity's so-called "free will" to turn to God is more accurately described as a "freed will," liberated by God's grace to receive faith. Faith is a pure, undeserved gift from God. As such, in the words of one theologian, it is time to "drop the charges" of Pelagianism against Arminius.[202] At the same time, underscoring that humanity is a willing recipient of that divine grace and faith, Arminius left space for responsiveness in the divine-human relationship. The relationship is one of mutuality; God takes the initiative, but salvation is a cooperative process. God desires the salvation of all; nothing can prevent the demonstration of God's mercy except a refusal to repent.[203] Arminius's dissent from Reformed theology was, in part, a reaction against the increasingly prevalent doctrine of unconditional predestination, as well as what he perceived as its practical effect—an aberrant doctrine of the assurance of salvation that resulted in either unwarranted security or hopeless despair. Arminius sought to articulate a doctrine of salvation that encouraged both true assurance and a desire to progress in sanctification.

---

202. McGonigle, "Arminius and Wesley," p. 100.

203. *Dec. sent.*, p. 92; *Works* 1: 637.

# Conclusion

*In our Arminius you have a living representation of that*
*scribe who was instructed in the kingdom of heaven, con-*
*cerning whom the Lord Jesus mentions in Matthew [13:52],*
*who as the opulent head of the household, brings forth*
*from his treasury things new and old.*

—ÉTIENNE DE COURCELLES, 1645

IN MANY CHRISTIAN circles, Jacob Arminius and the impact that he
had on Protestant theology remain completely unknown. In other contexts,
the term "Arminianism" is ubiquitous, though it is rarely accompanied by
engagement with the writings and thought of Arminius himself. In fact,
"Arminianism" often bears little resemblance to the views of Arminius,
but instead is taken broadly to include such versions of anti-Calvinism as
semi-Pelagianism or open theism. The aim of this book has been to present Arminius's thought to those who have not sufficiently known or have
simply misunderstood his most enduring theological contributions. This
brief story is not complete, though, without a survey of the subsequent history of Arminianism, including a summary of his thought and his legacy.

## I. The Rest of the Story
### A. Remonstrance and the Synod of Dordt

When Arminius died on 19 October 1609, the controversy surrounding his
theology did not die with him. The Twelve Years' Truce signed in 1609
between Spain and the United Provinces of The Netherlands seemed to give
the new country fresh energy for the battle within. Even before his death, the
controversies among the theological faculty at Leiden had spread through the
churches of The Netherlands like wildfire, sparked from the pulpits especially by the opponents of Arminius. In the early months of 1609, the printing
press, like a frenzied gale whipping a growing fire, ensured that the controversies would not be contained. Arminius's and Gomarus's disputations on

predestination (from five years earlier) were collected and printed together, translated for the first time from Latin into the Dutch vernacular.[1] This publication was the first shot fired in a pamphlet war carried out for the next decade between the followers of Arminius and his opponents.[2]

On 14 January 1610, less than three months after Arminius's death, forty-four supporters of Arminius's theology among the Dutch Reformed Church signed a statement of remonstrance, or protest, known thereafter as the Remonstrance of 1610.[3] This brief document laid out five articles which, though controversial, they believed are true and biblical and thus ought to be tolerated within the Reformed Church. These articles may be summarized as follows:

1. God chose to save through Jesus Christ all those who through grace would believe in him and persevere to the end.
2. Jesus Christ obtained forgiveness of sins sufficient for all.
3. Fallen humanity can think or do nothing that is truly good by free will.
4. God's grace, which is not irresistible, is necessary for thinking or doing any good.
5. True believers are enabled by grace to persevere to the end, and it may be possible to lose this grace.[4]

These points are consistent with the views of Arminius; indeed, some come verbatim from his *Declaration of Sentiments*. Those who signed this Remonstrance and others who supported its theology have since been known as Remonstrants.

The following year, 1611, a conference met at The Hague to allow the opposing sides to discuss the Remonstrance and to work toward resolving their differences. But the primary outcome was the opposition's rebuttal

---

1. Jacobus Arminius and Franciscus Gomarus, *Twee disputatien vande goddeliicke predestinatie* (Leiden: Jan Paedts Jacobszoon, 1609).

2. This pamphlet war is detailed in Van Itterzon, *Gomarus*, pp. 151–189; and Michael Abram Hakkenberg, "The Predestinarian Controversy in the Netherlands, 1600–20" (Ph.D. diss., University of California at Berkeley, 1989), pp. 320–379. Cf. G. Brandt, *History*, 2: 54–55, 68; Bangs, *Arminius*, pp. 322–323; Otterspeer, *Bolwerk*, p. 245. Israel, *Dutch Republic*, p. 439, has interesting statistics on the pamphlet publications.

3. Hoenderdaal, "Inleiding," p. 37 (along with other secondary sources) puts the number of signatories at forty-four. But Uytenbogaert, *Kerckelicke historie*, p. 529, lists forty-three and states that more signed the document in the following days.

4. See *Articuli Arminiani*, in Schaff, *Creeds of Christendom* 3: 545–549. Cf. the full text in Uytenbogaert, *Kerckelicke historie*, pp. 524–529.

to the five articles of the Remonstrance, and those opponents became known in the controversy as Counter-Remonstrants.[5] The Remonstrance and Counter-Remonstrance set the tone and agenda for other conferences and publications of the next decade. Along with Uytenbogaert, the most prominent leader of the Remonstrant party was Simon Episcopius (1583–1643), former student of Arminius and his successor at Leiden University.[6] Episcopius would be the leading voice of the Remonstrants at the national Synod of Dordt (Dordrecht, 1618–1619).

While at Leiden University, Arminius himself had called for a council to discuss the disputed issues within the church. Regional *classes* were not resolving the debates.[7] During his speech on religious divisions in 1606, Arminius had laid down ground rules that he hoped would prevail in the council. The Synod of Dordt, which came nearly a decade after his death, was not what he envisioned. The Counter-Remonstrants, now supported by Prince Maurits, summoned the council to discuss issues of church polity (particularly, issues of state and church, as well as commissioning a new Bible translation) and doctrine. The Remonstrants were invited to the synod not as equal participants, but as accused defendants. By the end of the deliberations in 1619, they were dismissed as false teachers, removed from their positions in the churches, and expelled from the country.[8]

The Canons of the Synod of Dordt again mirrored the five topics raised in the Remonstrance of 1610. In the canons, the synod offered its positive doctrine along with the rejection of the errors of the Remonstrants.[9] The original intention for the canons was simply to respond to the five articles

---

5. For a summary of The Hague Conference (1611) and previous scholarship on it, see Den Boer, *God's Twofold Love*, pp. 211–217.

6. On Episcopius, see Calder, *Memoirs of Episcopius*. G. J. Hoenderdaal, "Arminius en Episcopius," 203–235, compares and contrasts Arminius and his former student.

7. On Dutch church polity and synods, see Kooi, *Liberty and Religion*; Israel, *Dutch Republic*, pp. 367–372.

8. For more on the Synod of Dordt, see *Works* 1: 541–579; G. Brandt, *History*, vol. 3; Calder, *Memoirs of Episcopius*, pp. 265–368; De Jong, ed., *Crisis in the Reformed Churches*; G. J. Hoenderdaal, "De kerkordelijke kant van de Dordtse Synode," *Nederlands theologisch tijdschrift* 23/5 (1969): 349–363; Israel, *Dutch Republic*, pp. 433–477; Goudriaan and Van Lieburg, eds., *Revisiting the Synod of Dordt*.

9. See the canons in Schaff, *Creeds of Christendom*, 3: 550–597. And see the acts of the synod in *Acta synodi Dordrechti*; ET, *Articles of Dort*. See also the *Sententiae Remonstrantium*, in *Acta synodi Dordrechti*, trans. in *Crisis in the Reformed Churches*, ed. De Jong, pp. 221–229. The acronym "TULIP," the so-called five points of Calvinism, is a later English-language innovation and does not correspond exactly to the five heads of doctrine at Dordt.

of the Arminians. But since subscription to the canons immediately became compulsory for ministers (and even church staff, such as organists), the canons quickly evolved into a confessional standard that, along with the Belgic Confession and Heidelberg Catechism, comprises the third component of the Dutch Church's "three forms of unity."[10] Because the synod had delegates from other regions throughout Europe where the Reformed faith was strong, it had an international impact beyond The Netherlands as a statement of absolute predestination against all forms of conditional predestination. As for the Dutch Remonstrants, they maintained their community and, once permitted to return to The Netherlands, established their seminary in Amsterdam with Episcopius as its first professor of theology.

By the late seventeenth century, the Remonstrant Church had imbibed the spirit of Enlightenment rationalism as well as doctrinal latitudinarianism. Although there is some debate regarding the degree to which later Remonstrant thought was anticipated by Arminius, no one doubts the striking discontinuity between the theological assumptions, methods, and outcomes of Arminius and later Remonstrants such as Philip van Limborch.[11]

## B. Anglo-American Arminianism

Something closely akin to the theology of Arminius was also part of the Anglican communion. Although any direct links to the influence of Arminius himself are hard to trace and in the end of dubious importance, such theology is often labeled "Arminian."[12] The Thirty-Nine Articles of the Church of England (1563/1571) affirm predestination (Art. XVII), but nothing

---

10. On this process from judgment to confessional status, see Donald Sinnema, "The Canons of Dordt: From Judgment on Arminianism to Confessional Standard," in Goudriaan and Van Lieburg, eds., *Revisiting the Synod of Dordt*, pp. 313–333.

11. Hicks, "Theology of Grace," pp. 12–21, argues for sharp discontinuity. Ellis, *Episcopius' Doctrine*, pp. 182–185, is willing to see some of the discontinuities anticipated in Arminius. Cf. Lambertus Jacobus van Holk, "From Arminius to Arminianism in Dutch Theology," in Gerald O. McCulloh, ed., *Man's Faith and Freedom*, pp. 27–45; G. J. Hoenderdaal, "The Debate about Arminius Outside the Netherlands," in *Leiden University in the Seventeenth Century: An Exchange of Learning*, ed. Th. H. Lunsingh Scheurleer and G. H. M. Posthumus Meyjes (Leiden: Brill, 1975), p. 142.

12. See the definition of English Arminianism in Nicholas R. N. Tyacke, *Anti-Calvinists: The Rise of English Arminianism c. 1590–1640*, Oxford Historical Monographs (Oxford: Clarendon Press, 1987), p. 245: "It does *not* mean that the Dutch theologian Jacobus Arminius was normally the source of the ideas so labeled. Rather Arminian denotes a coherent body of anti-Calvinist religious thought, which was gaining ground in various regions of early seventeenth-century Europe. Arminianism itself can plausibly be understood as part of a more widespread philosophical skepticism, engendered by way of reaction to the dogmatic certainties of the sixteenth-century Reformation." Cf. Hoenderdaal, "The Debate about Arminius," p. 143: "The debate about Arminius was primarily held in England."

in the language rules out a conditional or broadly "Arminian" understanding of the doctrine. Indeed, the openness of Article XVII to various kinds of interpretation can be seen to account for the statements of the Lambeth Articles (1595) and the Irish Articles of Religion (1615). The Lambeth Articles teach a decidedly "Reformed" doctrine of predestination, and the fact that they are put forward as an addition to the Thirty-Nine Articles is an indication that Article XVII was not seen as "strong" enough to ensure Reformed theology and to rule out "Arminian" views. The presence of "Arminianism" in the Church of England was widespread and pervasive, and while some of these theologians followed more closely the trajectory of later Remonstrants such as Limborch than that of Arminius himself, other elements of Anglican "Arminian" theology were close to that of Arminius.[13]

Another type of Arminianism without direct links to Arminius himself is the Methodism of John and Charles Wesley. John and Charles, both of whom were Anglican until their deaths, serve as exemplars of a kind of Arminianism prevalent within the Anglican Church.[14] Like anti-Calvinists before them, the Wesley brothers reacted against "the horrible decree" of God as described by Calvin. Though they had no genealogical relationship to Arminius, early Methodist theologians consciously took up the Arminian mantle. John Wesley even called his magazine *The Arminian*.[15]

---

13. Disputes about predestination were carrying on in England before Arminius had any influence. E.g., see Peter Baro, *Summa trium de praedestinatione sententiarum*, in *Ep. ecc.* 15, pp. 29–32; *Works* 1: 91–100; Stanglin, "Arminius *avant la lettre*," 51–74. The rise and degree of Arminian dominance within the Anglican Church has been debated. See Tyacke, *Anti-Calvinists*; idem, "Debate: The Rise of Arminianism Reconsidered," *Past and Present* 115 (1987): 201–216; Peter White, "The Rise of Arminianism Reconsidered," *Past and Present* 101 (1983): 34–54; idem, "The Rise of Arminianism Reconsidered: A Rejoinder," *Past and Present* 115 (1987): 217–229; idem, *Predestination*. For emphasis on the period following the Restoration, see Stephen Hampton, *Anti-Arminians*. For the Arminian influence among eighteenth-century Presbyterians, see David Steers, "Arminianism amongst Protestant Dissenters in England and Ireland in the Eighteenth Century," in Th. Marius van Leeuwen, Keith D. Stanglin, and Marijke Tolsma, eds., *Arminius, Arminianism, and Europe*, pp. 159–200. For a more general survey, see Geoffrey F. Nuttall, "The Influence of Arminianism in England," in Gerald O. McCulloh, ed., *Man's Faith and Freedom*, pp. 46–63. See also Carl O. Bangs, "'All the Best Bishoprics and Deaneries': The Enigma of Arminian Politics," *Church History* 42 (1973): 5–16.

14. As noted by Hosea Hewitt, "Influence of James Arminius on Modern Religious Thought," *Methodist Review* 5th series, vol. 15 (September 1899): 792, Methodism would have been impossible under the domination of Calvinism.

15. Wesley never cited Arminius or claimed to have read him, but he encouraged others to do so, he read other Anglican theologians who read Arminius, and he probably was directly influenced by *Declaration of Sentiments*. See Alfred H. Pask, "The Influence of Arminius on John Wesley," *London Quarterly and Holborn Review* 185 (October 1960): 258–263; W. Stephen Gunter, "John Wesley, a Faithful Representative of Jacobus Arminius," *Wesleyan Theological Journal* 42/2 (2007): 65–82. Gunter argues for the overall faithfulness of Wesley's thought to Arminius's distinct soteriology.

In a sense, the Wesleys and later Wesleyan theologians were closer than the later Remonstrants to the evangelical thought of Arminius himself, who rejected all Pelagianism, insisting on salvation by grace alone through faith alone and the total inability of humanity to be saved. In fact, many of the early theologians of the Wesleyan movement held and defended a more robust doctrine of original sin than did Arminius himself (and certainly more so than the later Remonstrants). For where Arminius had insisted upon the corruption of original sin while denying guilt (strictly speaking, human sinners are guilty for what they *do*), John Wesley takes a different line. He defends the federalism of the Westminster Confession in insisting that Adam is a "public person" who made a "covenant" for himself and for his posterity.[16] As Barry Bryant points out, "In a well-known letter to John Newton dated 14 May 1765, Wesley indicated that there was not a 'hair's-breadth' separating him from Calvin" with respect to the doctrine of sin.[17] He insists that any denial of the doctrine of original sin "saps the very foundation of all revealed religion."[18] Many important theologians of early Methodism echo Wesley on this point: Richard Watson, Thomas Ralston, Luther Lee, Samuel Wakefield, and William Burt Pope (among others) resolutely deny all forms of both Pelagianism and semi-Pelagianism, and they all endorse federalist accounts of the doctrine of original sin.[19] The situation changes within Methodist theology in the latter part of the nineteenth century as John Miley

---

16. John Wesley, "The Doctrine of Original Sin," in *The Works of John Wesley*, vol. 9 (Grand Rapids, MI: Zondervan, n. d.), pp. 261–262.

17. Barry E. Bryant, "Original Sin," in *The Oxford Handbook of Methodist Studies*, ed. William J. Abraham and James E. Kirby (Oxford: Oxford University Press, 2009), p. 534.

18. Wesley, "Original Sin," p. 194.

19. E.g., Richard Watson, *Theological Institutes: Or, a View of the Evidences, Doctrines, Morals, and Institutions of Christianity*, vol. 2 (New York: N. Bangs and J. Emory, 1826), p. 215; Thomas N. Ralston, *Elements of Divinity: A Concise and Comprehensive History of Bible Theology; Comprising the Doctrines, Evidences, Morals, and Institutions of Christianity; with Appropriate Questions Appended to each Chapter* (New York: Abingdon Press, 1847), pp. 123–127; Luther Lee, *Elements of Theology: Or An Exposition of the Divine Origin, Doctrines, Morals, and Institutions of Christianity* (Syracuse: A. W. Hall, 1853), pp. 117–118; Samuel Wakefield, *A Complete System of Christian Theology: Or, A Concise, Comprehensive, and Systematic View of the Evidences, Doctrines, Morals, and Institutions of Christianity* (Cincinnati: Cranston & Stowe, 1858), pp. 292–293; William Burt Pope, *A Compendium of Christian Theology: Being Analytical Outlines of a Course of Theological Study, Biblical, Dogmatic, Historical*, 3 vols., 2nd ed. (New York: Hunt and Eaton, 1889), 2: 62–63. Lee's version is actually a mixture of federalism and a mediate account. Cf. Hynson, "Original Sin," 65–83.

and others come closer to Arminius's own position in holding that original sin is corruption only.[20] But this is not to be confused with Pelagianism or semi-Pelagianism, for all humanity has lost original righteousness, is corrupt by nature, is guilty for (actual) sins, and is always dependent upon divine grace to have freedom and power to choose the good. The conclusion of Wesley is appropriately descriptive: all who deny original sin "are but heathen still, in the fundamental point which differences [sic] heathenism from Christianity."[21]

The major theologians of the Wesleyan tradition also affirmed belief in the universal and prevenient grace of God as well as a conditional doctrine of predestination, and they were in continuity with Protestant doctrines of justification and regeneration.[22] For example, Wesley emphasized that "faith is the *necessary* condition of justification"—indeed, it is "the *only necessary* condition thereof."[23] In similar fashion, Wesleyan theologians insisted upon the gratuitous and genuine reality of the new birth.[24] In these ways they were largely consistent with the theology of Arminius himself.[25] The continuing theologies of classical Methodists and theologians of the holiness movement carry forward this legacy.[26]

In addition to Wesleyanism, many Christians from Baptistic (for example, General, Free Will, and many Southern Baptists) and Restorationist (for example, Stone-Campbell) traditions have long been inclined toward

---

20. E.g., John Miley, *Systematic Theology*, vol. 1 (New York: Methodist Book Concern, 1892), pp. 429–528. Cf. Henry C. Sheldon, "Changes in Theology among American Methodists," *American Journal of Theology* 10 (1906): 31–52.

21. John Wesley, *Fifty-two Standard Sermons* (Salem, OH: Schmul Publishing, 1988), p. 456.

22. E.g., see Kenneth Collins, *The Scripture Way of Salvation: The Heart of John Wesley's Theology* (Nashville, TN: Abingdon, 1997); Thomas C. Oden, *John Wesley's Scriptural Christianity: A Plain Exposition of His Teaching on Christian Doctrine* (Grand Rapids, MI: Zondervan, 1994), pp. 277–309.

23. John Wesley, "Justification by Faith," in *Fifty-two Standard Sermons*, p. 49. See the discussion in Collins, *The Scripture Way of Salvation*, pp. 69–100.

24. E.g., John Wesley, "The Scripture Way of Salvation," in *Fifty-two Standard Sermons*, pp. 438–447. Cf. Collins, *The Scripture Way of Salvation*, pp. 101–130.

25. Cf. Olson, *Arminian Theology*, pp. 179–220.

26. Among the theologians of the twentieth-century holiness movement, see the work of H. Orton Wiley, *Christian Theology*, 3 vols. (Kansas City: Beacon Hill Press, 1940); A. M. Hills, *Fundamental Christian Theology: A Systematic Theology* (Pasadena: C. J. Kinne, 1931); H. Ray Dunning, *Grace, Faith, and Holiness: A Wesleyan Systematic Theology* (Kansas City: Beacon Hill Press, 1988); J. Kenneth Grider, *A Wesleyan-Holiness Systematic Theology* (Kansas City: Beacon Hill Press, 1994).

Arminianism. Sometimes this theology is adopted in explicit awareness of the history of the Arminian and Remonstrant controversies and in conscious agreement with the theology of Arminius.[27] But very often there is little or no dependence upon, or even awareness of, the tenets and arguments of Arminius himself.[28] Perhaps in consequence, the terms "Arminian" and "Arminianism" have come to be applied to a vast range of views and ecclesial groups. In many cases, "Arminianism" simply means rejection of the Reformed doctrine of predestination. In some instances, the "Arminian" theology is refined and sophisticated; in others, it may be ill-formed and vague. Sometimes the theology espoused under the label of "Arminianism" bears little or no resemblance to that of Arminius— sometimes, especially at more popular levels, what is claimed as "Arminian" may be explicitly inconsistent with the theology of Arminius. If "Arminian" simply means some version of Protestantism that is not Reformed, then surely many theologies and ecclesial bodies count as such. But such a way of reckoning is insufficient; Lutheran theologians, for example, are neither "Arminian" nor "Reformed." On the other hand, if the theology of Arminius himself has any real connection with the term, then it is highly doubtful that, say, open or process theism, or views that deny the "classical" doctrine of God or the doctrines of original sin or justification by grace alone through faith alone (or many others) could rightly be considered "Arminian," despite the fact that, in popular understanding, such views may often be regarded as forms of Arminianism. Such diversity of "Arminian" theologies calls for a moment's reflection. Perhaps there are few neat and tidy answers to questions of definition. Without such definition, however, the label is not likely to be helpful in current discussions.

## C. Did Arminius "Lose"?

It is common for the opponents of Arminianism to point out that the judgment of history shows that Arminius, or at least Arminians, "lost" at the Synod of Dordt in 1618–1619. Of course, it is not possible that Arminius himself lost anything at Dordt—all that he "lost" was his battle with tuberculosis ten years earlier. A plausible case might be made that, had Arminius not died

---

27. E.g., see the work of Matthew Pinson, F. Leroy Forlines, Jack Cottrell, and John Mark Hicks.

28. Cf. Gerald O. McCulloh, "The Influence of Arminius on American Theology," in *Man's Faith and Freedom*, pp. 64–87.

prematurely, the decade leading up to the synod, and the national synod for which Arminius had hoped, would have turned out differently.[29] Such counterfactual reconstruction need not detain us here, but the salient point remains: *Arminius* did not "lose" the debate to his opponents. Of course, it is true that the national synod sided with his opponents and against the Remonstrants. But even here the situation is fairly complex. They clearly lost the vote, but the Remonstrants would claim that they lost due to political factors and manipulation, rather than on purely intellectual grounds (the Reformed, of course, held a different opinion of the situation); in other words, all they "lost" was a vote that was influenced by gamesmanship and political intrigue.[30]

Arminians would claim that they "lost" in the same sense that any other unjustly persecuted Christian group has lost. Such loss is gain. In retrospect, with the subsequent spread of Arminius's ideas throughout the Protestant world (whether or not those ideas came "from" him in any genealogical sense), one would be hard-pressed to substantiate the claim that he "lost."[31] Interestingly, even some Christians who are committed to Reformed ecclesial bodies will admit that the theology of Arminius should have been retained as a legitimate theological option and perhaps is theologically superior to the conclusions put forth by Dordt. Alvin Plantinga, for instance, recognizes that his very influential statement of the "Free Will Defense" to the problem of evil (as well as important aspects of his broader metaphysics of modality) bears very strong similarities to Arminius's theology.[32] When the "Arminian" elements of his philosophical theology are pointed out to him, he agrees: "That's substantially right."[33] Plantinga continues by opining that the Synod of Dordt simply made a mistake: "As for my view of the Synod of Dordt, I think that the Arminians should be thought of as Calvinists. They thought of themselves as Calvinists. The synod declared that they weren't, but this was probably a mistake

---

29. Gomarus and other Counter-Remonstrants were bolder in their opposition after Arminius's death. See *Works* 1: 78; Bangs, *Arminius*, p. 248.

30. Israel, *Dutch Republic*, p. 441: "The Arminians won the intellectual battle but lost the political."

31. As observed long ago by Johann Lorenz von Mosheim, *Institutiones historiae Christianae recentioris* (Helmstedt: Christ. Frid. Weygand, 1741), p. 630: "This is most certain, that after the time of the council of Dordt, the [Genevan sentiments] began to pass away (*fluere*) and to sink (*labi*) more and more."

32. Alvin Plantinga, *The Nature of Necessity* (Oxford: Oxford University Press, 1974).

33. Alvin Plantinga, "The Philosophy of Religion," in *God's Advocates: Christian Thinkers in Dialogue*, ed. Rupert Shortt (Grand Rapids, MI: Eerdmans, 2005), p. 53.

on the part of the Reformed or Calvinist community."[34] We need not endorse Plantinga's claim that the early Arminians should be considered Reformed to see the important point: it still may be argued that the theological proposals of Arminius seem to be "winning" the intellectual battle, even within some sectors of Reformed life and thought.

## II. Arminius the Theologian
### A. Summary of Key Themes

Arminius is situated in a long line of thinkers who have dealt with the most important questions of Christian theology and have attempted to communicate intelligible solutions to the people of their day. He also stands at the head of a theological trajectory that has had an enormous and abiding influence on Protestant Christianity. As we offer final reflections on Arminius's theology and legacy, we observe some recurring themes that continue to surface. Anyone who knows a little about Arminius will recognize predestination as one of these themes. But it is not the only one. This volume has revealed the many other aspects of his theology that not only shaped, but were also shaped by, his contested doctrine of predestination. One way to summarize Arminius's thought is to consider three motivating factors that drove his soteriology, all of which were at the same time deeply theological and pastoral.

First, Arminius sought to reconcile divine grace and human freedom. What is the relationship between divine sovereignty and the lives and destinies of humans? God is not passive and uninvolved with his creation, but neither are humans blocks of stone that have no will. If someone emphasized one side of the dialectic over the other, Arminius was there to bring the balance back. But what is the positive solution? This question is connected to all of his discussions of providence and predestination, including his articulation of middle knowledge.[35] He admitted that, if he could solve these problems, it would be worth more to him than the riches of King Midas.[36]

---

34. Alvin Plantinga, "The Philosophy of Religion," p. 53.

35. Dekker, *Rijker dan Midas*, p. 1. The question of grace and freedom is also what motivated Molina to articulate middle knowledge in the first place, as part of his *Liberi arbitrii cum gratiae donis, divina praescientia, providentia, praedestinatione et reprobatione concordia*.

36. *Ep. ecc.* 19, pp. 34–35.

Another motivating factor for Arminius, connected in many ways with the first, was the problem of evil, or, to put it another way, theodicy. Particularly important for Arminius in this respect is his concern for the glory and goodness of God. That God is not the author of sin is Arminius's constant assertion against his opponents' apparently deterministic, or at least inevitable, divine decree of the fall. But, given God's sovereignty, foreknowledge, and freedom in creating, to what degree is God responsible for sin? Whenever Arminius discussed the good pleasure (*beneplacitum*) and justice (*iustitia*) of God or the free will and contingency of human decision, this question of theodicy and its resolution was occupying Arminius's thoughts. Hoenderdaal claims that this issue "was the point of departure for Arminius and for Episcopius."[37]

Third, the assurance of salvation was an issue that motivated much of Arminius's dissent from the dominant Reformed positions. In his ministry he witnessed too many instances of both despair and carnal security, problems he viewed not as exceptions but as logical consequences of Reformed teachings. His teachings on the nature of God's love and grace, predestination, and the Christian life of sanctification were all shaped in part by his belief that godly assurance must navigate between the Scylla and Charybdis of hopelessness and carelessness.

These three motivating factors are points of departure, not foundations per se or central dogmas. They cannot bear the burden of explaining or determining everything about Arminius's system of theology.[38] What they do explain is how Arminius arrived at some of his conclusions and why he defended those conclusions so fervently. These motivating factors also confirm that Arminius was engaged in the same theological problems as the Christian tradition before him, especially the Western stream in the wake of Augustine. The answers he formulated to these pivotal questions (though not all theological questions) are consistent with a trajectory that runs from Irenaeus through Origen, Aquinas, and Molina, in contrast perhaps to the line from Augustine through Aquinas, Calvin, and Bañez. The upshot is that, on these key points of departure, Arminius came out with quite different answers

---

37. Hoenderdaal, "Arminius en Episcopius," p. 230: "Dit was het uitgangspunt van Arminius en van Episcopius." See also the analysis of God's justice provided in Den Boer, *God's Twofold Love*.

38. Den Boer, *God's Twofold Love*, comes as close as anyone to proposing such a dogma. He calls *iustitia Dei* the "all-determining leading motive" for Arminius's theology (p. 279), and claims that *iustitia* is "in the entire structure of Arminius's theology the fundamental concept. . . . God's essence is characterized by justice" (p. 325).

than most of his Reformed contemporaries. We may summarize the distinctive areas of Arminius's theology (vis-à-vis Reformed theology) in three points
which, once grasped, also summarize the content of the Arminian debate.
These three distinctive points hang together for Arminian theology, even as
their contraries logically cohere for Reformed theology. And each of these
three following points is rooted in the doctrines of God and creation.

First of all, Arminius stresses that God's act of creation is the communication of good only, intended for the creature's good. The act of creating
was God's first demonstration of free grace. Love means to will the good
of another; God, as holy love, created humanity for the purpose of eternal
communion with him. Arminius's Reformed colleagues could not express
God's purpose so plainly. According to his opponents, God does not love
all people for the purpose of salvation. In some Reformed accounts, a
great part of humanity was created for the purpose of destruction. In other
accounts, they were simply passed over with no hope or divine intention
of salvation. But for Arminius, God's desire for the salvation of "all people"
(1 Tim. 2:4) means that he desires the salvation of each individual person.
God's love for fallen humanity is not simply a love for justice or a vague
sense of affection toward reprobate humans; it is a desire to communicate
the eternal benefits of Christ to the entire race.

Second, election to salvation and reprobation to condemnation are conditional. God chooses those who are foreknown to be penitent believers, and he
condemns those he knows to be impenitent unbelievers. For the Reformed,
God's predestination has nothing whatsoever to do with any human condition. His reason for loving some sinners unto salvation while rejecting others
in their sin is—beyond the demonstration of mercy and justice—mysterious.
For Arminius, however, electing someone who is unwilling would be as
unjust as reprobating for any reason other than voluntary sin.

Finally, the grace that is necessary for salvation can be refused. God wills
for all people to be saved. The reason that some people will not be saved is
not any lack of divine love, but the *nature* of divine love. God's love is communicated not as an irresistible coercion, but as a tender persuasion that
will not finally override the human will. For the Reformed, God always gets
whom he elects, and humanity has no say about the reception of grace. For
Arminius, grace must still precede the human will to enable any turn
toward God. But salvation is received by those who refuse to resist God's
grace. It is offered, even if counterfactually, to all, but is resisted by some.

Summary of a whole theological system is an unenviable task, particularly when it is the summary of a summary. Focusing on a few theological

topics, as we have done, is bound to result in the omission of other important topics. Besides these motivating factors and distinctive points in
Arminius's thought, there are many other distinctively "Arminian" doctrines that flow naturally from them. In addition, there are nuances and
whole areas of Arminius's theology that have been left untouched in this
volume. But perhaps enough has been said to help readers understand his
theology better and to inspire them to examine his works on their own.

## B. Was Arminius "Reformed"?

In light of the discussion of Arminius's distinctive teachings, it is natural
to compare his thought with the shared theology of his colleagues and to
ask whether Arminius was Reformed. The extent to which this category
question has occupied popular-level and even scholarly discussions is remarkable. Some interpreters admit more complexity than others, but
many defend the opinion that Arminius was indeed Reformed.[39] At the
outset, two observations are in order. First, it is not hard to detect the influence of modern agendas on this question. For example, categorizing
Arminius as Reformed could encourage Remonstrant/Arminian and
Reformed Churches as they continue their ecumenical cooperation with
one another. For many who ask this question, there seems to be more at
stake with this label than a mere historical curiosity. A second and related
point has to do with the definition of "Reformed." For instance, the fact
that the Remonstrant Church is part of the World Communion of Reformed
Churches today is an interesting commentary on the evolution of the term
"Reformed," but it reveals little about the use of this word or what it meant
to be confessionally Reformed in the early seventeenth-century Dutch context. For the purposes of the present discussion, while applauding ecumenical gains, it is methodologically necessary to jettison modern
definitions of Reformed that would not be recognized in Arminius's time.[40]

---

39. E.g., see Carl O. Bangs, "Arminius as a Reformed Theologian," in *The Heritage of John
Calvin: Heritage Hall Lectures, 1960–70*, ed. John H. Bratt (Grand Rapids, MI: Eerdmans,
1973), pp. 209–222; Den Boer, "Met onderscheidingsvermogen," 269–272.

40. E.g., see D. Brent Laytham, "The Place of Natural Theology in the Theological Method
of John Calvin and Jacobus Arminius," *Church Divinity* 8 (1989–1990): 35, who claims that
Arminius rejects "natural theology," as does Calvin. He reasons that, since this rejection is
the touchstone of Reformed theology, Arminius is therefore to be regarded as a Reformed
theologian. See also Olson, *Arminian Theology*, pp. 51–54, who proposes the criteria of an
emphasis on God's glory and covenant theology, thus admitting Arminius under the
Reformed umbrella.

Let us rehearse only the most important points of the scholarly discussion.[41] On the one hand, Carl Bangs, following G. J. Hoenderdaal, asserts that to deny the label of Reformed to Arminius is to impose anachronistic definitions of the term based on the narrowing that took place at Dordt ten years after Arminius's death.[42] Richard Muller, on the other hand, argues that the definition of Reformed theology codified at Dordt was already the standard interpretation of the confession and catechism in Arminius's lifetime, an interpretation that was reinforced in previous synods that disciplined alternative viewpoints. Thus there is no anachronism involved in contrasting Arminius with the Reformed. Arminius's attempt to exploit the ambiguity of the confessional documents was unconvincing to his peers and out of step with their authorial intent.[43]

In the sense of social and ecclesiastical affiliations, there is no doubt that Arminius was Reformed. He ministered in the Reformed Church and taught in its seminary, subscribed to its confessional statements, and at the time of his death was officially in good standing with the Reformed Church. The only real question is about the relationship of his theology to that of the Reformed Church. When most modern readers encounter Arminius's actual teachings and writings for the first time, they are generally astonished to find him more "Reformed" (by most traditional definitions) than they previously thought. In much of his theology—prolegomena, Christology, ecclesiology, eschatology—there is no question about his connection to the Reformed tradition, and nearly every page of his writings betrays the Reformed context that gave birth to his theology. With respect to the more controversial doctrinal topics, Arminius sought wiggle room within the confessional statements to present his theology as a viable Reformed option. After all, he argued, if supralapsarianism, which was not endorsed in the confession or catechism (not to mention later at Dordt), was a viable Reformed option, then perhaps his view of conditional predestination would also be viable. Arminius could not have known

---

41. For a fuller analysis of the scholarly debate on this question, see Stanglin, "Arminius and Arminianism," pp. 10–13.

42. Bangs, "Arminius as a Reformed Theologian," pp. 212, 218; idem, "Review of Richard Muller, *God, Creation, and Providence.*" *Church History* 66/1 (1997): 118–120.

43. Richard A. Muller, "Arminius and the Reformed Tradition," *Westminster Theological Journal* 70/1 (2008): 19–48. The same point about synodical decisions is made in Fred van Lieburg, "Gisbertus Samuels, a Reformed Minister Sentenced by the Synod of Zeeland in 1591 for His Opinions on Predestination," in Goudriaan and Van Lieburg, eds., *Revisiting the Synod of Dordt*, pp. 3–19.

ahead of time that the lines would be drawn more precisely between conditional and unconditional predestination than between supra- and infralapsarianism, but, given the degree of the controversy and the opposition that he experienced in his own lifetime, he would not have been surprised at the outcome.

As noted above, with regard to the controversial questions, Arminius's connection to the Reformed tradition did not sever his genuine link to a different thread that had always been present in Christian history and was particularly dominant in the early church. Notwithstanding all of the similarities between Arminius and his Reformed contemporaries, he forged a new trajectory from within Reformed theology that veered in significant ways from it. Though the paths run parallel along much of the way, at crucial junctures they also turn in opposing directions. The differences between the two paths were too much to bear under one ecclesial umbrella— at least in early modern Holland.

Whether one desires to label Arminius as "Reformed" is not a question of great import to us. Either answer requires much qualification. What is important is to have a clear understanding of the similarities and differences. Roger Olson recognizes the depth of the differences when he emphasizes the impossibility of a hybrid between Arminianism and Calvinism.[44] Those who claim to be "Calminians" do not appear to recognize the incommensurability of these systems, and, if they did, we believe that they would probably discover themselves to be Arminian. There is no middle ground between (1) resistible and irresistible operations of grace; (2) conditional and unconditional predestination; and (3) God's saving intention for creation and his use of it as a means for destruction. In contrast to the standard Reformed theology of Arminius's day, Mark Ellis's evaluation of early Remonstrants, whose theology he sees as consistent with that of Arminius, is judicious: their many "unique doctrines . . . are per se reasons enough to declare that they represented an alien theological development."[45]

Our examination of Arminius's theology reveals that he was not just a Calvinist who tweaked one doctrine (predestination). A few key differences created a ripple effect throughout his theology. Recognizing these differences allows for a greater appreciation than is sometimes expressed

---

44. Olson, *Arminian Theology*, pp. 61–77.

45. Ellis, "Introduction," p. vi.

for Arminius as a significant thinker and contributor to the history of theology. Recognizing these differences need not obscure the similarities with Reformed theology; neither should it impede current efforts to build ecumenical bridges. Instead, clearer understanding should help facilitate current and future dialogue.

## III. The Arminian Legacy

In addition to the points mentioned above that have figured prominently in this book, there are many other aspects of Arminius's legacy that have been held dear by his theological descendants. Those who have embraced Arminianism, though, have highlighted some aspects of the legacy over other aspects. Bangs has recognized the contrast between, on the one hand, the Dutch Remonstrant legacy, which has underscored toleration, freedom of conscience and biblical interpretation, and universalism (corresponding to so-called "Arminianism of the head"), and, on the other hand, the received Anglo-American legacy of Arminianism, characterized by its emphasis on grace, evangelism, and holiness ("Arminianism of the heart").[46] These two traditions have certainly gone their separate ways over the centuries, but the overlap between them is traceable to Arminius.

### A. Scripture above Confession and Catechism

An enduring aspect of the Arminian legacy has been a pronounced emphasis upon what is sometimes called the "Protestant Principle." Arminius was remembered as a professor who directed his students primarily to Scripture.[47] Scripture, and Scripture alone, is finally authoritative as a source of theology. Arminius forthrightly recognizes his liability if he is found in violation of his stated allegiance to the Reformed confessions of his time (clearly, he thinks that he does *not* violate their wording). But he also insists that his ultimate responsibility is not to the creeds and confessions; rather, it is to God's revelation as found in Holy Scripture. This means that while confessional statements are very valuable, they simply cannot be used to coerce belief in propositions that run contrary to scriptural teaching. Indeed, to insist that the confessions have such priority is

---

46. Bangs, "Recent Studies," 424–426.

47. Bertius, *Oratio*, in *Opera*, fol. ooo1ᵛ; *Works* 1: 37.

to deny the (Protestant) confessions themselves (which confess belief in sola Scriptura).[48]

Confessions of faith, particularly as they become increasingly detailed, should have a subordinate priority in theology. Like their Protestant predecessors in the previous century, the Remonstrants soon discovered that confessions are necessary simply to proclaim openly the beliefs of a particular church. Their confession of faith, written by Episcopius, opens with a lengthy preface explaining the role of a confession and the Remonstrant rejection of obligatory subscription. The Remonstrants and evangelical Arminians follow Arminius in stating that Scripture is their only rule of faith and that confessions do not have incontrovertible authority.[49] This commitment to Scripture over confession and catechism—which does not devalue their importance but rather establishes it—also means in a practical sense that biblical scholarship should not be constrained by ideological pre-commitments.[50]

## B. Unity and Toleration

The tendency to minimize the hegemony of confessional statements in determining ecclesiastical boundaries leads to a spirit of ecumenical unity, which is accompanied by a willingness to allow a diversity of theological interpretations. Arminius dealt with the topic of discord within the Christian church most extensively in his oration as rector of Leiden University. When there is division among Christians, there is isolation and one group cannot derive any good from another.[51] Rather than focusing on the differences, Christians should consider all the doctrines that they hold in common.[52] Although Arminius himself was involved in doctrinal conflict, as Hoenderdaal writes, "He did not seek the dispute; he would have rather

---

48. Arminius agreed with many others in the Dutch Church that the Heidelberg Catechism and Belgic Confession should be subject to a revision process in an upcoming national synod, particularly if their interpretation is to remain narrow and their subscription obligatory. See *Dec. sent.*, pp. 126–136; *Works* 1: 701–730.

49. Episcopius, *Arminian Confession*, pp. 3–31. Cf. Gerrit Jan Heering and G. J. Sirks, *Het seminarium der Remonstranten driehonderd jaar, 1634–1934* (Amsterdam: Lankamp & Brinkman, 1934), p. 22.

50. Regarding the Remonstrant legacy of free, scholarly research and interpretation of Scripture, see Heering and Sirks, *Het seminarium*, p. 22: "Van Luther's vrijheid van den christen om zelf de Schrift te onderzoeken, maakten zij krachtig gebruik."

51. *Oratio de dissidio*, in *Opera*, p. 76; *Works* 1: 445.

52. *Oratio de dissidio*, in *Opera*, p. 87; *Works* 1: 472.

avoided it."[53] The Remonstrants became champions of ecumenism, unity, and toleration in The Netherlands. This emphasis, though not unique to Arminians among the Dutch, was strengthened by the plight of Arminius and his followers in the early seventeenth century. Promotion of religious freedom and toleration quickly became one of the distinguishing characteristics of Remonstrantism.[54] As the Remonstrant professor Arnold Poelenburg said in 1659, "But this is that badge of distinction (*insigne*) of Remonstrantism; this crown of our glory, because we neither have made this schism, nor have we admitted another, nor do we favor or approve of any: but we urge, call, and invite all who love Christ alone, who adhere to the gospel alone, to enter the same communion of peace with us."[55]

Connected with these themes is the call to epistemic humility. Arminius declared that Christians must acknowledge the difficulty of discovering the truth on all subjects of theology.[56] The Remonstrants point to Arminius as someone who, though he did not make a "radical break with all dogmatism," nevertheless represented a "departure from it."[57] For Arminius, there were clear boundaries to the Christian faith, and he certainly was a "dogmatist" when it came to the central doctrines of the faith. Arminius had in mind a unity built on the faith that C. S. Lewis would call "mere Christianity." The words of Peter Meiderlin, taken up by later Remonstrants and so many other groups, reflect the sentiment of Arminius: "In essentials, unity; in nonessentials, liberty; in both, charity."[58] The

---

53. Hoenderdaal, "Jacob Arminius," 62: "Er suchte den Disput nicht, er vermied ihn lieber."

54. On attitudes regarding religious freedom in The Netherlands, 1580–1600, as well as subsequent Arminian attitudes, see Lecler, *Toleration*, 2: 256–323. The Remonstrant case for religious toleration has also been documented in Gerrit Voogt, "Remonstrant–Counter-Remonstrant Debates: Crafting a Principled Defense of Toleration after the Synod of Dordrecht (1619–1650)," *Church History and Religious Culture* 89/4 (2009): 489–524. See also Christiane Berkvens-Stevelinck, et al., eds., *The Emergence of Tolerance in the Dutch Republic* (Leiden: Brill, 1997); Jeremy D. Bangs, "Dutch Contributions to Religious Toleration," *Church History* 79/3 (2010): 585–613.

55. Arnold Poelenburg, "Oratio funebris in obitum clarissimi viri D. Stephani Curcellaei," in Étienne de Courcelles, *Opera theologica* (Amsterdam: Daniel Elsevier, 1675), fol. oooo1ʳ.

56. *Oratio de dissidio*, in *Opera*, p. 86; *Works* 1: 471.

57. Groenewegen, *Jacobus Arminius*, p. 37: "Zijn arbeid is nog geen radicale breuk met alle dogmatisme, maar een duidelijke verwijdering daarvan." Likewise, Otterspeer, *Bolwerk*, p. 212, pits Arminius against the "dogmatist" Gomarus.

58. Cf. Groenewegen, *Jacobus Arminius*, p. 20. On the history of this slogan, see Hans Rollmann, "In Essentials Unity: The Pre-History of a Restoration Movement Slogan," *Restoration Quarterly* 39/3 (1997): 129–139.

Remonstrants eventually did make a radical break with dogmatism, and their anti-dogmatism came to mean not only the acceptance of all Christian confessions, but also eventually of all religious persuasions, so that toleration came to exclude the possibility of any judgment. The later Remonstrant forays into Cartesianism, Lockeanism, and various eclectic Enlightenment epistemologies have been traced by some scholars back to Arminius's open-minded call for peace.[59] However this part of his legacy has been received, Arminius was nevertheless a voice of Christian unity and toleration in an age when such was unpopular and even dangerous.

## C. Good Conscience

Arminius's personal motto was, "A good conscience is paradise" (*bona conscientia paradisus*). Good conscience refers to both religious belief and moral practice. First, with respect to religious beliefs, Christians must not violate their conscience by ignoring truth or confessing beliefs that they do not hold. Arminius's strong opposition to certain doctrines and his persistent advocacy of others reflect his personal commitment to pursuing theological truth and following it wherever it leads him. To later Remonstrants who embraced the Enlightenment endorsement of personal liberties, this religious conscience was considered to be absolutely "autonomous."[60]

In addition to religious conscience, Arminius's theology stresses the centrality of the moral conscience. Good deeds have no causal role in justification, but they are the necessary fruit. A true believer can apostatize either by rejecting the faith or by committing sins out of a malicious heart that is inconsistent with saving faith. Hence there is no place for carnal security in the Christian life. Sanctification is an ongoing process that must never stop in this life. Some interpreters have noted the strongly "practical" character that pervades Arminius's theology.[61] Although all Christians acknowledge the importance of a life of holiness, Arminians have given special emphasis to this doctrine. G. J. Heering speaks of the

---

59. E.g., Sirks, *Arminius' pleidooi*, p. 68.

60. E.g., see Heering and Sirks, *Het seminarium*, p. 22.

61. The "practical bias" of Arminius's theology was a recurring emphasis in Hoenderdaal's accounts of Arminius. See G. J. Hoenderdaal, "The Life and Thought of Jacobus Arminius," *Religion in Life* 29/4 (1960): 540–547; idem, "De theologische betekenis," 98; idem, "Inleiding," p. 34.

strong ethical character of Remonstrant theology,[62] and Wesleyan groups have been well known for their stress on holiness of life and pursuit of perfect love.

## D. God and Humanity: Holy Love, Sinful Creatures, and Free Grace

All these elements of Arminius's theology have had an important and enduring legacy. He is certainly not the first to hold these views, and they can be seen in the theology of many subsequent "Arminian" theologians. But his place is nonetheless crucial in their development and spread. Among all of these emphases, perhaps most important is the following theological conviction: his bedrock confidence in the sheer goodness of God and the beauty of the divine glory, the creation of humanity to share that goodness and to enjoy that glory, and the loving grace that is provided and offered to all.

First is the deep conviction in the utter goodness and benevolence of God. Within the simplicity of the Triune divine life, God necessarily *is* perfect goodness. Doctrines that purport to give an account of divine being and action must not undercut or contradict belief in God's goodness. God's goodness is finally the holy love of the Triune God, and we see it in the justice and mercy of his actions. His omnipotence and sovereignty should indeed be celebrated, but these divine attributes always must be considered in ways that are consistent with his essential goodness. God acts for his own glory, but his concern for his glory cannot be understood as a lack or need within God's own life. On the contrary, his concern for his glory is utterly consistent with his concern for humanity, for God intends that we may worship him and participate in his glory. God is glorified when his goodness and glory are shared with creation.

Divine action is always completely consistent with the divine nature; thus God creates to express and share his goodness. Humanity, made in the image of God, is created to know, love, and worship God. God has not created humans as tragically fated actors in some cosmic drama written and directed by God for God's own amusement. God has not created humans—any humans—as an outlet for a divine wrath that somehow must be expressed for God to be God. No, on the contrary, God has created humans—all humans—in his image and to share his goodness.

---

62. Heering and Sirks, *Het seminarium*, p. 24.

Second, Arminius and later Arminians (whose views are consistent with his) have been well aware that sin has brought destruction and alienation from God, and they resolutely deny that God is in any way the "author" of sin or the ultimate determining agent. Instead, there is a stout insistence on the "free will defense" with respect to the origin of sin and evil, along with a sober confession of the inability of humans to save or redeem themselves. God always acts in ways that are completely consistent with the perfection of God's simple goodness; therefore it is inconceivable that God would either perform evil actions or make it inevitable that human persons do so. Sin is *against* God's will and God's nature.

Finally, the Arminian theological legacy also maintains that the Triune God does not abandon us in our sin; instead, it celebrates the fact that the holy love of the Triune God is extended to sinners in the person of the incarnate Son. God's grace is grounded in the holy goodness of God, and the extent of his grace is the same as the extent of his creative work. Thus the work of the incarnate Son is intended for and available to *all* human sinners: God "so loved the world" (Jn. 3:16) and "is not willing that any should perish but that all should come to repentance" (2 Pet. 3:9). Some Remonstrants and latter-day "Arminians" (as well as many of their Reformed critics) understand this doctrinal commitment to entail the certainty of universal salvation, but the general Arminian theological tradition rejects such a conclusion for theological (as well as exegetical) reasons. For grace, while universal and prevenient, is not coercive. Humans are not forced or coerced or manipulated into sinful activity; nor are they forced or coerced or manipulated into salvation. On the contrary, God's grace is sufficient for all but also free to all. According to traditional Arminian theology, the sad truth is that God's grace is, in fact, sometimes rejected: "you always resist the Holy Spirit" (Acts 7:51). God's grace does not subdue nature and freedom, which are gifts of God, but is intended to perfect them. Unlike its Reformed counterpart, Arminianism is a theology dominated not by a sovereign, "perfect will," but permeated by perfect, free grace and love.

The task of theology is to articulate—in light of Scripture, tradition, and reason—an account of the nature of God, the nature of humanity, and the relation between the two. Arminius was a recipient of the orthodox tradition that systematized its thought and language about the Triune God in the early church. He also stood in a long line of Augustinian thought that wrestled with theological anthropology. Arminius built on these foundations laid before him and attended to their every feature. But his most enduring contribution lies in "the mutual relation between God and humanity," which he calls the foundation of religion.[63] The doctrine of God has important implications regarding God's intentions for humanity. The doctrine of humanity in turn has implications for the nature of salvation. Creation is in continuity with redemption, and both reflect God's character. Arminius bequeathed to Protestant churches a legacy that wrestles with divine sovereignty and human freedom without sacrificing either one on the altar of the other. Above all, Arminius highlighted a doctrine of grace based on Scripture and the most venerable traditions of the church. Among Protestant churches, the Arminian legacy declares that grace is an unmitigated, extravagant gift of God intended for the healing and restoration of all creation, a gift that liberates humanity to seek the beauty of God's face and to enjoy eternal fellowship with him.

---

63. *Disp. priv.* XI.1. This contribution of Arminius to Christian theology was observed by William Fairfield Warren, "Arminius," *Methodist Quarterly Review* 4th series, vol. 9 (July 1857): 345–361.

# Bibliography

PRE-1800 AUTHORS (ORIGINAL EDITIONS,
REPRINTS, AND TRANSLATIONS)

*Acta synodi nationalis, in nomine Domini nostri Iesu Christi . . . Dordrechti habitae anno M.DC.XVIII. et M.DC.XIX.* Dordrecht: Isaac Elzevir, 1620.

Anselm of Canterbury. De conceptu virginali et originali peccato. In PL 158.

Arminius, Jacobus. *Amica cum D. Francisco Iunio de praedestinatione, per litteras habita collatio.* In *Opera,* pp. 445–619.

Arminius, Jacobus. *Analysis cap. 9. ad Romanos ad Gellium Snecanum.* In *Opera,* pp. 778–807.

Arminius, Jacobus. *Apologia D. Iacobi Arminii adversus articulos quosdam [XXXI] theologicos in vulgus sparsos.* In *Opera,* pp. 134–183.

Arminius, Jacobus. *Articuli nonnulli diligenti examine perpendendi, eo quod inter ipsos Reformatae Religionis professores de iis aliqua incidit controversia.* In *Opera,* pp. 948–966.

Arminius, Jacobus. *Declaratio sententiae I. Arminii de praedestinatione, providentia Dei, libero arbitrio, gratia Dei, divinitate Filii Dei, et de iustificatione hominis coram Deo.* In *Opera,* pp. 91–133.

Arminius, Jacobus. *Disputationes privatae, de plerisque Christianae religionis capitibus, incoatae potissimum ab auctore ad corporis theologici informationem.* In *Opera,* pp. 339–444.

Arminius, Jacobus. *Disputationes publicae de nonnullis religionis Christianae capitibus.* In *Opera,* pp. 197–338.

Arminius, Jacobus. *Epistola ad Hippolytum a Collibus.* In *Opera,* pp. 935–947.

Arminius, Jacobus. *Examen modestum libelli, quem D. Gulielmus Perkinsius . . . edidit ante aliquot annos de praedestinationis modo et ordine.* In *Opera,* pp. 621–777.

Arminius, Jacobus. *Examen thesium D. Francisci Gomari de praedestinatione.* [Amsterdam,] 1645.

Arminius, Jacobus. *The Missing Public Disputations of Jacobus Arminius: Introduction, Text, and Notes.* Ed. Keith D. Stanglin. Brill's Series in Church History, vol. 47. Leiden: Brill, 2010.

Arminius, Jacobus. *Opera theologica.* Leiden: Godefridus Basson, 1629. [The following works appear in order as found in the *Opera*.]

Arminius, Jacobus. *Oratio de componendo dissidio religionis inter Christianos, habita ab auctore VIII. February 1605 cum rectoratum deponeret.* In *Opera*, pp. 71–91.

Arminius, Jacobus. *Oratio de sacerdotio Christi habita a D. Iacobo Arminio cum publice doctor s. theologiae crearetur.* In *Opera*, pp. 9–26.

Arminius, Jacobus. *Orationes tres de theologia, quas ordine habuit auctor cum lectiones suas auspicaretur.* In *Opera*, pp. 26–71.

Arminius, Jacobus. *Quaestiones numero novem cum responsionibus et anterotematis, nobiliss. DD. curatoribus Academiae Leidensis exhibite a deputatis synodi . . . mense Novembri anni 1605.* In *Opera*, pp. 184–186.

Arminius, Jacobus. *Quelques poésies de Jacques Arminius composées pendant son séjour en Suisse.* Ed. H. de Vries de Heekelingen. The Hague: Martinus Nijhoff, 1925.

Arminius, Jacobus. *Verclaringhe Iacobi Arminii saliger ghedachten, in zijn leven professor theologiae binnen Leyden: aengaende zyn ghevoelen.* Leiden: Thomas Basson, 1610.

Arminius, Jacobus. *Verklaring van Jacobus Arminius, afgelegd in de vergadering van de staten van Holland op 30 Oktober, 1608*, ed. G. J. Hoenderdaal. Lochem: De Tijdstroom, 1960.

Arminius, Jacobus. *De vero et genuino sensu cap. VII. Epistolae ad Romanos dissertation.* In *Opera*, pp. 809–934.

Arminius, Jacobus. *The Works of James Arminius*, London ed. Trans. James Nichols and William Nichols. 3 vols. 1825, 1828, 1875. Reprint, Grand Rapids, MI: Baker, 1986.

Arminius, Jacobus. *The Writings of James Arminius.* American ed. Trans. James Nichols and W. R. Bagnall. 3 vols. 1853. Reprint, Grand Rapids, MI: Baker, 1977.

Arminius, Jacobus, and Franciscus Gomarus. *Twee disputatien vande goddeliicke predestinatie.* Leiden: Jan Paedts Jacobszoon, 1609.

*The Articles of the Synod of Dort, and Its Rejection of Errors: With the History of Events Which Made Way for That Synod.* Trans. Thomas Scott. Utica, NY: William Williams, 1831.

*Articuli Arminiani sive Remonstrantia.* In Schaff, *Creeds of Christendom* 3: 545–549.

*Articuli XXXIX. Ecclesiae Anglicanae. A.D. 1562.* In Schaff, *Creeds of Christendom* 3: 486–516.

*The Auction Catalogue of the Library of J. Arminius.* Facsimile ed. with an intro. by Carl O. Bangs. Utrecht: HES, 1985.

Augustine of Hippo. *Confessionum libri tredecim.* In *PL* 32.

Augustine of Hippo. *Contra duas epistolas Pelagianorum.* In *PL* 44.

Augustine of Hippo. *De civitate Dei contra paganos.* In *PL* 41.

Augustine of Hippo. *De natura et gratia ad Timasium et Iacobum contra Pelagium*. In *PL* 44.

Augustine of Hippo. *Sermones ad populum omnes*. In *PL* 38.

Baro, Peter. *Summa trium de praedestinatione sententiarum*. In *Ep. ecc.* 15, pp. 29–32; *Works* 1: 91–100.

Bertius, Petrus. *De vita et obitu reverendi et clarissimi viri D. Iacobi Arminii oratio. Dicta post tristes illius exsequias XXII. Octob. Anno M.D.C.IX. in Auditorio Theologico*. In Arminius, *Opera theologica*, fols. 001ʳ–0004ᵛ.

Biel, Gabriel. *Collectorium circa quattuor libros sententiarum*. Ed. Wilfridus Werbeck and Udo Hofmann. 4 vols. Tübingen: Mohr, 1973–1984.

Brandt, Caspar. *Historia vitae Iacobi Arminii*. Amsterdam: Martinus Schagenius, 1724.

Brandt, Caspar. *The Life of James Arminius, D.D.* Trans. John Guthrie, with an intro. by T. O. Summers. Nashville: E. Stevenson and F. A. Owen, 1857.

Brandt, Gerard. *The History of the Reformation and Other Ecclesiastical Transactions in and about the Low-Countries*, 4 vols. London: T. Wood for Timothy Childe, 1720–1723.

Calvin, John. *Institutes of the Christian Religion*. Trans. Henry Beveridge. 1845. Reprint, Grand Rapids, MI: Eerdmans, 1994.

Calvin, John. *Institutio Christianae religionis* (1559). In *Ioannis Calvini opera quae supersunt omnia*. Ed. G. Baum, E. Cunitz, and E. Reuss, vol. 2. Brunswick: C. A. Schwetschke and Son, 1863–1900.

*Canons and Dogmatic Decrees of the Council of Trent*, in Schaff, *Creeds of Christendom*, 2: 77–206.

*Canons of the Council of Orange*, in *Creeds and Confessions of Faith in the Christian Tradition*, ed. Jaroslav J. Pelikan and Valerie R. Hotchkiss, vol. 1. New Haven, CT: Yale University Press, 2003.

*Canons of the Synod of Dort*. In Schaff, *Creeds of Christendom*, 3: 550–597.

Courcelles, Étienne de. "Praefatio Christiano Lectori." In Arminius, *Examen thesium Gomari*, fols. 02ʳ–04ᵛ.

Duns Scotus, John. *God and Creatures: The Quodlibetal Questions*. Trans. with an intro., notes, and glossary by Felix Alluntis and Allan B. Wolter. Princeton, NJ: Princeton University Press, 1975.

Episcopius, Simon. *The Arminian Confession of 1621*. Trans. Mark A. Ellis. Eugene: Pickwick, 2005.

Episcopius, Simon. *Institutiones theologicae privatis lectionibus Amstelodami traditae*. In *Opera theologica*. Amsterdam: Joannes Blaev, 1650.

Erasmus, Desiderius. *On the Freedom of the Will: A Diatribe or Discourse*. Trans. E. Gordon Rupp. In *Luther and Erasmus: Free Will and Salvation*. Library of Christian Classics, vol. 17, pp. 35–97. Philadelphia: Westminster Press, 1969.

Eusebius Pamphili of Caesarea. *Historia ecclesiastica*. In *PG* 20.

Featley, Daniel. *Parallelismus nov-antiqui erroris Pelagiarminiani*. London: Robert Mylbourne, 1626.

Featley, Daniel. *Pelagius redivivus: Or Pelagius Raked out of the Ashes by Arminius and His Schollers.* London: Robert Mylbourne, 1626.

Gomarus, Franciscus. *Bedencken over de lyck-oratie van Meester P. Bertius.* In *Verclaringhe, over de vier hooftstucken, der leere, waer van hy met sijn weerde mede— Professore D. Iacobo Arminio, gheconfereert heeft, voor de E.E. moghende Heeren Staten van Hollandt ende Westvrieslandt: overghelevert den achtsten Septembris,* pp. 41–49. Leiden: Jan Jansz. Orlers, 1609.

Gomarus, Franciscus. *Disputationum theologicarum decima-quarta, de libero arbitrio.* Samuel Gruterus respondens. 19 March 1603. Leiden: Joannes Patius, 1603.

Gomarus, Franciscus. *Disputationum theologicarum vigesima-tertia, de fide iustificante.* Henricus H. Geisteranus, Jr., respondens. 15 October 1603. Leiden: Joannes Patius, 1603.

Gomarus, Franciscus. *Theses theologicae de iustificatione hominis coram Deo.* Isaacus Diamantius respondens. 20 March 1604. Leiden: Joannes Patius, 1604.

Gomarus, Franciscus. *Waerschouwinghe over de vermaninghe aen R. Donteclock.* Leiden: Jan Jansz. Orlers, 1609.

Irenaeus of Lyon. *Adversus haereses.* In *PG* 7.

John Chrysostom. In Epistolam ad Romanos homiliae. In *PG* 60.

John of Damascus. *Expositio accurata fidei orthodoxae.* In *PG* 94.

Kuchlinus, Johannes. *Theses theologicae de divina praedestinatione.* M. Gerardus Vossius respondens. Leiden: Joannes Patius, 1600.

Limborch, Philip van. *Historical Relation Concerning the Origin and Progress of the Controversies in the Belgic League, upon Predestination and Its Connected Heads.* In L.W.P., "Arminian Controversy in the Low Countries." *Methodist Review* 26 (1844): 425–460, 556–587.

Luther, Martin. *D. Martin Luthers Werke: Kritische Gesamtausgabe,* 66 vols. Weimar: Hermann Böhlau, 1883–1987.

Luther, Martin. *De captivitate Babylonica Ecclesiae praeludium.* In *Luthers Werke,* 6: 497–573.

Migne, J.-P., ed. *Patrologiae cursus completus, series Graeca.* 161 vols. Paris, 1857–1866.

Migne, J.-P., ed. *Patrologiae cursus completus, series Latina.* 221 vols. Paris, 1878–1890.

Molhuysen, P. C. *Bronnen tot de geschiedenis der Leidsche Universiteit.* 7 vols. The Hague: Martinus Nijhoff, 1913–1924.

Molina, Luis de. *On Divine Foreknowledge (Part IV of the Concordia).* Trans. Alfred J. Freddoso. Ithaca, NY: Cornell University Press, 1988.

Mosheim, Johann Lorenz von. *Institutiones historiae Christianae recentioris.* Helmstedt: Christ. Frid. Weygand, 1741.

Moulin, Pierre du. *Anatome Arminianismi seu, enucleatio controversiarum quae in Belgio agitantur, super doctrina de providential, de praedestinatione, de morte Christi, de natura et gratia.* Leiden: Abraham Picard, 1619.

Moulin, Pierre du. *The Anatomy of Arminianisme: or The Opening of the Controversies Lately Handled in the Low-Countryes.* London: T.S. for Nathaniel Newbery, 1620.

Novatian. *De Trinitate*. In *PL* 3.

Origen. *De principiis*. In *PG* 11.

Origen. *In Epistolam ad Romanos*. In *PG* 14.

Perkins, William. *A Golden Chaine: Or, the Description of Theologie*. In *Workes of Perkins* 1: 9–116.

Perkins, William. *De praedestinationis modo et ordine: et de amplitudine gratiae divinae . . . desceptatio*. Cambridge: John Legatt, 1598.

Perkins, William. *The Workes of That Famous and Worthy Minister of Christ . . . Mr. William Perkins*, 3 vols. London: John Legatt, 1631–1635.

Peter Lombard. *Sententiarum libri quatuor*. In *PL* 192.

Poelenburg, Arnold. "Oratio funebris in obitum clarissimi viri D. Stephani Curcellaei." In Étienne de Courcelles, *Opera theologica*, fols. 002ʳ-00003ᵛ. Amsterdam: Daniel Elsevier, 1675.

*Praestantium ac eruditorum virorum epistolae ecclesiasticae et theologicae*. 2nd ed. Preface by Philip van Limborch. Amsterdam: H. Wetstenium, 1684.

Prynne, William. *Anti-Arminianisme: Or The Church of Englands Old Antithesis to New Arminianisme*. 2nd ed. [London,] 1630.

Schaff, Philip, ed. *The Creeds of Christendom, with a History and Critical Notes*. 3 vols. 6th ed. 1931. Reprint, Grand Rapids, MI: Baker, 1998.

*Sententiae Remonstrantium*. In *Acta synodi Dordrechti*; also trans. in *Crisis in the Reformed Churches*, ed. Peter Y. de Jong, pp. 221–229. Grand Rapids, MI: Reformed Fellowship, 1968.

Tertullian of Carthage. *Adversus Praxeam*. In *PL* 2.

Theodotus, Salomon. Ἑνοτικον *dissecti Belgii, in quo historica relatio originis et progressus eorum dissidiorum continentur*. Ursel: Wendelinus Iunghen, 1618.

*Thomas Aquinas. Summa theologiae*. 61 vols. London: Blackfriars, 1964–1981.

Trelcatius, Lucas, Jr. *Disputationum theologicarum quarto repetitarum vigesima-septima de bonis operibus et meritis eorum*. Ricardus Janus Neraeus respondens. 4 March 1606. Leiden: Joannes Patius, 1606.

Ursinus, Zacharias, and Caspar Olevianus. *The Heidelberg Catechism*. In *The Creeds of Christendom*, ed. Philip Schaff, 3: 307–355. Reprint, Grand Rapids, MI: Baker, 1998.

[Uytenbogaert, Joannes.] *Kerckelicke historie, vervatende verscheyden gedenckwaerdige saecken*. S. l., 1646.

Wesley, John. "The Doctrine of Original Sin." In *The Works of John Wesley*, vol. 9. Grand Rapids, MI: Zondervan, n.d.

Wesley, John. *Fifty-two Standard Sermons*. Salem, OH: Schmul Publishing, 1988.

MODERN SOURCES

Adams, Robert M. "An Anti-Molinist Argument." *Philosophical Perspectives* 5 (1991): 343–353.

Adams, Robert M. "Middle Knowledge and the Problem of Evil." *American Philosophical Quarterly* 14 (1977): 109–117.

Ashby, Stephen M. "A Reformed Arminian View." In *Four Views on Eternal Security*, ed. J. Matthew Pinson, pp. 135–187. Grand Rapids: Zondervan, 2002.

Asselt, Willem J. van. *The Federal Theology of Johannes Cocceius (1603–1669)*. Leiden: Brill, 2001.

Asselt, Willem J. van, et al., eds. *Reformed Thought on Freedom: The Concept of Free Choice in Early Modern Reformed Theology*. Texts and Studies in Reformation and Post-Reformation Thought. Grand Rapids, MI: Baker Academic, 2010.

Atkinson, Lowell M. "The Achievement of Arminius." *Religion in Life* 19/3 (1950): 418–430.

Ayres, Lewis. *Nicea and Its Legacy: An Approach to Fourth-Century Trinitarian Theology*. Oxford: Oxford University Press, 2004.

Babcock, William S. "Grace, Freedom and Justice: Augustine and the Christian Tradition." *Perkins Journal* 26/4 (1973): 1–15.

Bac, J. Martin. *Perfect Will Theology: Divine Agency in Reformed Scholasticism as against Suárez, Episcopius, Descartes, and Spinoza*. Brill's Series in Church History, vol. 42. Leiden: Brill, 2010.

Bangs, Carl O. "'All the Best Bishoprics and Deaneries': The Enigma of Arminian Politics." *Church History* 42 (1973): 5–16.

Bangs, Carl O. *Arminius: A Study in the Dutch Reformation*. 2nd ed. Grand Rapids, MI: Zondervan, 1985.

Bangs, Carl O. "Arminius and Reformed Theology." Ph.D. diss., University of Chicago, 1958.

Bangs, Carl O. "Arminius and Socinianism." In *Socinianism and Its Role in the Culture of the XVIth to XVIIIth Centuries*, ed. Lech Szczucki, pp. 81–84. Warsaw: Polish Academy of Sciences, 1983.

Bangs, Carl O. "Arminius and the Reformation." *Church History* 30 (1961): 155–170.

Bangs, Carl O. "Arminius as a Reformed Theologian." In *The Heritage of John Calvin: Heritage Hall Lectures, 1960–70*, ed. John H. Bratt, pp. 209–222. Grand Rapids, MI: Eerdmans, 1973.

Bangs, Carl O. "Introduction." In *Works* 1: vii–xxix.

Bangs, Carl O. "Recent Studies in Arminianism." *Religion in Life* 32/3 (1963): 421–428.

Bangs, Carl O. "Review of Richard Muller, *God, Creation, and Providence*." *Church History* 66/1 (1997): 118–120.

Bangs, Jeremy D. "Dutch Contributions to Religious Toleration." *Church History* 79/3 (2010): 585–613.

Bangs, Nathan. *The Life of James Arminius, D.D., Compiled from His Life and Writings, as Published by Mr. James Nichols*. New York: Harper and Brothers, 1843.

Berkhof, Louis. *Systematic Theology*. 2 vols. Grand Rapids, MI: Eerdmans, 1938.

Berkouwer, G. C. *Faith and Justification*. Trans. Lewis B. Smedes. Studies in Dogmatics. Grand Rapids, MI: Eerdmans, 1954.

Berkvens-Stevelinck, Christiane, et al., eds. *The Emergence of Tolerance in the Dutch Republic*. Leiden: Brill, 1997.

Bieber-Wallmann, Anneliese. "Remonstrantenstreit." In *Augustin Handbuch*, ed. Volker Henning Drecoll, pp. 627–633. Tübingen: Mohr Siebeck, 2007.

*Biografisch lexicon voor de geschiedenis van het nederlandse protestantisme*, ed. D. Nauta, et al., 6 vols. Kampen: Kok, 1978–2006.

Blacketer, Raymond A. "Arminius' Concept of Covenant in Its Historical Context." *Nederlands archief voor kerkgeschiedenis* 80/2 (2000): 193–220.

Boer, William A. den. *God's Twofold Love: The Theology of Jacob Arminius (1559–1609)*. Trans. Albert Gootjes. Reformed Historical Theology, vol. 14. Göttingen: Vandenhoeck & Ruprecht, 2010.

Boer, William A. den. "Met onderscheidingsvermogen: Arminius' waardering voor en kritiek op Calvijn en diens theologie." *Theologia Reformata* 52/3 (2009): 260–273.

Bosch, L. J. M. "Petrus Bertius (1565–1629)." Ph.D. diss., Katholieke Universiteit te Nijmegen, 1979.

Brower, Jeffrey E. "Simplicity and Aseity." In *Oxford Handbook of Philosophical Theology*, ed. Thomas P. Flint and Michael C. Rea, pp. 105–128. Oxford: Oxford University Press, 2009.

Bryant, Barry E. "Original Sin." In *The Oxford Handbook of Methodist Studies*, ed. William J. Abraham and James E. Kirby, pp. 522–539. Oxford: Oxford University Press, 2009.

Calder, Frederick. *Memoirs of Simon Episcopius, the Celebrated Pupil of Arminius, and Subsequently Doctor of Divinity*. London: Hayward and Moore, 1838.

Casiday, Augustine M. C. "Grace and the Humanity of Christ according to St Vincent of Lérins." *Vigiliae Christianae* 59/3 (2005): 298–314.

Clarke, F. Stuart. "Arminius's Understanding of Calvin." *Evangelical Quarterly* 54 (January–March 1982): 25–35.

Clarke, F. Stuart. "Arminius's Use of Ramism in His Interpretation of Romans 7 and 9." In *Interpreting the Bible: Historical and Theological Studies in Honour of David F. Wright*, ed. Anthony N. S. Lane, pp. 131–146. Leicester: Apollos, 1997.

Clarke, F. Stuart. *The Ground of Election: Jacobus Arminius' Doctrine of the Work and Person of Christ*. Studies in Christian History and Thought. Waynesboro, GA: Paternoster, 2006.

Clarke, F. Stuart. "The Theology of Arminius." *London Quarterly and Holborn Review* 185 (October 1960): 248–253.

Clotz, Henrike L. *Hochschule für Holland: Die Universität Leiden im Spannungsfeld zwischen Provinz, Stadt und Kirche, 1575–1619*. Stuttgart: Steiner, 1998.

Collins, Kenneth J. *The Scripture Way of Salvation: The Heart of John Wesley's Theology*. Nashville, TN: Abingdon Press, 1997.

Cossee, Eric H. "Arminius and Rome." In *Arminius, Arminianism, and Europe*, ed. Th. Marius van Leeuwen, Keith D. Stanglin, and Marijke Tolsma, pp. 73–85. Brill's Series in Church History, vol. 39. Leiden: Brill, 2009.

Craig, William Lane. "Middle Knowledge: A Calvinist-Arminian Rapprochement?" In *The Grace of God, the Will of Man*, ed. Clark H. Pinnock, pp. 141–164. Grand Rapids, MI: Zondervan, 1989.

Craig, William Lane. "Middle Knowledge, Truth-Makers, and the 'Grounding Objection.'" *Faith and Philosophy* 18 (2001): 337–352.

Cross, Richard. *Duns Scotus on God*. Aldershot, UK: Ashgate, 2003.

Dekker, Evert. "Jacobus Arminius and His Logic: Analysis of a Letter." *Journal of Theological Studies* 44 (1993): 118–142.

Dekker, Evert. *Rijker dan Midas: Vrijheid, genade en predestinatie in de theologie van Jacobus Arminius, 1559–1609*. Zoetermeer, The Netherlands: Boekencentrum, 1993.

Dekker, Evert. "Was Arminius a Molinist?" *Sixteenth Century Journal* 27/2 (1996): 337–352.

Deursen, A. T. van. *Bavianen en slijtgeuzen: Kerk en kerkvolk ten tijde van Maurits en Olde[n]barnevelt*. Assen: Van Gorcum, 1974.

Dorner, Isaak August. *History of Protestant Theology Particularly in Germany Viewed according to Its Fundamental Movement*. 2 vols. Trans. George Robson and Sophia Taylor. Edinburgh: T & T Clark, 1871.

Dunning, H. Ray. *Grace, Faith, and Holiness: A Wesleyan Systematic Theology*. Kansas City: Beacon Hill Press, 1988.

Eekhof, Albert. *De theologische faculteit te Leiden in de 17de eeuw*. Utrecht: G.A.J. Ruys, 1921.

Ellis, Mark A. "Introduction." In Simon Episcopius, *The Arminian Confession of 1621*, trans. Mark A. Ellis, pp. v–xiii. Eugene: Pickwick, 2005.

Ellis, Mark A. *Simon Episcopius' Doctrine of Original Sin*. American University Studies, Series 7: Theology and Religion, vol. 240. New York: Peter Lang, 2006.

Fesko, J. V. "Arminius on Union with Christ and Justification." *Trinity Journal* n. s. 31 (2010): 205–222.

Flint, Thomas P. *Divine Providence: The Molinist Account*. Ithaca, NY: Cornell University Press, 1998.

Flint, Thomas P. "The Problem of Divine Freedom." *American Philosophical Quarterly* 20/3 (1983): 255–264.

Foxgrover, David. "'Temporary Faith' and the Certainty of Salvation." *Calvin Theological Journal* 15/2 (1980): 220–232.

Frame, John M. *The Doctrine of God: A Theology of Lordship*. Philipsburg: P & R, 2002.

Freddoso, Alfred J. "Introduction." In Molina, *On Divine Foreknowledge (Part IV of the Concordia)*, trans. Alfred J. Freddoso, pp. 1–81. Ithaca, NY: Cornell University Press, 1988.

Freddoso, Alfred J. "Medieval Aristotelianism and the Case Against Secondary Causation in Nature." In *Divine and Human Action: Essays in the Metaphysics of Theism*, ed. Thomas V. Morris, pp. 74–118. Ithaca, NY: Cornell University Press, 1988.

Gavrilyuk, Paul. *The Suffering of the Impassible God: The Dialectics of Patristic Thought.* New York: Oxford University Press, 2006.

Goudriaan, Aza. "'Augustine Asleep' or 'Augustine Awake'? Arminius's Reception of Augustine." In *Arminius, Arminianism, and Europe,* ed. Th. Marius van Leeuwen, Keith D. Stanglin, and Marijke Tolsma, pp. 51–72. Brill's Series in Church History, vol. 39. Leiden: Brill, 2009.

Goudriaan, Aza. "Justification by Faith and the Early Arminian Controversy." In *Scholasticism Reformed: Essays in Honour of Willem J. van Asselt,* ed. Maarten Wisse, et al. Studies in Theology and Religion, vol. 14, pp. 155–178. Leiden: Brill, 2010.

Goudriaan, Aza. "The Synod of Dordt on Arminian Anthropology." In *Revisiting the Synod of Dordt,* ed. Aza Goudriaan and Fred van Lieburg, pp. 81–106. Brill's Series in Church History, vol. 49. Leiden: Brill, 2011.

Goudriaan, Aza, and Fred van Lieburg, eds. *Revisiting the Synod of Dordt (1618–1619).* Brill's Series in Church History, vol. 49. Leiden: Brill, 2011.

Graafland, C. *Van Calvijn tot Barth: Oorsprong en ontwikkeling van de leer der verkiezing in het Gereformeerd Protestantisme.* The Hague: Boekencentrum, 1987.

Grider, J. Kenneth. *A Wesleyan-Holiness Theology.* Kansas City: Beacon Hill Press, 1994.

Groenewegen, H. Y. *Jacobus Arminius op den driehonderd-jarigen gedenkdag van zijnen dood.* Leiden: S. C. van Doesburgh, 1909.

Gross, Julius. *Entwicklungsgeschichte des Erbsündendogmas.* 4 vols. Basel: Ernst Reinhardt Verlag, 1960–1972.

Gunter, W. Stephen. *Arminius and His Declaration of Sentiments: An Annotated Translation with Introduction and Theological Commentary.* Waco: Baylor University Press, 2012.

Gunter, W. Stephen. "John Wesley, a Faithful Representative of Jacobus Arminius." *Wesleyan Theological Journal* 42/2 (2007): 65–82.

Hakkenberg, Michael Abram. "The Predestinarian Controversy in the Netherlands, 1600–1620." Ph.D. diss., University of California at Berkeley, 1989.

Halverson, James. "Franciscan Theology and Predestinarian Pluralism in Late-Medieval Thought." *Speculum* 70/1 (1995): 1–26.

Hampton, Stephen. *Anti-Arminians: The Anglican Reformed Tradition from Charles II to George I.* Oxford Theological Monographs. Oxford: Oxford University Press, 2008.

Harrison, A. W. *The Beginnings of Arminianism to the Synod of Dort.* London: University of London Press, 1926.

Hart, David Bentley. "No Shadow of Turning: On Divine Impassibility." *Pro Ecclesia* 11/2 (2002): 184–206.

Hasker, William. *God, Time, and Knowledge.* Cornell Studies in Philosophy of Religion. Ithaca, NY: Cornell University Press, 1989.

Heering, Gerrit Jan, and G. J. Sirks. *Het seminarium der Remonstranten driehonderd jaar, 1634–1934.* Amsterdam: Lankamp & Brinkman, 1934.

Hewitt, Hosea. "Influence of James Arminius on Modern Religious Thought." *Methodist Review* 5th series, vol. 15 (September 1899): 779–793.

Hicks, John Mark. "Classic Arminianism and Open Theism: A Substantial Difference in Their Theologies of Providence." *Trinity Journal* n. s. 33 (2012): 3–18.

Hicks, John Mark. "The Righteousness of Saving Faith: Arminian versus Remonstrant Grace." *Evangelical Journal* 9 (Spring 1991): 27–39.

Hicks, John Mark. "The Theology of Grace in the Thought of Jacobus Arminius and Philip van Limborch: A Study in the Development of Seventeenth-Century Dutch Arminianism." Ph.D. diss., Westminster Theological Seminary, 1985.

Hillerbrand, Hans J. "Was There a Reformation in the Sixteenth Century?" *Church History* 72/3 (2003): 525–552.

Hillerbrand, Hans J., ed. *The Oxford Encyclopedia of the Reformation*. 4 vols. New York: Oxford University Press, 1996.

Hills, A. M. *Fundamental Christian Theology: A Systematic Theology*. Pasadena: C. J. Kinne, 1931.

Hoenderdaal, G. J. "Arminius en Episcopius." *Nederlands archief voor kerkgeschiedenis* 60 (1980): 203–235.

Hoenderdaal, G. J. "The Debate about Arminius Outside the Netherlands." In *Leiden University in the Seventeenth Century: An Exchange of Learning*, ed. Th. H. Lunsingh Scheurleer and G. H. M. Posthumus Meyjes, pp. 137–159. Leiden: Brill, 1975.

Hoenderdaal, G. J. "Inleiding." In *Verklaring van Jacobus Arminius, afgelegd in de vergadering van de staten van Holland op 30 Oktober, 1608*, ed. G.J. Hoenderdaal, pp. 8–41. Lochem: De Tijdstroom, 1960.

Hoenderdaal, G. J. "Jacob Arminius." In *Orthodoxie und Pietismus*, ed. Martin Greschat, pp. 51–64. Stuttgart: W. Kohlhammer, 1982.

Hoenderdaal, G. J. "De kerkordelijke kant van de Dordtse Synode." *Nederlands theologisch tijdschrift* 23/5 (1969): 349–363.

Hoenderdaal, G. J. "The Life and Struggle of Arminius in the Dutch Republic." In *Man's Faith and Freedom*, ed. Gerald McCulloh, pp. 11–26. New York: Abingdon Press, 1962.

Hoenderdaal, G. J. "The Life and Thought of Jacobus Arminius." *Religion in Life* 29/4 (1960): 540–547.

Hoenderdaal, G. J. "De theologische betekenis van Arminius." *Nederlands theologisch tijdschrift* 15/2 (1960): 90–98.

Holk, Lambertus Jacobus van. "From Arminius to Arminianism in Dutch Theology." In *Man's Faith and Freedom*, ed. Gerald O. McCulloh, pp. 27–45. New York: Abingdon Press, 1962.

Horton, Michael S. *God of Promise: Introducing Covenant Theology*. Grand Rapids, MI: Baker Books, 2006.

Hughes, Christopher. *On a Complex Theory of a Simple God: A Study in Aquinas' Doctrine of Divine Simplicity*. Cornell Studies in Philosophy of Religion. Ithaca, NY: Cornell University Press, 1989.

Hynson, Leon O. "Original Sin as Privation: An Inquiry into a Theology of Sin and Sanctification." *Wesleyan Theological Journal* 22/2 (1987): 65–83.

Israel, Jonathan. *The Dutch Republic: Its Rise, Greatness, and Fall, 1477–1806.* Oxford: Clarendon Press, 1995.

Itterzon, Gerrit Pieter van. *Franciscus Gomarus.* The Hague: Martinus Nijhoff, 1929.

Itterzon, Gerrit Pieter van. "Gomarus, Franciscus." In *Biografisch lexicon voor de geschiedenis van het nederlandse protestantisme,* 2: 220–225. Kampen: Kok, 1978–2006.

Jong, Peter Y. de, ed. *Crisis in the Reformed Churches, Essays in Commemoration of the Great Synod of Dort, 1618–1619.* Grand Rapids, MI: Reformed Fellowship, 1968.

Jorgenson, James. "Predestination according to Divine Foreknowledge in Patristic Tradition." In *Salvation in Christ: A Lutheran-Orthodox Dialogue,* ed. John Meyendorff and Robert Tobias, pp. 159–169. Minneapolis: Augsburg, 1992.

Jowers, Dennis W. "Introduction." In *Four Views on Divine Providence,* ed. Dennis W. Jowers. Grand Rapids, MI: Zondervan, 2011.

Kooi, Christine. *Liberty and Religion: Church and State in Leiden's Reformation, 1572–1620.* Studies in Medieval and Reformation Thought, vol. 82. Leiden: Brill, 2000.

Krivocheine, Basil. "The Simplicity of the Divine Nature and Distinctions within God, According to St. Gregory of Nyssa." *St. Vladimir's Theological Quarterly* (1977): 76–104.

Kuyper, Abraham. *De Leidsche professoren en de executeurs der Dordtsche nalatenschap.* Amsterdam: J. H. Kruyt, 1879.

Lake, Donald M. "He Died for All: The Universal Dimensions of the Atonement; Jacob Arminius' Contribution to a Theology of Grace." In *Grace Unlimited,* ed. C. H. Pinnock, pp. 223–242. Minneapolis: Bethany Fellowship, 1975.

Lamberigts, Mathijs. "Le mal et le péché. Pélage: La rehabilitation d'un hérétique." *Revue d'histoire ecclésiastique* 95 (2000): 97–111.

Lamberigts, Mathijs. "Pelagianism: From an Ethical Religious Movement to a Heresy and Back Again." Trans. John Bowden. In *'Movements' in the Church,* ed. Alberto Melloni, pp. 39–48. London: SCM Press, 2003.

Lamping, A. J. "Kuchlinus (Cuchlinus), Johannes." In *Biografisch lexicon voor de geschiedenis van het nederlandse protestantisme,* 5: 317–319. Kampen: Kok, 1978–2006.

Landgraf, Artur Michael. *Dogmengeschichte der Frühscholastik.* 4 vols. Regensburg: Verlag Friedrich Pustet, 1952–1956.

Laytham, D. Brent. "The Place of Natural Theology in the Theological Method of John Calvin and Jacobus Arminius." *Church Divinity* 8 (1989–1990): 22–44.

Lecler, Joseph. *Toleration and the Reformation.* 2 vols. Trans. T. L. Westow. New York: Association Press, 1960.

Lee, Luther. *Elements of Theology: Or An Exposition of the Divine Origin, Doctrines, Morals, and Institutions of Christianity.* Syracuse, NY: A. W. Hall, 1853.

Leeuwen, Th. Marius van, Keith D. Stanglin, and Marijke Tolsma, eds. *Arminius, Arminianism, and Europe: Jacobus Arminius (1559/60–1609)*. Brill's Series in Church History, vol. 39. Leiden: Brill, 2009.

Lieburg, Fred van. "Gisbertus Samuels, a Reformed Minister Sentenced by the Synod of Zeeland in 1591 for His Opinions on Predestination." In *Revisiting the Synod of Dordt*, ed. Aza Goudriaan and Fred van Lieburg, pp. 3–19. Brill's Series in Church History, vol. 49. Leiden: Brill, 2011.

Lillback, Peter A. *The Binding of God: Calvin's Role in the Development of Covenant Theology*. Texts and Studies in Reformation and Post-Reformation Theology. Grand Rapids, MI: Baker Academic, 2001.

Linde, S. van der. "De Dordtse Synode, 1619–1969." *Nederlands theologisch tijdschrift* 23/5 (1969): 339–348.

McCall, Thomas H. "I Believe in Divine Sovereignty." *Trinity Journal* n. s. 29 (2008): 205–226.

McCall, Thomas H. "We Believe in God's Sovereign Goodness: A Rejoinder to John Piper." *Trinity Journal* n. s. 29 (2008): 235–246.

McCall, Thomas H., and Keith D. Stanglin. "S. M. Baugh and the Meaning of Foreknowledge." *Trinity Journal* n. s. 26 (2005): 19–31.

McCulloh, Gerald O. "The Influence of Arminius on American Theology." In *Man's Faith and Freedom: The Theological Influence of Jacobus Arminius*, ed. Gerald O. McCulloh, pp. 64–87. New York: Abingdon Press, 1962.

McCulloh, Gerald O., ed. *Man's Faith and Freedom: The Theological Influence of Jacobus Arminius*. New York: Abingdon Press, 1962.

McGonigle, Herbert. "Arminius and Wesley on Original Sin." *European Explorations in Christian Holiness* 2 (2001): 96–108.

McKenna, S. J. "Semi-Pelagianism." In *New Catholic Encyclopedia*. 2nd ed. Vol. 12: 899–901. Detroit: Thomson/Gale, 2003.

McSorley, Harry J. "Was Gabriel Biel a Semipelagian?" In *Wahrheit und Verkündigung*, ed. Leo Scheffczyk, et al., pp. 1109–1120. Munich: Verlag Ferdinand Schöningh, 1967.

Maronier, Jan Hendrik. *Jacobus Arminius: Een biografie*. Amsterdam: Y. Rogge, 1905.

Miley, John. *Systematic Theology*. Vol. 1. New York: Methodist Book Concern, 1892.

Moltmann, Jürgen. *The Crucified God: The Cross of Christ as the Foundation and Criticism of Christian Theology*. Trans. R. A. Wilson and John Bowden. Minneapolis: Fortress Press, 1974.

Moltmann, Jürgen. *The Trinity and the Kingdom: The Doctrine of God*. Trans. Margaret Kohl. Minneapolis: Fortress Press, 1993.

Morsink, Gerrit. *Joannes Anastasius Veluanus (Jan Gerritsz. Versteghe, levensloop en ontwikkeling)*. Kampen: Kok, 1986.

Muller, Richard A. "Arminius and the Reformed Tradition." *Westminster Theological Journal* 70/1 (2008): 19–48.

Muller, Richard A. "Arminius and the Scholastic Tradition." *Calvin Theological Journal* 24/2 (1989): 263–277.

Muller, Richard A. "The Christological Problem in the Thought of Jacobus Arminius." *Nederlands archief voor kerkgeschiedenis* 68 (1988): 145–163.

Muller, Richard A. *Dictionary of Latin and Greek Theological Terms: Drawn Principally from Protestant Scholastic Theology.* Grand Rapids: Baker, 1985.

Muller, Richard A. "The Federal Motif in Seventeenth-Century Arminian Theology." *Nederlands archief voor kerkgeschiedenis* 62 (1982): 102–122.

Muller, Richard A. *God, Creation, and Providence in the Thought of Jacob Arminius: Sources and Directions of Scholastic Protestantism in the Era of Early Orthodoxy.* Grand Rapids, MI: Baker, 1991.

Muller, Richard A. "God, Predestination, and the Integrity of the Created Order: a Note on Patterns in Arminius' Theology." In *Later Calvinism: International Perspectives,* ed. W. Fred Graham. Sixteenth Century Essays and Studies, vol. 22, pp. 431–446. Kirksville, MO: Truman State University Press, 1994.

Muller, Richard A. "Grace, Election, and Contingent Choice: Arminius' Gambit and the Reformed Response." In *The Grace of God and the Bondage of the Will,* ed. Thomas Schreiner and Bruce Ware, 2 vols., 2: 251–278. Grand Rapids, MI: Baker, 1995.

Muller, Richard A. "A Note on 'Christocentrism' and the Imprudent Use of Such Terminology." *Westminster Theological Journal* 68 (2006): 253–260.

Muller, Richard A. *Post-Reformation Reformed Dogmatics.* 4 vols. 2nd ed. Grand Rapids, MI: Baker Academic, 2003.

Muller, Richard A. "The Priority of the Intellect in the Soteriology of Jacob Arminius." *Westminster Theological Journal* 55 (1993): 55–72.

Muller, Richard A. *The Unaccommodated Calvin: Studies in the Foundation of a Theological Tradition.* Oxford Studies in Historical Theology. New York: Oxford University Press, 2000.

Nuttall, Geoffrey F. "The Influence of Arminianism in England." In *Man's Faith and Freedom,* ed. Gerald McCulloh, pp. 46–63. New York: Abingdon Press, 1962.

Oberman, Heiko A. *The Harvest of Medieval Theology: Gabriel Biel and Late Medieval Nominalism.* 1963. Reprint, Grand Rapids, MI: Baker, 2000.

O'Brien, T. C. "Appendices." In *Thomas Aquinas, Summa theologiae,* Volume 26, *Original Sin (1a2ae.81–85),* pp. 105–161. New York: McGraw-Hill, 1965.

O'Conner, Timothy. "The Impossibility of Middle Knowledge." *Philosophical Studies* 66 (1992): 139–166.

Oden, Thomas C. *John Wesley's Scriptural Christianity: A Plain Exposition of His Teaching on Christian Doctrine.* Grand Rapids, MI: Zondervan, 1994.

Oden, Thomas C. *The Justification Reader.* Grand Rapids, MI: Eerdmans, 2002.

Olson, Roger E. *Arminian Theology: Myths and Realities.* Downers Grove, IL: IVP Academic, 2006.

Olson, Roger E. *The Story of Christian Theology: Twenty Centuries of Tradition and Reform.* Downers Grove, IL: IVP, 1999.

Otte, Richard. "A Defense of Middle Knowledge." *International Journal for Philosophy of Religion* 21 (1987): 161–169.

Otterspeer, Willem. *Groepsportret met Dame I. Het bolwerk van de vrijheid: De Leidse universiteit, 1575–1672.* Amsterdam: Bert Bakker, 2000.

Pask, Alfred H. "The Influence of Arminius on John Wesley." *London Quarterly and Holborn Review* 185 (October 1960): 258–263.

Peterson, Robert A., and Michael D. Williams. *Why I Am Not an Arminian.* Downers Grove, IL: InterVarsity Press, 2004.

Pinnock, Clark H. "Systematic Theology." In *The Openness of God: A Biblical Challenge to the Traditional Understanding of God,* pp. 101–125. Downers Grove, IL: InterVarsity Press, 1994.

Pinson, J. Matthew. "Will the Real Arminius Please Stand Up? A Study of the Theology of Jacobus Arminius in Light of His Interpreters." *Integrity* 2 (2003): 121–139.

Piper, John. "I Believe in God's Self-Sufficiency." *Trinity Journal* n. s. 29 (2008): 227–234.

Pitkin, Barbara. "The Protestant Zeno: Calvin and the Development of Melanchthon's Anthropology." *Journal of Religion* 84/3 (2004): 345–378.

Plantinga, Alvin. *Does God Have a Nature?* Milwaukee: Marquette University Press, 1980.

Plantinga, Alvin. *God, Freedom, and Evil.* Grand Rapids, MI: Eerdmans, 1974.

Plantinga, Alvin. *The Nature of Necessity.* Oxford: Oxford University Press, 1974.

Plantinga, Alvin. "On Ockham's Way Out." *Faith and Philosophy* 3 (1983): 235–269.

Plantinga, Alvin. "The Philosophy of Religion." In *God's Advocates: Christian Thinkers in Conversation,* ed. Rupert Shortt, pp. 43–66. Grand Rapids, MI: Eerdmans, 2005.

Plantinga, Richard, Thomas R. Thompson, and Matthew D. Lundberg. *An Introduction to Christian Theology.* Cambridge: Cambridge University Press, 2010.

Platt, John E. *Reformed Thought and Scholasticism: The Arguments for the Existence of God in Dutch Theology, 1575–1650.* Studies in the History of Christian Thought, vol. 29. Leiden: Brill, 1982.

Pope, William Burt. *A Compendium of Christian Theology: Being Analytical Outlines of a Course of Theological Study, Biblical, Dogmatic, Historical.* 3 vols. 2nd ed. New York: Hunt and Eaton, 1889.

Praamsma, Louis. "The Background of the Arminian Controversy (1586–1618)." In *Crisis in the Reformed Churches,* ed. Peter Y. De Jong, pp. 22–38. Grand Rapids, MI: Reformed Fellowship, 1968.

Radde-Gallwitz, Andrew. *Basil of Caesarea, Gregory of Nyssa, and the Transformation of Divine Simplicity.* Oxford: Oxford University Press, 2009.

Raitt, Jill. "Harmony of Confessions." In *The Oxford Encyclopedia of the Reformation,* ed. Hans J. Hillerbrand, 2: 211–212. New York: Oxford University Press, 1996.

Ralston, Thomas N. *Elements of Divinity: A Concise and Comprehensive View of Bible Theology; Comprising the Doctrines, Evidences, Morals, and Institutions of Christianity; with Appropriate Questions Appended to each Chapter.* New York: Abingdon Press, 1847.

Rieu, W. du, ed. *Album studiosorum Academiae Lugduno Batavae MDLXXV–MDCCCLXXV, accedunt nomina curatorum et professorum.* The Hague: Martinus Nijhoff, 1875.

Rogge, H. C. *Caspar Janszoon Coolhaes, de voorloper van Arminius en der Remonstranten.* 2 vols. New ed. Amsterdam: Y. Rogge, 1865.

Rogge, H. C. *Johannes Wtenbogaert en zijn tijd.* 3 vols. Amsterdam: Y. Rogge, 1874–1876.

Rollmann, Hans. "In Essentials Unity: The Pre-History of a Restoration Movement Slogan." *Restoration Quarterly* 39/3 (1997): 129–139.

Rorem, Paul. "Augustine, the Medieval Theologians, and the Reformation." In *The Medieval Theologians*, ed. G. R. Evans, pp. 365–372. Oxford: Blackwell, 2001.

Sarx, Tobias. *Franciscus Junius d.Ä (1545–1602): Ein reformierter Theologe im Spannungsfeld zwischen späthumanistischer Irenik und reformierter Konfessionalisierung.* Reformed Historical Theology, vol. 3. Göttingen: Vandenhoeck & Ruprecht, 2007.

Schreiner, Susan E. "Pelagianism." In *The Oxford Encyclopedia of the Reformation*, ed. Hans J. Hillerbrand, 3: 238–241. New York: Oxford University Press, 1996.

Schweizer, Alexander. "Sebastian Castellio als Bestreiter der calvinischen Prädestinationslehre, der bedeutendste Vorgänger des Arminius." *Theologische Jahrbücher* 10 (1851): 1–27.

Sheldon, Henry C. "Changes in Theology among American Methodists." *American Journal of Theology* 10 (1906): 31–52.

Sinnema, Donald. "The Canons of Dordt: From Judgment on Arminianism to Confessional Standard," in *Revisiting the Synod of Dordt*, ed. Aza Goudriaan and Fred van Lieburg, pp. 313–333.

Sirks, G. J. *Arminius' pleidooi voor de vrede der kerk.* Referatenreeks uit Remonstrantse Kring, vol. 11. Lochem: Uitgave de Tijdstroom, 1960.

Slaatte, Howard A. *The Arminian Arm of Theology: The Theologies of John Fletcher, First Methodist Theologian, and His Precursor, James Arminius.* Washington, DC: University Press of America, 1978.

Stanciu, Diana. "Re-interpreting Augustine: Ralph Cudworth and Jacobus Arminius on Grace and Free Will." *Zeitschrift für antikes Christentum* 11/1 (2007): 96–114.

Stanglin, Keith D. "Arminius and Arminianism: An Overview of Current Research." In *Arminius, Arminianism, and Europe*, ed. Th. Marius van Leeuwen, Keith D. Stanglin, and Marijke Tolsma, pp. 3–24. Brill's Series in Church History, vol. 39. Leiden: Brill, 2009.

Stanglin, Keith D. "'Arminius *avant la lettre*': Peter Baro, Jacob Arminius, and the Bond of Predestinarian Polemic." *Westminster Theological Journal* 67 (2005): 51–74.

Stanglin, Keith D. *Arminius on the Assurance of Salvation: The Context, Roots, and Shape of the Leiden Debate, 1603–1609.* Brill's Series in Church History, vol. 27. Leiden: Brill, 2007.

Stanglin, Keith D. "Johannes Kuchlinus, the 'Faithful Teacher': His Role in the Arminian Controversy and His Impact as a Theological Interpreter and Educator." *Church History and Religious Culture* 87/3 (2007): 305–326.

Stanglin, Keith D. "Methodological Musings on Historiography (A Rejoinder)." *Church History and Religious Culture* 92 (2012): 121–129.

Stanglin, Keith D. *The Missing Public Disputations of Jacobus Arminius: Introduction, Text, and Notes.* Brill's Series in Church History, vol. 47. Leiden: Brill, 2010.

Stanglin, Keith D. "The New Perspective on Arminius: Notes on a Historiographical Shift." *Reformation & Renaissance Review* 11/3 (2009): 295–310.

Stanglin, Keith D. "Review of William den Boer, *Duplex Dei Amor: Contextuele karakteristiek van de theologie van Jacobus Arminius (1559–1609)* (Apeldoorn: Instituut voor Reformatieonderzoek, 2008)." *Church History and Religious Culture* 90/2–3 (2010): 420–425.

Stanglin, Keith D., and Richard A. Muller. "*Bibliographia Arminiana*: A Comprehensive, Annotated Bibliography of the Works of Arminius." In *Arminius, Arminianism, and Europe,* ed. Th. Marius van Leeuwen, Keith D. Stanglin, and Marijke Tolsma, pp. 263–290. Brill's Series in Church History, vol. 39. Leiden: Brill, 2009.

Steers, David. "Arminianism amongst Protestant Dissenters in England and Ireland in the Eighteenth Century." In *Arminius, Arminianism, and Europe,* ed. Th. Marius van Leeuwen, Keith D. Stanglin, and Marijke Tolsma, pp. 159–200. Brill's Series in Church History, vol. 39. Leiden: Brill, 2009.

Steinmetz, David C. *Luther in Context.* Grand Rapids, MI: Baker, 1995.

Stump, Eleonore. *Aquinas.* New York: Routledge, 2003.

Tjalsma, D. *Leven en strijd van Jacobus Arminius.* Lochem: Uitgave de Tijdstrrom, 1960.

Trueman, Carl R. *Histories and Fallacies: Problems Faced in the Writing of History.* Wheaton: Crossway, 2010.

Trueman, Carl R. *John Owen: Reformed Catholic, Renaissance Man.* Great Theologians. Burlington, VT: Ashgate, 2007.

Tyacke, Nicholas R. N. *Anti-Calvinists: The Rise of English Arminianism c. 1590–1640.* Oxford Historical Monographs. Oxford: Clarendon Press, 1987.

Tyacke, Nicholas R. N. "Debate: The Rise of Arminianism Reconsidered." *Past and Present* 115 (1987): 201–216.

Venemans, B. A. "Junius, Franciscus (François du Jon)." In *Biografisch lexicon voor de geschiedenis van het nederlandse protestantisme,* 2: 275–278. Kampen: Kok, 1978–2006.

Visser, Arnoud S. Q. *Reading Augustine in the Reformation: The Flexibility of Intellectual Authority in Europe, 1500–1620.* Oxford Studies in Historical Theology. New York: Oxford University Press, 2011.

Voogt, Gerrit. "Remonstrant—Counter-Remonstrant Debates: Crafting a Principled Defense of Toleration after the Synod of Dordrecht (1619–1650)." *Church History and Religious Culture* 89/4 (2009): 489–524.

Wakefield, Samuel. *A Complete System of Christian Theology: Or, a Concise, Comprehensive, and Systematic View of the Evidences, Doctrines, Morals, and Institutions of Christianity.* Cincinnati: Cranston & Stowe, 1858.

Warren, William Fairfield. "Arminius." *Methodist Quarterly Review* 4th series, vol. 9 (July 1857): 345–361.

Watson, Richard. *Theological Institutes: Or, a View of the Evidences, Doctrines, Morals, and Institutions of Christianity.* Vol. 2. New York: N. Bangs and J. Emory, 1826.

Weaver, Rebecca Harden. *Divine Grace and Human Agency: A Study of the Semi-Pelagian Controversy.* Patristic Monograph Series, 15. Macon, GA: Mercer University Press, 1996.

Weinandy, Thomas. *Does God Suffer?* Notre Dame: University of Notre Dame Press, 2000.

White, Peter. *Predestination, Policy, and Polemic: Conflict and Consensus in the English Church from the Reformation to the Civil War.* Cambridge: Cambridge University Press, 1992.

White, Peter. "The Rise of Arminianism Reconsidered." *Past and Present* 101 (1983): 34–54.

White, Peter. "The Rise of Arminianism Reconsidered: A Rejoinder." *Past and Present* 115 (1987): 217–229.

Wierenga, Edward R. *The Nature of God: An Inquiry into the Divine Attributes.* Ithaca, NY: Cornell University Press, 1989.

Wijminga, P. J. *Festus Hommius.* Leiden: D. Donner, 1899.

Wiley, H. Orton. *Christian Theology.* Vol. 1. Kansas City: Beacon Hill Press, 1940.

Witt, William Gene. "Creation, Redemption and Grace in the Theology of Jacob Arminius." Ph.D. diss., University of Notre Dame, 1993.

Woltjer, J. J., and M. E. H. N. Mout. "Settlements: The Netherlands." In *Handbook of European History, 1400–1600: Late Middle Ages, Renaissance, and Reformation.* 2 vols., ed. Thomas A. Brady, Jr., et al., 2: 385–415. Leiden: Brill, 1994–1995.

Wood, Arthur Skevington. "The Declaration of Sentiments: The Theological Testament of Arminius." *Evangelical Quarterly* 65 (April 1993): 111–129.

# Index

CPSIA information can be obtained at www.ICGtesting.com
Printed in the USA
BVOW02s2113201113

336884BV00001B/4/P